BELIEF AND MAKE-BELIEVE

BELIEF AND MAKE-BELIEVE

Critical Reflections on the Sources of Credulity

G. A. WELLS

Open ✸ Court
La Salle, Illinois

OPEN COURT and the above logo are registered in the U.S. Patent and Trademark Office.

© 1991 by Open Court Publishing Company

First printing 1991

Printed and bound in the United States of America.

Library of Congress Cataloging-in-Publication Data

Wells, George Albert, 1926–
    Belief and make-believe : critical reflections on the sources of
credulity / G.A. Wells.
        p.   cm.
    Includes bibliographical references and indexes.
    ISBN 0-8126-9187-3 (cloth).—ISBN 0-8126-9188-1 (pbk.)
    1. Thought and thinking. 2. Reason. 3. Instinct. 4. Emotions.
    5. Apologetics—History. 6. Religion and poetry. I. Title.
  B105.T54W45   1991
  121'.6—dc20   91-40296
                                                            CIP

CONTENTS

PREFACE

In the first part of this book I have tried to give a reasonable account of the nature of belief. In the second, I turn to criticism of a particular system of beliefs, as they are revealed in the writings of some modern Christian apologists. In the third part I discuss the role of make-believe in Christian apologetics, and in particular the ways in which genuine ideas commonly get lost in a jungle of meaningless verbiage. The fourth part is concerned with the relation between religion and the arts.

My opening chapter begins by inquiring into what ideas must be like if they are to be used profitably in the process of thinking and reasoning. Next, I try to counter attempts to represent the historian's thinking—so important for Christianity—as significantly different from that of the scientist and the man of common sense; and finally I discuss how abuse of the thinking process is avoided.

The second chapter considers the parts played, in the formation and development of beliefs, by reason on the one hand and by instinct and emotion on the other. The role of instinct in human behaviour was of course inconspicuous as long as instinct was understood to mean only the most stereotyped responses. I try to show that instinct and emotion (a state of excitement associated with an instinct) are particularly relevant factors in the relation between leaders and followers. Fundamentalist groups—Christian and other—illustrate the willingness of millions to trust in the authority of individual leaders.

What I say throughout Part One (Chapters 1 and 2) about the reasoning process, and how it is often detrimentally influenced by language, follows in the footsteps of my old teacher, F.R.H. (Ronald) Englefield. His three posthumously published books are listed in my bibliography, and I hope that the present book will help to make them more widely known and appreciated. They are a more than adequate reply to the view which, according to Paul and Linda Badham (who do not share it) is "deeply entrenched among many of the leading biologists of today"—the view, namely, that "man alone can think, with man's use of language being taken as the key behavioural evidence of this unique ability" (Badham 1984, p. 49). I do not see how any fair-minded person who reads Englefield's account of the thinking process, and who studies the authorities to whom he there refers, can persist in such a view. Language and thought are not inseparable, but they are forms of human behaviour that have developed together, and their mutal influence is of great importance for human belief.

My Part Two shows how difficult plausible defence of the traditional Christian creed has become. The apologists discussed here are concerned either to establish a sufficient historical basis for Christian faith (Chapters 3 and 4), or to come to terms with the scheme of salvation and damnation unequivocally set forth in the New Testament (Chapter 5). Many readers may be surprised and shocked by the extent to which these apologists reject traditional items of Christian faith, and by their readiness to admit how little—how very little—can be reliably known about the character, the views, and the activities of Jesus.

One result of the difficulty of defending traditional positions in a straightforward way is that they are now commonly defended in the manner discussed in Part Three, that is by raising the plane of discussion to such a level of abstraction that the ideas offered are attenuated to meaninglessness. The Oxford theologian Maurice Wiles indicates what I have in mind:

It is sometimes argued that Christian belief is impaled inescapably
on the horns of a dilemma. It can either be stated in a strong form,
in which it is interesting but almost sure to be false. Or it can be
stated in a weak form, in which it has some chance of being true but
ceases to be interesting. A robust incarnational faith which speaks
of a God who has lived a human life and died a human death; that
would be a faith which had bite to it, a faith worth believing—if one
could. But hedge and qualify that understanding of incarnation and
the faith will die, if not of the thousand qualifications themselves,
then of the boredom of its own attenuated claims. (1974, p. 115)

Wiles does not himself accept "this dichotomy", but he
recognizes that it is not easy for the apologist to avoid
either the one or the other of the alternatives he here
specifies. It is not without ground that Professor Lewis,
whose Christology is (in Wiles's terminology) of the 'robust
incarnational' kind, complains of colleagues who retain
"only a form of words, without any of the substance of
what would normally be understood by talk of the divinity
of Jesus or of his being also Christ" (1981, pp. 33–34).

It is not only in religious contexts that such purely
verbal thinking occurs, and its frequency there and elsewhere justifies my inquiry in Part One into the nature of
ideas and the thinking process. What has to be explained is
that aplogists can themselves be satisfied and can impress
people with what to others appears to be no more than 'a
form of words'; that, as Huxley put it, "on even the most
solemn and important of questions, men are apt to take
cunning phrases for answers" (1894, p. 236). It is understandable that an apologist might shift his ground from the
specific to the abstract in order to get the better of an
opponent, and for that purpose it may not matter over-
much to him that some of his ideas are unintelligible. But it
would be absurd for the apologist himself to believe in
something he knew to be unintelligible, for propositions
that are not understood cannot be believed. All that can
happen in such cases is that a form of words is assented to
as if it stood for something intelligible—as when the
Athanasian creed speaks of "the Father incomprehensible,
the Son incomprehensible and the Holy Ghost incomprehensible", declares these to be "not three incompre-

hensibles but one", and insists that "he that will be saved must thus think of the Trinity". It is perhaps appropriate to recall in this connection that George Orwell, in his novel *Nineteen Eighty-Four*, defined doublethink as "the power of holding two contradictory beliefs in one's mind simultaneously, and accepting both of them".

A schoolboy, faced with the need to attach a meaning to the symbol 'i'—a quantity which when multiplied by itself yields 'minus one'—may suspect that his instructors are taking advantage of his innocence. Only later, when he has grasped the rules by which i can be made to yield firm mathematical truths, can his initial distrust be overcome. In this instance, what appears at first sight to be a piece of trickery turns out to provide valuable results. At a later stage, the inquiring schoolboy may find the basic assumptions of the theory of Relativity hard to swallow. But belief and trust are in time established—partly from the evidence of astronomical and other physical observations, and partly from the inner coherence and aesthetic beauty of the theory itself. Sadly, such instances do not provide a general justification for the practice of make-believe. The aesthetic charms of a belief, or even its internal coherence, do not by themselves establish truth or reliability. Too often, beliefs are found to depend on little more than wishful thinking. And the answer to the question: 'Is it possible to believe anything which one does not understand?' is that it depends on what one means by 'believe'.

Part Four discusses the links—real and fanciful—between religion and poetry. It also discusses recent tendencies towards make-believe of a non-religious kind in literature and literary criticism. The relevance of the arguments of Part One will again be apparent here. Religion and art, because specifically human, are often linked as affording insights into aspects of reality not accessible to science, and are widely regarded as inexplicable by principles which have been established as explanations of mammalian behaviour generally. One aim of this book is to question these assumptions; and one thing which its four parts have in common is a rejection of mystification and of comforting inspirational answers to questions about man and his place in the universe.

Since I completed his book, publications relevant in particular to its first and last chapters have appeared. Maurice Bloch, in his article 'Language, Anthropology and Cognitive Science' (*Man*, 26 [1991], 183–198), shares my view that there is no inevitable connection between ideas and words. He refers to R. Brown's *The First Language: the Early Stages* (Harmondsworth: Penguin Books, 1973) for "many examples of conceptual thinking in pre-linguistic children", and says that, for example, "children have the concept 'house' before they can say the word". Bloch also mentions other "studies which show that the acquisition of lexical semantics by children is very largely a matter of trying to match words to already formed concepts." His conclusion is that "much knowledge is fundamentally non-linguistic", and that "concepts involve implicit networks of meanings which are formed through the experience of, and practice in, the external world" (pp. 185–86). This may seem obvious, but in the present-day climate of opinion Bloch has to argue the case in detail. I would add that, in the course of man's history, he formed his notions first and invented words for them afterwards. Admittedly, today many notions arise through the misunderstanding of words, and every individual must learn the majority of his words before he forms clearly the notions they conventionally stand for. But in the history of language we must expect to see language follow in the train of developing thought and not lead the way. Words multiply as the progressing analysis of the world gives rise to a larger number of ideas, new words being made necessary by new discoveries and inventions, new ways of understanding and explaining things.

It is not possible in this connection to avoid some discussion of the origin of human language. In the same issue of *Man*, Adam Kendon contributes an article entitled 'Some Considerations for a Theory of Language Origins'

(199–221), in which he expresses long overdue appreciation of Köhler's truly masterly descriptions (on which I
have drawn in my opening chapter) of "just what it is that
chimpanzees do when they go about solving a problem
they have been set". Köhler, he adds, "showed that they
could arrive at novel solutions by combining in new ways
diverse features of objects already well-known in other
contexts" (pp. 208, 217 n.20). Kendon justly notes that
these animals have nevertheless "not developed a system
of language-like communication because they do not need
to. The kind of social life they lead is one that does not
require it", for with them "co-operation involving a *complementary* relationship between the behaviour of two or
more individuals is largely absent" (p. 212). It is still
sometimes said, dismissively, that there is no evidence
concerning the origin of language, by which *documentary*
evidence is meant. It is true that it would be futile to look
for that. One can, however, show, with the help of Köhler,
that reasoning is quite possible without language; and one
can argue that a small improvement in the mental capacity
of the chimpanzee, combined with that physical inferiority
which compelled men to organize themselves in society or
perish, will have given the conditions for the invention of
language.

Kendon also supposes (what I too argue here and
elsewhere: see below, pp. 223–24, 240f) that "language
began as a sort of pantomine", and this, he says, "obviously means that the first kind of behaviour that could be said
to be functioning in anything like a linguistic fashion
would have to have been gestural" (p. 215). In her review of
my 1987 book on *The Origin of Language* (in *Histo-
riographia Linguistica,* 17 [1990], 411–17), Professor
Julie Andresen points out that this view that communication depended initially on gesture and pantomine now
commands sizable assent. She refers to R. W. Wescott's
review (in *Language in Society,* 14 [1985]) of a recent
symposium on language's origin and development where
he notes a growing tendency to favour the views that

"language probably shifted in prehistoric times from a predominantly visual to a predominantly auditory channel", and that "speech movements probably began as imitations or accompaniments of manual gestures" (Wescott, p. 128). The strongest argument in this regard is that, whereas verbal languages must depend very largely on convention, the first modes of communication must have been 'natural' in the sense that the signs, to have been intelligible, must have had some obvious relation to their meaning. These primitive, self-explanatory signs would be abridged and stylized through use and then be virtually conventional and no longer self-explanatory. In due course the possibility of using *arbitrarily* invented signs (whether gestural or vocal) would be realized.

In the final chapter of the present book, I suggest that, when conventional oral speech had supplanted older forms of communication (gesture, pantomine, picture writing, modelling, and drawing), these older forms were put to new uses and developed into what we know as art. Models and drawings came to be made for their own sake, and miming dances became a form of recreation or entertainment. Models were also used for magical purposes and, much later, for scientific ones. Pantomine survives today in various forms of religious ritual. Poetry is a specialized form of conventional oral language, and the connection between the two is a little more complicated, as oral language retains, as its principle function, communication. With poetry, as with language, there can be no documentary evidence as to origins—nothing of the earliest compositions can now remain—yet it is possible, as I try to show, to make relevant inferences from extant data. The inquiry may perhaps be resented. But because the poet deals unscientifically with his subject, it does not follow that the action of the poet in so doing is not a fit subject for scientific investigation. Englefield's account of the origin of poetry, on which I draw in Chapter 7, is an answer to those who find in religion and art the meeting place of mystery. My debt to him, here as elsewhere, is considerable.

I am grateful, too, to Professor Carl Lofmark for very helpful comments on an early draft of my manuscript, and to the late Dr. David Oppenheimer (who died suddenly in June 1991) for valuable criticism of repeated drafts and revisions. I dedicate this book to the memory of this true scholar and true friend.

I trust the reader will not be irritated, and mutter, about what has been called 'the scholar's vice of self-citation', when he finds himself referred to earlier publications of mine where they cover topics mentioned in this one. In a few instances I have drawn—with editorial permission which I gratefully acknowledge—on material that I have recently had published in article form. The details are:

'Burke on Ideas, Words and Imagination', *British Journal for Eighteenth-Century Studies,* 9 (1986).

'Wilhelm Wundt and Cultural Origins', *Quinquereme,* 11 (1988).

'Criticism and the Quest for Analogies', *New German Studies,* 15 (1989).

'The Bible With or Without Illusions?', *New Humanist,* 105 no.1 (1990).

Other books are frequently referred to, in both text and notes of this one, by the author's name and the date of publication. The bibliography (on pp. 285ff. below) lists these authors in alphabetical order and gives full details of the relevant publications.

Scripture quotations are (except where otherwise indicated) from the Revised Version (RV), published 1881–85, of the Authorised Version (AV) or King James Bible of 1611. Other English versions are referred to as follows:

NEB   *The New English Bible,* copyright of Oxford and Cambridge University Presses.

RSV   *The Revised Standard Version,* copyright of the Division of Christian Education, National

Council of the Churches of Christ in the United States.

In some cases, brief scriptural phrases have been rendered literally or adapted to the syntax of my sentences.

I use the terms Matthew, Mark, etc., sometimes to designate the author of the relevant gospel and sometimes to designate that gospel itself. Which meaning is intended will be clear from the context.

PART ONE

THINKING AND BELIEF

1

IDEAS, WORDS, AND THE THINKING PROCESS

i. IDEAS: PARTICULAR, GENERAL, AND ABSTRACT

Belief, of any kind, presupposes that we have some ideas in which we believe. The process of thinking which has led to beliefs is itself a process of manipulating ideas. Consequently it is vital, if we are to understand anything about either thinking or belief, that we are quite clear as to what we understand by ideas.

The idea of an individual object is a multiple representation that has been constructed out of a variety of different data about that object. Thus my idea of a particular cat is composed of the various *aspects* which it has presented to me—the feel of its fur, the various postures it adopts, the movements and sounds it makes, and so on. These aspects cohere in the sense that, when I experience any one of them in the presence of the animal, I know that I can easily put myself in positions from which I can successively experience others. My brain links the memories of such individual aspects so as to form an idea which more completely represents the real thing. As a result of this mental activity, man—and other animals—can often recognise an object or situation from a small number of presented aspects, perhaps even from a single one, and it is this ability that constitutes perception, as against mere sensation. A dog, for instance, may recognise an intruding cat when what it actually sees is no more than a small black patch behind the garden bushes. The sensation gives rise in his mind to an *idea* of the cat, and his behaviour is determined by that idea.

To let all the aspects of an object well-known to me pass through my mind would require many hours and make constructive thinking impracticable. But if, in order to think about that object, I have to consult my memory, it is usually enough to recall just that set of aspects which are relevant to my problem. We have a way of introducing a topic by saying: 'You know old so-and-so?' or 'You remember my apartment in town?' When our partner in conversation replies affirmatively, he may have in his mind old so-and-so's red hair, his harsh voice, or his Yorkshire accent. But whatever first comes into his mind, he is ready to switch to other of his memories of the gentleman lurking in the background of his mind as they are required by what I go on to say. These memories are on the alert, ready for duty, but not yet actually on parade.

Awareness that ideas are derived from sensory impressions has sometimes served to obscure the very great difference between the two. Hume, for instance, said that ideas are "nothing but copies and representations" of sensory impressions, and differ from them "only in their strength and vivacity".[1] But our ideas represent things, and in consequence they are much more than copies of sensations. Two persons may have similar sensations and yet not by any means the same idea. Even a dog may in a particular situation have sensations similar to those of a man, but can hardly have the same ideas. An individual thing is never presented to an observer except in some particular aspect. It is the memory of all these aspects, all the forms which the thing has ever assumed in his experience, all the events in which it has participated, all the uses to which it has been put, all the contexts in which it has appeared—it is this collection of associated memories that constitutes the idea of the thing in his mind. Thus an idea is a highly organised system of memories derived from impressions, and the extent and range of such an organised system depends very much on the capacity of the individual's brain, as well as on his experience.

This is equally true of ideas of classes of things. Some philosophers have had great difficulty in seeing wherein such ideas consist. Berkeley argued that he could envisage in his mind's eye a particular triangle or man, but not triangles or mankind in general.[2] He supposed that the idea of a particular thing is just a single image in the mind; whereas he could find no clear image in his mind when he thought of a generality. But this difficulty disappears if we allow that even an idea of a particular thing is not one remembered image but a great number of them, recalled in sequence. It is the *source* of the general idea (built up from the many individuals which make up the generality), and not the nature of the mental construction, which makes it different from the particular idea (built up from experience of only one individual). By way of illustration we may think of two collections of photographs—one comprising views of a particular church, and the other a similar number of views, but each of a different church. There may be as much variety of form and colour in the one collection as in the other, and what distinguishes the two is their different origin. If, at any given moment, we could obtain a 'still' in order to inspect what is in our mind, we should as often as not find nothing by which we could recognize whether it was an aspect of a general or of a particular idea. If a general idea, as represented in the mind at a particular moment, is indistinct, this may well be because the numerous elements of which it is composed are competing for a place in consciousness.

Even the idea of some particular thing may be quite indistinct for the same reason. The chief difference between thinking about an object or situation in its absence and actually perceiving it is that, when it is presented to our senses, we perceive one particular aspect which is changed in a definite manner by our own movements (unless, of course, the object is either a perfect sphere or, like the sun, too far away for our movements to affect the aspect it presents); whereas when we recall or imagine an object, many different aspects may compete for a place in our consciousness, and in consequence we may have a mixed or intermittant image; so that even if the several images are each clear, the total effect of the confused recall of many is vagueness and lack of distinctness.

A general idea, then, is the idea of a large number of related particulars, and the more general the idea, the larger the number of particulars from which it is derived. Statements about a general idea are understood to apply to all those individuals which are included in the group. Having constructed the general idea 'fish', I must not say that a fish is a marine animal, because there are some fish which never go into the sea. If I say that mammals suckle their young, then this has to be true of cats, mice, monkeys, and so on. To use the term 'mammal' accurately and understand propositions about it, I must be acquainted with many different species selected from all the most divergent types. If, as I have argued, even the idea of an individual thing can often be very composite, then the general idea—an idea of all the members of a group with their resemblances and differences—may be infinitely more composite; and highly general ideas can be formed and employed adequately only in the most clear-thinking and gifted minds.

Admittedly, adequacy is relative and depends on the thinker's purpose. To grow potatoes in the garden, a flimsy idea of them will suffice. It will not matter if the idea does not include all the available data. But to find a cure for potato disease requires an idea that is based on the fullest knowledge, with a much closer correspondence between the idea and the complex reality. Unless the thinker's purpose is very restricted, he will always find it necessary to supplement the momentary memories which spring into his mind when he thinks of a thing or a class of things. But many authors, ancient and modern, betray, when they write of ideas, that they suppose an idea to be one precise and particular image which can be recalled in a moment and contemplated entirely. Even Bertrand Russell at times suggests that this is what he understands by an idea. He writes for instance of *"the* image (if any) employed in thinking of William the Conqueror" (my italics), and says that, unlike the name 'William the Conqueror', it will "differ from person to person and is sure to be too concrete. If (e.g.) we think of him on horseback, that will not suit 'William was born at Falaise' because he was not born on horseback" (1948, p. 112). He evidently supposes that the "image employed in thinking" is something fixed and invariable for each person, or at least for each particular thinking operation. The name is the same for all, but the image is peculiar to each. But it is not in fact the case that someone must think of William either on a horse or in his cradle, but not both. No useful idea is ever of this nature.

The following pronouncement which Thomas Brown made in his *Lectures on the Philosophy of the Human Mind* (1830, p. 290) indicates one source of the strange belief to the contrary, namely that it is a consequence of the supposed oneness of the mind:

> I trust I need not repeat to you that, in itself, every notion, however seemingly complex, is and must be truly simple—being one state or affection of one simple substance, mind. Our conception of a whole army, for example, is as truly this one mind existing in this one state, as our conception of any one of the individuals that compose an army.

Perhaps also involved in this misconception is the feeling that our ideas of the most complicated things are really extraordinarily simple. They are certainly apt to be.

A distinction can be made between abstract and general ideas. If it is true that all the creatures included in the general group 'butterflies' have a number of common characters, we may think of these characters separately without thinking about a butterfly. Any set of qualities or characters found in a number of distinct objects may, for the purposes of thought, be dealt with apart. We may, with an effort, confine our thoughts to this set of characters *in abstraction* from all the other characters which are to be found in the objects. This becomes increasingly difficult as the group of objects from which the abstraction is derived becomes more diverse, for the abstraction then becomes more intangible, less like the idea of any actual object. Butterflies, for instance, constitute one family of the order Lepidoptera, and these have fewer features in common than those common to all butterflies, so that the abstraction 'Lepidopteron' is less descriptive, less suggestive of any existing creature. The Lepidoptera are in turn one of many orders which constitute the class 'insects', and the characters common to all insects add up to something resembling even less any existing creature. The insects are themselves one of several classes which constitute the phylum 'arthropods'. It is obvious that this is a term which only a zoologist could hope to use properly. Fortunately it is not well-known, so that few people are tempted to use it at all, otherwise it is certain that they would mostly talk nonsense. Although abstractions are formed by cutting out many particulars, insofar as they play a part in practical behaviour they are not empty but full. The proposition which refers to abstract qualities is but a condensed formula which stands for a large number of propositions about different particulars which have the qualities in common.

In sum, 'butterfly', 'lepidopteron', and so forth may be a general idea, in which case it is an idea about individuals belonging to the group, or it may be abstract, that is, an idea of the features common to all members of the group. Abstract ideas designate qualities which we recognize in things, but which do not exist independently.

General and abstract ideas can be represented in the mind at any one moment only by some part or aspect or member—even only the word the idea is called by—and the remaining components will remain on call, as we saw to be the case even with ideas of individual things. But with generalities there is infinitely more to be recalled, and with abstractions their remoteness from actual existences militates against cohesion of their components. If an expert in the field thinks of the characters common to all mammals, he forms in his mind what may be called the abstract mammal, and this may be said to be imageless both because it bears very little resemblance to any real mammal (which will possess many additional characters, many of which are much easier to observe and hence to envisage with a clear image) and also because it consists of numerous elements which compete for the place in consciousness (as we saw to be the case even with the much more tangible memories of the different aspects of a single object). It is true that certain simple qualities can easily be represented, even pictured, in isolation in our thoughts. We can abstract the redness of red objects, the sweet taste of sweet foods, the wetness of fluids, and think of such qualities apart from any particular object which possesses them. They have no shape or pattern, and are easy to envisage also because our sense organs are specifically adapted to distinguish colours, tastes, and so on. But we cannot readily think of the vertebrateness of vertebrates, the birdness of birds, or the fishiness of fishes in the same way.[3]

It is such abstract ideas that cause most trouble. Different people's ideas of individual things can be checked against the common standard of the tangible thing. But abstractions such as 'life' and 'virtue', not being the names of any concrete objects, cannot be tested in this way. However, life is that which is common to all living things, and these are concrete. To convey the idea of life to somebody who lacks that idea, we have to present not one particular thing, but a large number of representative things in such a way as to call attention to the feature or property common to all. This is how abstractions are formed naturally, and it is by the same method that they are conveyed by one person to another. We may use abstract terms, and what we say may correspond with something real, but we can explain ourselves to somebody who has not abstracted in the same manner as ourselves only if we can refer to the realities from which the abstraction is derived, or to already familiar abstractions. Explanations and arguments which involve nothing but abstractions and highly general ideas must remain unintelligible to anyone who cannot supply the particular foundations for himself. The only safeguard against mental incoherence is the constant referring of abstract ideas to the concretes from which they have been (or should have been) derived. Schopenhauer rightly insisted that he "could not too often repeat that all abstract ideas are to be checked in the light of experience".[4]

ii. THE ROLE OF WORDS

The poet and literary critic S.T. Coleridge wrote to his friend William Godwin (22 September, 1800):

> I wish you to write a book on the power of the words. . . . Is thinking impossible without arbitrary signs? And how far is the word 'arbitrary' a misnomer? Are not words, etc., parts and germinations of the plant? And what is the law of their growth? In something of this sort I would endeavour to destroy the old antithesis of Words and Things; elevating, as it were, Words into Things and living things too.

The last of these sentences reveals the metaphysical bias which prompted these questions. What Coleridge really meant to ask was: can we not find a way of making words seem more important? For words are the stock in trade of the poet and the critic, and it is therefore important for both these to feel that words constitute a specially valuable commodity.

It is not, then, surprising that the importance of language in the thinking process has often been exaggerated. Bertrand Russell says: "all fairly elaborate thoughts require words" (1948, p. 74). It depends, of course, on what is meant by elaborate. The thought of a human face or voice, or of a landscape, may be quite elaborate and yet not dependent on words. Admittedly, I cannot describe or explain something without the use of language of some kind, but this is a question of communicating, not of thinking, and it does not follow that the ideas which are thus communicated can exist in the mind only in the form in which we have to communicate them. That even abstract ideas can be formed without words is illustrated by Rignano's discussion of what he calls "affective classification", by which he means the classification of things according to their practical equivalence for an animal and not according to their objective resemblances:

> By 'house', for example, we understand a group of objects, different as much as one pleases from one another, but all fitted to shelter us from bad weather. . . . By the word 'clothing' we denote a whole group of objects fitted to protect our bodies taken as a whole from the cold. . . . Furs, woollen stuffs, cotton fabrics satisfy in varying degrees and in different fashions our need to be covered. Beds, divans, armchairs, chairs and stools satisfy to a varying extent and in different ways our need for repose. (1923, pp. 106–07; p. 147 of the French original)

In the last case there seems to be no word in English, French, or German to denote all the relevant things indifferently. The 'affectivity' is all that is required to establish the classification and create the abstract idea. When I am weary, I seek a place of repose. I certainly do not need to have a word in order to know what I want. Rignano is not concerned with the function of language at this point, otherwise he would perhaps have adverted to this.

One reason why the importance of language in thinking has been exaggerated is that often nothing but words seem to be present to the mind. Edmund Burke discusses this matter in his *A Philosophical Inquiry into the Origin of our Ideas of the Sublime and the Beautiful* (1757), saying:

> If I say 'I shall go to Italy next summer' I am well understood. Yet I believe that nobody has by this painted in his imagination the exact figure of the speaker passing by land or water or both; sometimes on horseback, sometimes in a carriage . . . Still less has he any idea of Italy . . . or of the greenness of the fields, the ripening of the fruits, and the warmth of the air, with the change to this from a different season, which are the ideas for which the word *summer* is substituted . . . In short, we converse even of particular real beings . . . without having any idea of them excited in the imagination.[5]

He wonders "if they may properly be called ideas which present no distinct image to the mind" (p. 190). But an idea is the potentiality of a large number of images, not one particular image. When we are reflecting to some purpose, we select from those that are relevant. If we have no immediate purpose, the competing images may inhibit one another completely.

The substitution of mere words for ideas is permissible and harmless when we are concerned with matters perfectly familiar to us, as we are when we speak of 'summer' or 'travel'. Campbell noted in his *Philosophy of Rhetoric,* which late in the eighteenth century became a standard handbook, that in such cases "almost all the possible applications of the terms . . . have become customary" to us, so that "an unusual application of any term is instantly detected; this detection breeds doubt, and this doubt occasions an immediate recourse to ideas", that is, to the knowledge we have of the things signified by the words, so that we immediately see the meaning or the unmeaningness of what is said.[6]

Burke also discusses the effect on the mind of terms such as 'virtue', 'persuasion', 'docility'. They may, he says, have emotional effects, but they excite no clear image, no "representation . . . of the things for which they stand" (p. 177). It is obvious that he does not realise why. If a word is specifically associated with one particular image, as the name of a picture or a tune, then the word will evoke the image unless this is inhibited by some simultaneous stimulus. But most words, especially of the type which Burke is discussing, are associated with far too many different images to be able to elicit a particular one. Moreover—and of this Burke is well aware (p. 181)—in listening to speech, that is to say a rapid succession of words, no single word has time to evoke any image before the process is interrupted by the solicitations of the words which follow. The kind of word Burke is here discussing produces a certain attitude of mind which can be described as involving a certain bias towards a class or system of images which are associated and are liable to be recalled. What in fact arises in the mind will depend on the attendant circumstances. It is the same with every other single impression. The sight of a flower, the smell of a workshop, the sound of a bell, all these impressions *may* give rise to an image of something definite. But if there are a number of different memories stirred at the same time by the stimulus, they may inhibit one another and the mind remains blank. That does not mean that the impression has been without effect. The effect may be seen as a contribution, combined with the effects of other impressions, in the composite result which comes only after an interval.

When Burke discusses the emotional effect of words, he notes that from childhood we have associated certain words with approval or disgust, and that they continue ever after to arouse similar reactions. As examples he gives "wise, valiant, gracious, good and great", and says that "these words, by having no application, ought to be inoperative" (p. 179). He is, then, puzzled that they can produce emotional effects even though they suggest no particular images or ideas. Such definite association with one or other of two emotional attitudes, to the exclusion of all others, differs entirely from the associations between words and images, of which, as we have seen, a word can suggest a great variety. Words like 'valiant' or 'good' may be associated with all kinds of different images according to the chances of each man's experience, in spite of their common emotional colouring as a pleasant and yea-saying impulse. It is not possible to describe this emotion except by enumerating the very different situations which produce it. It is therefore not difficult to see how a word may evoke an emotional attitude, but will seldom be able to evoke a particular image.

If general or abstract ideas, such as of cats as a class, or mammals, vertebrates, or even animals in general are to be of any adequacy, they have to be slowly and laboriously built up in the mind, from progressively more particulars as the idea increases in generality, although it is as easy to *talk* about animals as about cats. The conventions of language make no difference between such words, all of which can equally well be made the subject or object of a sentence; but the similarity of grammatical form does not correspond to any similarity of conceptual content. There is, of course, no reason why it should, and language would be impossibly complex if such correspondence were aimed at. Real capacity, intellectual or practical, varies widely between individuals, but the power of speech is much more evenly distributed; and whereas ideas of any considerable compass may take years to form, a word is learned in a few minutes.

I do not mean to deny the advantages which language confers in thinking (quite apart from its use as a means of communication). When a clear idea has been linked to a verbal formula, the latter has only to be recalled to revive the former; and since long strings of verbal sequences can be committed to the memory comparatively easily, this is a convenient way of memorising complex ideas—ideas which require time to develop, but which do so readily once the process has been initiated. 'William the Conqueror became king of England in 1066' is an easily remembered formula which I can expand into full and significant ideas when required. But formulas which are linked with complicated and extensive ideas in some minds can be learned by others without the ideas. Provided the terms are not wholly unfamiliar to them, they may not realize their failure to understand the relevant ideas, and in trying to assimilate these, they will distort and simplify them.

This situation is a familiar one in schools and colleges. If at the outset the solution is presented with the problem to a student, the knowledge he acquires is often merely verbal. But as the period of instruction is short and the syllabus extensive, this is commonly what is done; and the students of today will be the professors of tomorrow.

In such cases, no deliberate deception is involved. However, as soon as there is any merit attached to the possession of knowledge, there will be a tendency to claim more than one has; and if one knows a little more than the majority, there exist techniques for giving this little the appearance of much. Voltaire says somewhere (I have lost the reference): "C'est le défaut de la jeunesse de croire que les choses communes peuvent recevoir un caractère de nouveauté par des expressions obscures". Alas! In the eighteenth century it may have been an error of youth; in the twentieth it has become almost universal. But although an error in the logical sense, it is no error from the business point of view, and many a lasting reputation has been built up by these means.

It is possible for an honest attempt at explanation to become combined with an affectation of knowledge when a theory is partly the result of a serious effort to explain something, but has its weak points disguised by a little plausible verbosity. The confusion need not be deliberate. When someone's thinking processes are sufficiently vague and confused, he is not really capable of knowing when he is speaking or writing coherently.

Different again is the hocus-pocus of inspiration. When someone believes he is giving voice to some mysterious knowledge imparted by superior beings, he may not try to understand, being content to act as a passive instrument. But the impressive circumstances of the utterance may have a persuasive effect even on those who are capable of superior intellectual processes, who may try very hard to interpret and make sense of what they hear. We then get a theory framed to satisfy two requirements: it must justify the revelation and be not too unplausible in itself. The same happens when, instead of the audible words of the visible prophet or seer, there exists an ancient and venerable tradition to be interpreted, perhaps by interpreters who are more intelligent than the propounder of the old tradition and who seek to adapt their theories to his inferior formula. However, plausible ideas are not readily achieved by this process, as we see from arguments about 'the spirit' (disagreement as to whether it proceeds from the Father or from the Father and the Son—'filioque' in the Nicene creed—helped to cause the split between eastern and western Christianity in 1054), and from the endless reinterpretations of "this is my body" (Mark 14:22 and parallels) and of Pauline statements about the relation between baptism and 'the spirit'. Recent forms of words on these two matters have been said by some candid apologists to be unintelligible to them.[7] Such protests would surely be more common but for the widespread belief that impressive-sounding formulations necessarily represent complex ideas; and this belief is in turn encouraged by the common assumption that words and ideas belong inseparably together.

Theologians are certainly apt to take this view. Sanders and Davies, in a book which will occupy us in a later chapter, declare that "we cannot think without words", even that someone's thoughts are indistinguishable from his words (1989, pp. 222–23). And G.B. Caird, in a book on the language of the Bible, likewise holds that "language is the indispensable vehicle of thought", so that "thinking may be described as talking to oneself" (1980, pp. 7, 12, 19). Theologians naturally form their views on thinking by reflection only on the type of thinking that is their professional concern. But this is not good enough. Until the comparative method is accepted as essential—until, that is, we take cognisance of what human thinking has in common with that of other mammals—we shall not understand how man comes by his ideas and his delusions. For this reason I shall devote some attention in the next section of this chapter to the thinking process in animals.

It has often been supposed that general ideas cannot be formed without words, and that animals other than man can therefore have no such ideas.[8] But we saw that there is no fundamental distinction between the particular and the general idea; and although animals do not talk, they react to things in other ways. A dog is obviously able to distinguish between the generality of cats, towards whom he is hostile, and the particular cat who is his housemate. And if animals react in the same way to a number of distinct objects or situations, this is often because they are abstracting the common features of those situations.[9]

iii.   THE THINKING PROCESS IN SCIENTIST, LAYMAN, AND CHIMPANZEE

The process of thinking, as something distinct from day-dreaming, involves representing to oneself some real situations or actions, some actual things in relation to one another; and if the process is not to be futile, these representations must behave in relation to other thoughts in the same manner as the things they represent behave in relation to their environment. The only guarantee that my thoughts will fulfil this condition is that I remember correctly what I have experienced. For instance, I hear a sound, and need to think out what event it signals. Is it a burglar fingering the door-handle, a mouse in the wainscot, a hedgehog snoring in the garden or a tap dripping in the bathroom? For each of these experimental theories some kind of test can be applied by recalling in greater detail the character of the imagined event. It cannot be a burglar, the rhythm is too regular, nor a hedgehog, for the sound is too shrill. Suddenly I remember the frozen pipes in the roof and realise that water is dripping through a ceiling. My reaction to the situation is thus delayed by a process of trial and error which goes on in the mind. Karl Popper sees in this the essence of scientific thinking, as well as of ordinary deliberation: "Deliberation always works by trial and error, or, more precisely, by the method of trial and of error-elimination" (1975, p. 234); we tentatively put forward some theory to explain something, and then envisage what this theory implies. If these implications are not fulfilled, we eliminate the theory (1972, p. 51). He notes that what is called today 'negative feed back' is only an application of this "general method of learning from our mistakes" (p. ix); and "the growth of scientific knowledge may be said to be the growth of ordinary human knowledge *writ large"* (p. 216). Science simply uses the method more consciously, deliberately seeks out evidence that will discredit a theory, and accepts the theory (and then only as provisional) only if it survives such rigorous testing. Knowledge thus progresses "by guesses, by tentative solutions to our problems, by *conjectures.* These conjectures are controlled by criticism; that is, by attempted *refutations,* which include severely critical tests" (p. vii). He holds that, if a theory is not testable, it is not scientific, although it may nevertheless be true.

Some (particularly the so-called 'creationists' who defend the accounts of the origin of life given in Genesis) have said that the theory of evolution is unscientific in this sense, a dogma which no conceivable evidence could refute. Geologists (for instance Strahler 1987, p. 76) have replied that the theory would be refuted if human fossils were found in the company of, say, dinosaur ones in such a way that the contemporaneity of the two life forms was beyond reasonable doubt. Although no such finding has occurred, it is a conceivable possibility.

Popper also notes that the "method of learning from our mistakes" is "fundamentally also the method used by living organisms in the process of adaptation" (p. 312), and is the same "whether practised . . . by chimpanzees or by men of science" (p. 216). But it is important to stress—as earlier writers had done—the distinction between on the one hand actually making trials or experiments and observing whether the results expected from them materialise, and on the other merely envisaging in the mind the implications of theories.[10] The latter process may, as in the case of interpreting a noise, consist in a series of experimental extrapolations: part of the situation is given, visually or audibly, and the mental experimentation supplies what is lacking, being in such cases akin to the simpler phenomenon of perception. The difference is that perception may be almost instantaneous because of the extremely strong and relatively restricted associations involved—a black streak passing through undergrowth can immediately be recognised as a dog—while mental experimentation is a protracted process in which associated memories can be evoked only one at a time. It is a process that is helpful not only *vis-à-vis* situations which affect us when we merely attend to them passively, but also in relation to those where we intervene actively in order to modify them. How, for instance, can I cross the river that is facing me? Can I jump or swim across, wade it, or find a ford? Is there a bridge or a fallen tree trunk over which I could walk? The river may be presented to my senses in an aspect which does not answer any of these questions. Actual experimentation on the ground would mean trying the activities in question in random order. But if I have met this river before in different places, I may be able—by recalling one of the aspects experienced at that time—to decide on a course of action which takes advantage of some feature not now immediately discernible.

The process of converting the present situation into another and more helpful one may involve all kinds of actions envisaged in the mind and only then carried out. Wolfgang Köhler, who investigated the thinking process in chimpanzees, claimed that they are capable of a great deal in this regard. In his experiments, these animals were under some kind of instinctive impulse—in particular, hunger—but in a situation where they had no appropriate immediate reaction to deal with the case. Sometimes they did not attempt any immediate physical experimentation, but were quiet and inactive, although apparently attending to the situation. After an interval they set to work and performed the appropriate series of actions which achieved the result aimed at, without any groping or experimentation. It looks as if they had carried out experiments in their imagination with the aid of memory. In ourselves we know that this is what happens.

Let me detail some of Köhler's examples. When food is presented outside the bars of the cage and out of reach, the chimpanzees recognize a situation that can be exploited with a pole, and so go in search of one. In one experiment the animal, during his search, came across an old box in which he recognized a potential pole and accordingly broke off a slat, with which he returned to the cage bars and drew in the food. That mental experimentation is involved in all this is shown by his behaviour. There is no actual physical trial in the presence of the initial situation: he does not try out various possibilities at random on the ground until he happens to hit upon some action that helps him. The focus of the situation, the food, is ignored, and the animal turns away from it under the guidance of a new goal, the pole. We assume therefore that he was able, in the presence of the first situation, to supply in his imagination the feature missing in it and to see himself, in his mind's eye, converting this situation into a favourable one with the aid of this feature. The box is not a pole, but a deliberate effort to detach a slat suggests that the ape has realised that he can extract a pole from it, and this also implies thinking. It shows that these animals can not only use but also make tools for a preconceived purpose. They can use a box as a ladder and improve the ladder by putting one box on another. In a paper originally published in 1921 Köhler pointed, apropos of tool making, to the way in which Sultan, one of the more intelligent apes, would "labour long to sharpen one end of a wooden board so that it will afterwards fit into a tube", thus providing him with a stick of double length with which to reach fruit that cannot be reached with either the board or the tube alone (1927, p. 272). Substitutes for sticks which these animals sought out included not only slats torn from boxes, but also branches from trees, bars broken from a shoe-scraper and screwed-up bundles of straw. It is as if the animal had formed for himself a definition of the tool required, not of course in any kind of language, but in terms of the task to be accomplished. He knows, from comparison of visual aspects, that it must be of a certain length; and from his muscular and tactile experience, he knows that it must have a certain weight and rigidity, so that a rope or a blanket will not do. He seems, then, to carry in his mind something which may permit him to recognize the essential characters of what he requires, in whatever combination with other characters it may happen to be presented; and this something may fairly be called an abstract idea. In Köhler's words: the stick "has acquired a certain functional value for certain situations, and . . . this effect extends to all other objects which have certain highly general qualities of form and consistency objectively in common with the stick, whatever they may otherwise look like" (1921, pp. 23–26, 73). The animal of course does not always have in mind all the relevant features of what he needs, and so sometimes chooses inappropriate tools — returning, for instance, in triumph with a stick, only to find that it is not quite long enough.

Köhler's findings have been amply confirmed by Jane van Lawick Goodall, who observed chimpanzees over a period of years in their natural African habitat. She saw that they chew a handful of leaves, so making them more absorbent, and then use them as a sponge to soak up water to drink from a place not directly accessible, such as the bottom of a hollow in a tree. They not only get termites to eat by pushing a long grass stem or twig into their nest, but also make a given twig more usable for this purpose by first stripping off its leaves (1971, pp. 47–48, 104). Such behaviour presupposes mental experimentation.

It is hardly surprising that a capacity which so obviously confers advantages on animals possessing it should have been evolved. "To find a way of getting from tree A to tree B whilst still sitting safely in tree A is far better than tackling the problem in a trial-and-error fashion on the ground, with the risk of being attacked by predators" (Davey 1981, p. 320). Nevertheless, that any creatures other than man are capable of such thinking is not generally acknowledged, and many still treat Köhler's conclusions with considerable reserve. Walker, for instance, allows only that his observations "should stand for evidence for sophisticated spacial memory and object manipulation in the chimpanzee" (1987, p. 348). Köhler of course claimed that the animals can manipulate not merely objects, but also ideas of objects, that they can, as Davey puts it, "shuffle around cognitively the elements of the problem until the correct solution is reached" (1981, p. 305). Davey thinks that this is "perhaps an overstatement", for two reasons; first, it has been shown that "previous experience with some of the objects in a problem-solving situation aided solution of the problem". This is surely not surprising: the experience gained in actual trial on the ground provides the material on which thinking can work. Indeed, it cannot work from any other basis: even we human beings do not imagine processes or events which we have not, at least in their elements, experienced. Davey's second objection is that chimpanzees can "generate quite sophisticated forms of behaviour" (such as fitting sticks together and piling boxes on top of each other) "during their play"; and elements of such behaviour that are relevant to a solution "may well occur 'by chance' in a problem-solving situation" (p. 308). Köhler's observations convinced him that chance was often not involved, that experience that had been gained elsewhere, whether in play or business, was deliberately exploited. As Davey is aware, Köhler was impressed by the fact that so often the animals appeared to hit on the correct solution "very suddenly—one moment they would be completely baffled by the problem, the next moment they would very suddenly and spontaneously execute the correct sequence of responses" (p. 305).

Of great significance is that this abrupt transition could occur when the problem situation was no longer actually visible to the animal. On one occasion, for instance, fruit had been attached to the roof and could easily be reached by standing on a box, but the only available box was out of sight in an adjacent corridor. Sultan made some futile attempts to reach the fruit, and Köhler then took him along the corridor and back to make sure he knew that the box was there, but did not attempt to point it out to him. The only immediate effect was that after the return from this little journey, Sultan clasped Köhler's hand firmly and tried to drag him to under the fruit, apparently intending to jump onto his back. When Köhler pushed him away, Sultan looked round for something that would serve him as a tool, and lighted upon a long bolt fastened to a door. While trying to detach it he hung upon the door in such a position that he could not see the fruit; and the box in the corridor was completely out of sight round a corner. This is Köhler's account of what then happened:

> Abruptly and without external occasion, Sultan stops working at the bolt, remains for an instant motionless, then jumps to the ground, gallops along the corridor and returns immediately with the box. (1921, p. 38)

Clearly, at the moment when Sultan stopped motionless, although both box and fruit were invisible to him, they were represented in his brain; and, in his mind's eye, he saw himself moving the former to under the latter. In other words, he carried out, in imagination, a manipulation which he then proceeded to carry out in fact.

The mistakes which Köhler's animals sometimes made in their quests for tools bring home the fact that what can be done in the imagination depends on memory and association, and these may represent the nature of objects in the real world only very imperfectly. With human beings, replacing concrete memories and associations with words constitutes an additional hazard, putting the whole process at one further remove from reality. But quite apart from the problems introduced by language, any representation of the real world in any mind, animal or human, can be but flimsy compared with the reality, and behaviour based on such an inadequate mental picture may lead to serious error, particularly since effective action must be based on confidence. When we have reviewed all our relevant beliefs, and found some favourable and others not to a course of action, we have to make our choice; and unless we can at this crucial moment suppress all the contrary tendencies, our action will be half-hearted, even if it occurs at all. Man is here most at risk, for he exceeds all other creatures in his capacity to build up representations in his brain and orientate his behaviour towards them.

Many men, for instance, are prompted to deal with a particular situation facing them by some mental representation of, say, Christianity in the first century or the Russian Revolution in the twentieth—a representation that may correspond only very imperfectly to what actually happened at these past times and remote places—or of some distant future prospect, such as eternal salvation.[11]

Men who harbour quite flimsy notions on such issues may have perfectly adequate and highly complex ones on matters where beliefs can be immediately tested by practical applications. The geologist Strahler has noted, apropos of the fact that technicians highly competent in their own fields side with the 'creationists' in the Evolution/Creation controversy:

> Much, if not all, of applied science, including engineering and technology, can be practiced with a narrow framework of specialisation that does not come into relevant contacts of any kind with religious beliefs or, for that matter, with any intellectual activities. A person who designs dams, or computers, or aircraft, is free to pick and choose from what the arts and humanities have to offer and to place those objects in a different mental compartment from that of the daily job (1987, p. 70).[12]

In sum, a belief is a hypothesis: it supplies the remainder of a situation of which only an aspect or phase is either directly present to the senses or represented by some remaining trace such as a historical document. If the hypothesis is wrong or inadequate, behaviour based on it may be ineffectual. In the field of daily domestic business and in the practical arts and crafts, where the results of every measure are quickly seen, false theories can soon be eliminated. But where verification is difficult, the construction of hypotheses is much freer, and the choice may be determined by some factor other than adequacy—such as their tendency to flatter or comfort the believer. That religious beliefs are describable in such terms is admitted even by those who maintain their correctness. For instance Alan Richardson (Dean of York from 1964 until his death in 1975) finds it "adequate from an anthropological or sociological standpoint" to define religion as man's quest for "security, status and permanence", a means of making the realities of his condition "more bearable" and of assuring himself that "there is significance in his existence" (1966, p. 16). The importance of comforting emotions for doctrinal developments is acknowledged, as when, for instance, Wiles shows that the decisive factor in Athanasius's victory over Arius was the need felt by popular Christian piety for a saviour who was fully divine (1967, pp. 96–97). "If the issues at stake had been matter for intellectual argument alone, the pattern of development would have been very different" (p. 87).

iv. THE HISTORIAN'S THINKING

Historians who repudiated any suggestion of providential control of human affairs have repeatedly been subjected to abusive criticism: Herder, for instance, in the eighteenth century, H.T. Buckle in the nineteenth, and J.M. Robertson in the twentieth. The whole burden of the opening sections of Herder's principal work is to show, by comparing man, body and mind, with other animals, that he is a natural species, and that his behaviour must be understood in the same way as that of any other natural thing. Herder argued on these lines long before the theory of evolution was well established to support him. Buckle, who accepted Herder's naturalistic views and sought inductive generalizations from historical facts, was subjected to almost unparalleled abuse, as J.M. Robertson (1895) ably showed. Robertson himself, who defended Buckle's method while correcting some of his mistakes, fared no better, as Andreski (1987) and others have shown in a volume assessing Robertson's achievement.

Historians hostile to Herder's method have explicitly denied that history is a science. "The concept of cause", says Croce, "must and should remain outside history because it was born in the realm of natural science and its place is there" (1941, p. 28). The implication of this "simple and fundamental truth", as he calls it, is that there is a linkage between the events with which science is concerned, but not between those of history; that the relation between, for example, heat and the vaporization of water is not for a moment to be compared with that between, say, the character of a ruler and the warlike activities of his country.

The basis of this distinction between history and science is that, to say that one thing is the cause of another implies a generalization (whenever the one is given, the other occurs); and generalization can be based only on the observation of regularity and recurrence, so that if the event and the circumstances in question are unique—and this is the case with historical phenomena—there can be no generalisation.

In Britain this view that there can be no science of history because the events of history are not repeated has been popularized by Collingwood. He objected to "the very idea of a science of human nature" (1946, pp. 224–25) and said:

> History is its own criterion; it does not depend for its validity on something outside itself, it is an autonomous form of thought with its own principles and its own methods. Its principles are the laws of the historical spirit and no others; and the historical spirit creates itself in the work of historical inquiry. (1946, p. 140)

This is a convenient doctrine since it makes the historian sole judge of the credibility of any alleged occurrence, however little he may know of anything but history. Thus mere astronomical probabilities need not be considered when the story of the Magi and their guiding star is criticised. If the 'historical spirit' pronounces favourably, the matter is settled.

I have shown elsewhere (Wells 1959, pp. 223ff) that a distinction between history and science was first influentially argued by Schopenhauer, whose motive was certainly not religious. As a philosopher, he despised the historians and their mere narrating of historical facts, and pleaded for a philosophical interpretation of these in the light of general principles of human behaviour. Many modern writers have, however, appealed to him in order to justify their conviction that history deals with things that have very little in common, whereas scientific ideas are formed by ignoring the respects in which a number of objects differ and concentrating on their shared qualities. Such views were very widespread at the beginning of the present century. "A scientific conception of the Germans", said Rickert, "may contain only what is common to all Germans," and must ignore their "incomparable" features, these being, however, historically the most important (1913, p. 263). This argument assumes that science is concerned exclusively with the kind of ideas which, in the first section of this chapter, I have called abstract, and never with those that I have called general. It has nevertheless been widely held. Xénopol, for instance, said in 1899 (p. 214):

> To arrive at generalizations from historical sequences, it is necessary to suppress their differences—to suppress, that is, the essential element, destroying the distinctive character of the event studied.

And Dilthey:

> History . . . ignores the traits in the life of individuals and societies which, in the epoch under consideration, are the same as those of all other epochs. History looks for what is individual and distinctive (1923, p. 28).

Max Weber commented on this kind of argumentation that to assess the historical significance of Bismarck by ignoring all that he had in common with other persons would entail concentrating on his fingerprints (1949, p. 129). Even these can hardly be said to have absolutely nothing in common with those of others. But the argument that generalizations cut out particulars was so widely accepted that those historians who believed it their function to generalize declared that this made them independent of historical facts! Thus Lamprecht spoke of "modern historical science" as having "brought the historian the independence from scientific material that characterises all advanced sciences" (1897, p. 38). "What is individual", he said, "is accessible only to artistic perception", and so "its comprehension can therefore only be a secondary matter in historical science" (1899, p. 49). The more sober historians naturally regarded this as ridiculous; Eduard Meyer said it makes learning historical facts "almost superfluous" and gives its practitioners a quite unjustified sense of superiority over "the conservative spirits who still tread the old paths, unable to get away from the facts" (1924, p. 12).

Major historical occurrences, such as the career of Bismarck or the 1914 war, are of course unique. But they admit of analysis into simpler events, concerning which generalizations are possible; and if we thus know the behaviour of the components, we may be able to deduce that of the composite. The non-recurrence of the greater events is due to the endless new combinations of their components. Perhaps even no game of chess is ever repeated, but every one is composed of the same few moves. Wars characteristically include battles, sieges, negotiations, and so forth, each one of which resembles, to some extent, the others, and so gives scope for generalization.

Even simple events are not repeated exactly. Breakfast varies from one occasion to another, but can be analysed into components that are less variable. Again, he started up the car, put up his umbrella, lit a cigarette: the sequence of movements for each of these actions may never be exactly the same on successive occasions, but we reckon it to be so because, for all the purposes that concern us, it is effectively the same. Equivalence is thus what is important, not equality. A particular fact or event is defined in relation to some human interest or need, and in this relation a good deal of variation between facts does not destroy their equivalence.

The more our powers of observation and measurement are increased, the less do we find exact recurrence or perfect equality. Seen from afar, riots are all much alike, but if one is interested in the participants, each one is unique. However, the character of a thing can sometimes be better discerned when detail is obliterated.

Science is familiar enough with the ideas of growth, development, metamorphosis, evolution, and other cumulative processes. No generalizations are possible concerning them unless they are recurrent or compounded of constituent processes that are recurrent. If we found the germ of a hitherto unknown organism and were able to watch it develop, we could at no stage predict the next unless we could detect some analogy or resemblance between that part of the development already observed and the development of some other organism previously known. By assuming certain fundamental functions, such as respiration and nourishment, we might sometimes be able to guess the destiny of a particular rudimentary organ, but that would be only an inference from our knowledge of organisms in general. If in the development of human society we can observe, in the same way, a continuous, new and non-recurrent process, it is not possible for us to infer the later stages from an observation of the earlier unless we have experience of other analogous processes. There are of course so many variables that prediction of any historical developments can never be more than tentative. Admittedly, both the severance of the American colonies from the motherland and the French Revolution were repeatedly foretold. But even a simple event, like the fall of a tile from a roof, is not an instance of one general principle or law, but the result of the interaction of several such laws, and often the way they combine cannot be foreseen and may be hard to establish even in retrospect. To make predictions about human social organization is so rash that one could venture on it only with the aid of very comprehensive ignorance.[13]

In all historical reconstructions we have to infer the past from the present, from the documents or other evidence now before us. And our inferences can have no other basis but observation of the normal course of things.

There can be no ground for inferring an ancient salt lake from the present distribution of the New Red Sandstone, with its lack of fossils, its deposits of salt, its ripple-marked surfaces with reptilian footprints, except on the strength of such generalizations as: fishes cannot live in water of a certain degree of salinity; soft sand on the shores of extensive waters is moulded by the waves and often retains the traces of animals that prowl across it; and when waters created by inland drainage dry up they leave deposits of salt. Thus, inferences from the present to the past, like those from the present to the future, depend on generalizations. These may be explicit and clearly formulated, or they may be vaguely assumed, but every inference, logical or illogical, implies some assumed correlation between facts.

The objection to historical generalization is not normally held to veto the use by historians of any generalizations at all, for no reasoning is possible without them. Every common noun denotes an idea derived from a more or less wide induction. If the historian tells us that Alfred was king of the West Saxons, he assumes that we shall attach some notion to the words 'king' and 'West Saxons', and this would be impossible if we had not met them in other contexts, from which we had extracted the general notion by which we are able to understand these words. Again, when the historian pronounces on the motives of his hero or the causes of some event, he has at his command a mass of naive psychology, made up of knowledge of his own mental processes and motives, and those of the people he knows, and a mass of everyday knowledge of what conditions produce what effects. This knowledge I call naive because it is based on very limited experience, and is also unsystematized, not clearly formulated in principles; and so when he applies it deductively to the persons or events of the past, he often fails to realize that any principles are involved. Nevertheless, when he infers, in some historical episode, a man's purposes from his actions, he can do so only on the assumption of some generalization. When, for instance, Froude observes that "it is incredible that the King would have persevered in the appointment of Becket to the See of Canterbury if he had been made distinctly to understand what Becket meant to do", this presupposes the generalization that circumspect persons do not appoint to positions of power men who intend to do them down. When, elsewhere, Froude explains the popularity among the clergy of Newman's movement by saying that "sacerdotalism gave them professional consequence", he implies the generalization that persons tend to be attracted to that which increases their kudos. It is only when assertions are made about the behaviour of things less familiar to us that we are bound to be aware that generalizations are implied. The geologist who explains the past with the aid of laws formed inductively from study of the present course of nature is fully conscious of doing so. He does not know from common everyday experience what effects are correlated with glacial or lagoonal conditions, but has to find this out by patient observation.[14]

When the historian or philosopher objects to historical generalizations, he is thinking of generalizations of this kind, those that are not obvious enough to be taken for granted; he is objecting to such 'laws' as Bury's, that "pressure from without, whether on a nation or a race, tends to promote unity and cohesion within", and that "in the case of a nation the danger of foreign attack increases the sense of unity among individual citizens and strengthens the central power" (1913, p. 322; cf. below, p. 68). It is noteworthy that historians who protest that there can be no such laws, because the important events of history are not repeated, are apt to make generalizations of precisely this kind when they write history instead of philosophizing about it. Collingwood, for instance, implies in his *Roman Britain* that when two nations come into steady contact and cross their stocks, both will benefit, unless perhaps there is a very great disparity between their respective culture-stages or between their stocks. He even expresses the hope that his study of Roman Britain will reveal principles which may be found useful in interpreting other periods of history (1934, pp. 7, 13).

Some historians who have formulated laws in accordance with which historical events are to be understood have been as hostile to regarding history as a science and as concerned to defend religion as those who have held the quest for historical generalizations to be impossible. A.J. Toynbee, for instance, begins his *The Study of History* by declaring that "the scientific method of thought . . . has been devised for thinking about Inanimate Nature" and is inapplicable to "historical thought, which is a study of living creatures" (1934, i, 7). In fact, scientific methods differ in every branch of scientific study, not all of which are restricted to the inanimate. There are, of course, general principles of evidence and reasoning that apply universally, and these are binding even on the historian.

Toynbee tries to uphold the distinction he is making by adding: "No practical man . . . would think of conducting a nursery garden on the principles of a factory" or vice versa; "and in the world of ideas, the corresponding misapplications of method ought to be avoided by scholars." Hence we should not "treat living creatures as though they were inanimate" (p. 8). What, then, are the principles of a nursery garden? Its manager has to procure materials and distribute them to the places where they are to be used, and must employ persons and machines for this purpose. The former must be paid and the latter kept in good repair. In all these respects he has the same problems as the manager of a factory. If by 'principles' we are to understand business or technical methods, then these will have certain similarities in both concerns because of the universal requirements of business in modern society— advertisement, account keeping, and so forth—and certain differences due to the different kinds of product. The contrast between the study of animate and that of the inanimate is not necessarily much greater than that between any one study and another. Toynbee's view is motivated in part by the natural desire of the specialist not to be beholden to some other kind of specialist whose work he cannot criticize. If a historian's conclusions have to be based on principles established in any of the sciences, then they are apt to be upset when the latter are changed; and he is naturally reluctant to build on foundations whose strength he is himself quite unable to judge. But this tendency of the investigator to claim that his conclusions cannot be called in question by appeal to facts and theories outside his jurisdiction results in an unscientific segregation of domains. Science is one, in that no theory in one field is acceptable if incompatible with accepted theories in all others.

Toynbee's historical 'laws' turn out to be entirely nugatory. His technique consists in using a word without any precise meaning and applying it with the aid of metaphor, analogy or equivocation to as many diverse things as possible. Vague, often merely verbal parallels are taken for universal principles. These are not applicable to anything, but as there is no thought of applying them, this defect is overlooked. He writes, for instance, of "the law of progressive simplification", a "correlation between improvement in technique and simplification in apparatus." Examples: the steam engine was replaced by the internal combustion engine; electric telegraphy and telephony no longer require metal wires; Egyptian and Babylonian writing systems became partially simplified, and alphabetic writing is distinctly simpler; many languages have abandoned elaborate inflections; clothes have become simpler since Louis XIV. He then decides that "etherialisation" is a better term for all these tendencies, for the process of simplification "liberates forces that have been imprisoned in a more material medium and thereby sets them free to work in a more etherial medium with a greater potency." There is "a transfer of energy, or shift of emphasis, from some lower sphere of being or sphere of action" to a higher one. Examples: Socrates transferred his interest from the physical to the psychic sphere, and the "etherialisation of our modern Western Art" when "the sceptre passed from . . . Architecture to . . . Music", so that the *élan* of artistic impulse "was thus, as it were, translated from the grosser medium of stone into the subtler medium of sound" (1934, iii, pp. 176–187).

Toynbee's account of the rise of Christianity illustrates his methods:

> The essence of the Christian Church, which at once differentiates it as an institution from the Roman Empire and explains how it was able to go on living and growing when the Empire perished, was the germ of creative power which it harboured, under apparently unfavourable conditions, in a social environment where the once potent indigenous forces of creation had failed. (1934, i, p. 57)

'Germs of creative power' are not very promising as ideas with which to explain cultural developments, and one cannot have the slightest confidence in such metaphorical expressions. If this is to rank as an explanation, we should have to know what this creative power is and how it is related to Christianity, and this is made no clearer by saying that it was the "essence" of the Christian Church.

Toynbee's fundamental method is little different from that of Marx and Engels, who summarize past events in a formula consisting of very ambiguous words, and then extrapolate: the formula is projected into the future and made to yield whatever seems convenient. A good example is Engels's claim, in his *Anti-Dühring,* that practically the whole of what exists develops in accordance with what he calls the law of negation of the negation: a phenomenon is followed by its negation, and this is in turn negated, giving some kind of better edition of the original phenomenon. To carry this argument through he has to give 'negation' so broad a meaning that any event or set of circumstances can be so regarded. He supposes that property is negated when it changes hands, that a seed is negated when it germinates, an egg when it is broken, and an algebraical quantity when it is multiplied by -1.[15] It is always possible to describe all manner of different processes by the same word, but no real generalization can be reached in this way.

v. THE ROLE OF ANALOGIES

My discussion of Toynbee and of Engels raises the questions: what place can the search for analogies have in thinking and in arguments that are really meaningful, and how does it come so often to be abused?

If an animal learns to deal with a particular situation, he must be able to apply his acquired knowledge or skill in other similar ones. The fox learns that guinea-fowl is good to eat by catching certain individuals whom he can never hope to see again. If what he has thereby acquired is to be described as knowledge or habit, he must transfer this behaviour to similar individuals whom he later encounters. My friend's dog, having on a few occasions met me coming along a particular path through the wood at a particular time of day, is on subsequent days on the look out for me at the same time and place if she happens to be there. She does not express herself in words, but her action implies the belief that this sequence of events is normal and can be relied on. She has generalized and is anticipating a consequent from a known antecedent.

This process of extending to many new cases what has been learned with one or a few implies that the same situation recurs and that the same reaction to it can be repeated. But as we saw, events never repeat themselves exactly, and so in acting on such generalizations an animal must not be too particular. Pavlov showed that in fact a similar situation suffices, and that the similarity need not be at all close. When his dogs were shown circles immediately before being fed, they soon began to salivate in expectation of food, and did so even when shown ellipses of varying eccentricity. He called this stage, when a fairly wide range of similar stimuli evokes the same reaction, the phase of generalization, and showed that further experience gradually narrows this range by eliminating the relevant responses in the case of those situations which lie outside certain limits of variation. If the dogs were presented with food only after the appearance of a circle, they rapidly ceased to salivate when they were shown an ellipse. Thus the phase of generalization is followed by the phase of concentration. At first, then, most differences in the situation are overlooked if certain conspicuous features are present, while later only those differences are overlooked which do not in fact affect the situation in relation to the animal, who thus learns to recognise what, for his purposes or needs, are its essential features.[16] But for the phase of generalization (the possibility of reacting to a new situation as if it were an old one) there could be no learning and no intelligent behaviour. But if this phase were not followed by the phase of concentration, the learning would often be disadvantageous to the animal.

Scientific thinking follows the same sequence, and passes from a first rough generalization, which is no more than an approximation, to specifying only the essential factors. The important thing is to multiply observations with varying conditions so as to establish the real correlations. In some cases this can be done by constructing the conditions in the laboratory, but in others—biology, geology, astronomy, for example—one can with patience and time establish correlations and generalizations by merely accumulating observations and recording as exactly as possible the conditions.

Generalization based on seeing likenesses is thus inevitable in thinking. The most valuable likenesses are those which are correlated with many others. When the older zoologists noticed some respect in which a bat resembles a mammal rather than a bird, they were encouraged to investigate further to see whether it resembles a mammal in other less conspicuous features. In this way generalization aids and encourages inquiry. It is very much easier to explore and experiment when there is a definite question to answer. Similarities are thus suggestive.

Science may be said to begin when both observation and experiment become deliberate and conscious. And there is no clear line of distinction between these two. The experiment is a set of observations in which the observer exercises a greater amount of control. The aim in either case is to discover correlations, to find out what events go together, whether in space or time. All mammalian behaviour depends on knowledge of correlation, so that scientific activity involves nothing new except awareness of the purpose. Science is only a refined form of the ordinary practical methods of dealing with the world and with ourselves. There is no difference, in principle, between learning to open a ginger-beer bottle and learning to prepare hydrogen gas. Knowledge and manipulative skill are needed in both cases. One cannot, then, make any distinction between science and knowledge; science is not a branch of knowledge, but the discipline of all thought. There is no domain of the human intellect not amenable to scientific treatment.

It is quite easy to see superficial analogies. The psychologist and physiologist Alexander Bain noted, apropos of Lorenz Oken's suggestion that the skull consists of a number of modified vertebrae, that such "brilliant identifications" are not always useful. Oken, he said, had "a fertile analogical brain", but "never took any steps to prove the reality of a supposed identification." "Of the many hundreds of analogies that he set forth . . . , there are probably not twenty that are sound" (1894, pp. 527–28).

Oken was like an animal that could perform only Pavlov's phase of generalization. If a modern scientist were to follow his example by generalizing freely and failing to narrow his generalizations by recourse to control experiments, he would find plenty of other scientists only too willing to criticize and correct him. On such matters, a much greater, and quite unwarranted tolerance is shown towards historians, political writers, and religious apologists.

Without some expectation of uniformity in the environment (including the behaviour of other animals), no animal could ever confidently interpret the situations facing it, for the number of possible interpretations would then be unlimited. Since animals other than man do in fact anticipate events from known antecedents; since things are linked in their experience, so that when the one happens, the other is looked for, it is ridiculous to claim that theism, let alone Christianity, is responsible for the belief in order in nature on which science rests. Yet such a claim has often been made. A.E. Taylor writes:

> The conception of God as perfect and flawless intelligence is manifestly the source of our rooted belief in the presence of intelligible order and system throughout nature; it has created the intellectual temper from which modern science itself has arisen. (1945, p. 2)

Similarly Richardson, although he admits that scientific knowledge "is basically ordinary 'common sense', . . . in germ as old as the first attempts of primitive men to devise an instrument—an axe head or a flint", nevertheless holds that "the Christian view of the world was a necessary precondition of science's emergence", as it rests on "the principle of the uniformity of nature"—an assumption that "has been made in Europe for hardly more than three or four hundred years" (1957, pp. 5–7, 12). Raven too believes that "the Christian schema, though plainly defective in its details as to the origin and the end of creation, yet had established a belief in an order and movement in the course of events which, if expressed in too crude a teleology, yet gave scientists their impulse towards the discovery of evolutionary developments" (1943, p. 25). He thinks it significant that very few of "the thousands who were done to death by the Inquisition or the lawcourts" were scientists, and that "the early scientists . . . were Christians" (p. 24). He fails to note what severe inconveniences they would have suffered, had they not been. It is significant that Copernicus carefully refrained from publishing his book for 36 years until he was on his death-bed (see Draper, 1923, p. 168). And if the Christian world-view was, as Richardson claims, "a necessary precondition of science's emergence", we shall have to deny that Archimedes, among many others, were scientists.

Popular apologists continue to make irresponsible

claims—not by incorrectly stating details (a thing too easily detected and corrected), but by broad superficial views and plausible-seeming generalizations. For instance, Malcolm Muggeridge believed that the symbol of the crucifix "has stimulated audacities of thought and exploration which have carried the human race forward with immense strides towards understanding and mastering their material circumstances" (1969, p. 46). In fact it was with the Renaissance and under the stimulus of a superior Arabic civilization that the material advance of Western Europe began, and every step forward toward an understanding of the material world was taken against the stubborn opposition of the Church.

2

REASON AND INSTINCT

i. REASON IN THE IDEAS OF
UNCIVILIZED PEOPLES

Just as the nature of the more complex ideas is best understood if one first studies simpler ones, so the role of reasoning in the formation of beliefs will be clearer if we begin with those of uncivilized peoples.

To some it has seemed absurd to attribute rational processes to the primitive mind at all when we find them playing only a subordinate role in the mental operations of civilized persons. Of course, the savage is not likely to be perplexed by everyday occurrences that are obviously harmless, any more than are the great majority of civilized people. His interest will be aroused only by abnormal things and by those which have an obvious relation to his wellbeing and are therefore capable of exciting his emotions. In such cases he will be concerned only with avoiding the evil that threatens or with achieving the wished-for success, not with questions 'How?' and 'Why?' as such; and this has been felt to distinguish him from the scientist, who, it has been held, faces these questions and seeks knowledge for knowledge's sake.[1]

If this is true of the scientist, it means only that the motive has changed, not the method, and this happens already at the uncivilized stage of human development. At first the hunter is impelled by the need to feed himself and his family, but when he experiences the joy of the chase, the admiration of his fellows at his skill and cunning, and also the possibility of exchanging his booty for something he cannot make himself, then he hunts from different motives and will not desist as soon as his own needs are satisfied. It is the same with every other occupation, and it is characteristic of man that he can learn to devote as much energy to the pursuit of means as to ends, and that the emotional drive which has its ultimate source in the fundamental instincts can become attached to all the secondary activities which originally were mere means of reaching a final goal. No doubt in the conditions of civilization these have become more elaborate, but even among savages they may be considerable, at least when compared with what is possible for apes. Even they are quite able to pursue the means while temporarily turning their back on their goal the better to achieve it (cf above, p. 20).

The importance of reasoning in early religion is apparent in primitive ideas of the soul. Guyau argues that the soul was meant to account (among other things) for the difference between the living and the dead and for dreams. The breath, he said, was the most tangible thing, other than the blood, with which life could be definitely associated. It can even be heard leaving the body at the last gasp. It is no hypothetical entity but fact, yet as a rule immaterial and invisible, so that it is not surprising that in many languages words for soul or spirit are derived from words meaning the breath or the wind. As for dreams, Guyau points out that the dreamer experiences adventures, yet is assured by his companions that he did not leave the room or tent at all during the night, and that this can be explained by supposing that there is a soul which can leave the body, roam the country and then return to its normal corporeal abode. In dreams one not only goes on adventures, but also meets friends and talks with them, yet thereafter they know nothing of the meeting. Some semblance of them had therefore been separated from their bodies without their knowledge. Sometimes these simulacra belong to the dead and must therefore represent some portion of those persons that survived death. Guyau added that this idea of an insubstantial soul which bears some resemblance to what the body in which it is housed looks like is strengthened by experience of shadows: "Ne semble-t-il pas qu'on voie l'esprit marcher à côté des corps sous cette forme de l'ombre, changer de place, même quand les corps sont immobiles?" (1927, p. 55). The development of theories of the soul (as of other theories) is but the continual revision of rational inferences in the light of accumulating experience—a revision prompted by such emotions as the desire for reunion, the sense of justice that requires the unfair balance of happiness here to be redressed hereafter, and the dread of annihilation. Under the perpetual urge of such desires and fears, reason works out its provisional theories, revises and replaces them as new phenomena attract attention or new explanatory models become available.[2]

When in this manner one thing is explained by assuming the existence of another, the process may be deliberate, in which case we speak of a theory or hypothesis and are aware of its provisional and uncertain nature. In other cases the assumption is involuntary and there may be no awareness that any is involved. The difference lies not in the mental process itself but in the degree to which we are able to realize its nature. When the savage recalls that the man he saw and spoke to in his dreams is dead, he feels impelled to try and account for these apparently incompatible experiences. We need not suppose that the whole community consisted of theorists, as there are marked differences in intellectual capacity among modern individuals and, as Köhler's experiments with apes have shown, among the members of other mammalian species, so that such differences may be presumed to have existed among primitive men—differences in the power of solving problems, in curiosity and power of observation. If we say that primitive men did in fact speculate and invent, we should mean that there were individuals among them who could and did accomplish these feats; the rest repeated what they were taught to believe. Uncivilized peoples are certainly not irrational, but their experience is restricted and unsupported by the accumulated knowledge of ages. Hypotheses can be constructed only from the materials of experience, and when these are limited, the hypotheses must be crude.

As Bowra has said (1962, p. 13): "Man advances through the acquisition, accumulation and intelligent application of experience. In truly primitive conditions this takes an enormous time".

Many students of myth have recognized that mythopoesis often personifies phenomena and supposes them to be animated. This animistic tendency can be explained if it can be shown to be a special case of some more general tendency, or the effect of the combination of two or more tendencies otherwise well known. Hence anthropologists such as Volney and Tylor tried to show that it is a special case of false reasoning. Volney (1822, p. 169) supposed that it was the spontaneous movement of the sun which led men to believe that it has an intelligence or will like their own: resemblance in one significant respect was thus taken to imply resemblance in others, and this is a perfectly familiar kind of reasoning from analogy. The scientist, confronted with an unfamiliar phenomenon, sees a certain analogy with something better known. He inquires how the present phenomenon would develop, how it could be made to change, how it could be cancelled, and so forth, if it did in fact behave like that other phenomenon already known, and he then investigates to see whether it does in fact fulfil such expectations; if not, he looks for another analogy, and out of scores thus noted, only rarely is one found to be fruitful.

One of the most uncompromising believers in the irrationality of uncivilized man was Wilhelm Wundt, the German physiologist, philosopher, and psychologist who lived from 1832 to 1920. His *Völkerpsychologie* or 'social psychology', published in ten volumes between 1900 and 1920, includes such an immense amount of anthropological data that he may fairly be called also an anthropologist. When in this work he discusses the 'Märchen' or folk tale, he obviously thinks that, for uncivilized man, the magic world of such tales was identical with the real world (1923, pp. 400, 405, 407). But it is really not necessary to suppose that only what was believed possible and plausible was put into such stories. If their purpose was entertainment—and that is surely obvious—why should the story-teller have been any more inclined to restrict himself to strict naturalism than his modern counterpart, even if he was, as Wundt says, less clear about the frontiers between fantasy and fact? Many stories go out of their way to stagger the audience with the incredible: Siegfried who cleaves the anvil; the swordsman who wields his blade with such rapidity that he can ward off the rain; the book of magic which gives power over heaven and earth. The very effort at exaggeration here warns us not to accept everything as an indication of what was believed possible. However, Wundt's attitude was very common among anthropologists of his time. Andrew Lang, for instance, refers (1899, p. 43) to a number of versions of a very widespread tale of a frog which swallowed up all the water so as to cause a universal drought which lasted until the water was vomited up. In the Australian version the animals play the jester before the frog in the hope of making him disgorge the water by laughing, and success is finally attained when the eel dances on the tip of its tail. For Lang, this story is simply a myth like any other, and no worse than the kind of nonsense one would expect from the thinking of uncivilized man. It is of course possible that drought was explained as due to frogs, who are obviously fond of water. Since they sometimes occur in very great numbers, the idea might arise that they could between them drink it all up. In times of drought they may be seen lying by dried up pools with distended bodies. But out of such a quasi-scientific belief it requires another motive to construct a tale in which a single frog achieves the feat and is thwarted by a dancing eel. The composers of such old folk tales may have utilized current ideas as far as it suited them, but allowed themselves as much licence as did H.G. Wells when he suggested a semi-plausible scientific basis for his time-machine so as to discourage critical doubts from disturbing our enjoyment of the romantic consequences of his assertions.

Instead of just comparing stories with one another in regard to their form and material, we need to ask what part they played in the social life of the native community. As Wundt is well aware, such communities commonly also possess elaborate verse compositions, and before phonetic writing was available, these could be recited only by specially gifted persons who had made a business of learning them. But the simple tales about sun and moon, and about the origin of this or that which form the substance of the 'Märchen', could have been told by mothers or nurses to children, perhaps to keep them quiet in the long winter nights or in periods of rain. If so, the stories could well display certain characteristics which could be called childish even in relation to the primitive ideas of the time. The anthropologist, who is apt to expect the most naive and fantastical beliefs to be held by primitive folk, finds it difficult to distinguish serious theory from childish make-believe. But there is no reason to suppose that even in the most primitive times this distinction did not exist.

I have elsewhere (Wells 1987 A, p. 107) had occasion to note, apropos of Wundt's view of the origin of language, that he will have nothing to do with any theory which attributes it to human inventiveness, and that he was thereby reacting against an older error of neglecting the impulsive and instinctive elements in human behaviour. But I can see no more sensible way of interpreting primitive beliefs and achievements than that which rests on the assumption that the minds of early men are in all essentials similar to our own and their motives like ours, although even 'rationalistic' anthropologists have had hesitations over this. Tylor, for instance, seems to accept the view that there was a period in the development of human culture especially favourable to the creation of myths; for he writes of the 'mythological period', and concludes the relevant chapter with the words:

> From first to last, the processes of *phantasy* have been at work; but where the savage could see *phantasms,* the civilised man has come to amuse himself with *fancies.* (1891, p. 315)

I have argued that the division here suggested existed at all stages: creations of the imagination for entertainment were just as possible and probable in the earliest ages as today. People today believe impossible things with as much confidence as their more primitive ancestors, only they are not quite the same things. (Tylor himself records some modern myths two chapters after the above quotation.[3]) And they amuse themselves with what they know to be fiction in the same way as their ancestors will have done.

The principal omission on both sides, with Tylor as with Wundt, concerns, I would suggest, the division of labour. It is misleading to talk, as Wundt does (1910, p. 32) of "the myth-forming consciousness". The formation of a myth is the work of a number of people—inventor, repeater, hearer—who do not all contribute the same elements to the final result; and this division of labour is surely responsible for some of the absurdities in primitive ideas. The beliefs of a people are beliefs of a large number of individuals who have had different experiences and are unequally endowed mentally. One more intelligent person may observe things and contrive theories which are unobserved or not understood by the majority of his fellows, and if he tries to describe what he has seen or thought he is very likely to be misunderstood. It follows that many of the beliefs we meet may be corrupted rather than rudimentary ones. This state of affairs is to be met with at every stage in intellectual history. In the case of beliefs which have obvious practical consequences when acted on, such as how to obtain and cook food or what constitutes an effective weapon, even unintelligent people can be kept from error by the discipline of results. In such matters of daily practice, where a belief can be tested at once by direct application, men give up their beliefs readily enough, otherwise the race would long since have become extinct. The notion that men are naturally credulous arises from the fact that, in many conspicuous matters, such as those pertaining to religion, there are no direct ways of putting beliefs to the test. And if there is no action that will be affected by the belief, but only some emotional condition, then that story or theory may be preferred which produces the most acceptable emotion (cf. above, p. 24). When we

look for a continuous process of intellectual advance, we
have to select a small number, sometimes a very small
number, of individuals in each generation as the bearers of
the authentic tradition. Scientific theory does not advance
like a majestic river, but rather like one of those choked
and silted streams that lose their waters in stagnant
swamps and advance only here and there in meandering
currents whose general direction is hard to determine.

That Wundt is aware (against what he so often says)
that primitive peoples can, in some contexts, be perfectly
rational, becomes apparent when he discusses primitive
inventions. The first step towards *any* invention, he says, is
accidental (1923, p. 513). For instance, we cannot suppose
that stringed musical instruments originated because men
first conceived the emotional effect of twanging strings and
then contrived an instrument in order to realize it. It is
necessary first to be led by some chance to note the effect,
and then attempts can be made to reproduce it by repro-
ducing the conditions. The experience must come before
the deliberate quest for it. Thus the string on the bow
employed in hunting and fighting gave ample occasion for
the creation of unintended sound effects. Next, an enhancement ('Steigerung') of the effect which has been
found pleasurable can be sought by improving the conditions, and on this basis stringed instruments were developed from stringed weapons. Again, he notes that the clash
of spear on shield in ritual dancing will have added to the
excitement (pp. 478–79). This will have led to an effort to
enhance the noise. Under such conditions new methods are
found of creating noise, not depending on weapons or
other implements, but on special percussion contrivances
which have no other use except that of creating a din (p.
514). Thus once the first impetus had been given, new
combinations and complications would follow until in the
end accidental discovery was replaced by planned invention. The human mind, then, does not work in a completely arbitrary fashion: if it did, it would be unlike the mind of
any other animal, and man could never have survived, to
say nothing of achieving civilization.

ii. GENERALIZED INSTINCTS AND THE REASONING THEY PROMPT

When a need cannot be immediately satisfied, locomotion —for example getting to the right place to satisfy hunger or thirst—and perhaps also manipulation of the surrounding objects, or even more complex and protracted behaviour may be required to produce the situation that will satisfy the need. Then there is generated in the animal an emotion, a feeling, or, to use the expression of J.P. Guilford (1939, p. 223), a state of tension, as if the organism were tensed like a stretched coil spring or a taut bow; and this state has the effect of maintaining the activity of the animal until the situation is found in which the tension can be released. It is because, in the higher animals, immediate response is not generally possible that emotion plays so large a part. There is plenty of evidence that the higher mammals can form ideas of desired situations and seek to modify their actual situation so as to bring it nearer to these.

Paulhan (1930, pp. 14–16) points out that emotion arises also when some normal instinctive or habitual tendency is arrested by a conflicting desire, fear, or purpose. He gives as an illustration the man who pays his first social call in a state of great nervousness. When he has grown used to such experiences, he is able to perform exactly the same operation without emotion, but on the first occasion his intention to pay the call is opposed by various fears which delay or inhibit his response. When, however, an impulse can be realized in accordance with the normal constitution of the animal, and no contrary or interfering impulse exists at the same time, then action follows not only without emotion, but often without consciousness. The reflex or habitual act may be performed unconsciously, but if, owing to any external or internal obstacle its performance is checked or diverted in some way from its normal form, then the movement at once becomes conscious.

Human emotions are characterized by the extreme indeterminacy of the actions which they evoke. When a man is hungry or sexually motivated, we cannot predict exactly what he will do, but if we are sufficiently acquainted with his behaviour, we can say what *kind* of things he may do. In fact the instincts of all the higher animals do not lead to specific actions, but have a more generalized influence on their behaviour. If, on this basis, one distinguishes what Englefield (1985, pp. 57ff) calls generalized instincts from specialized ones, then what psychologists call intelligent behaviour is prompted by the former type. When I desire something, I mentally review the possible ways of obtaining it, and then select one of these upon which to act. The initial items in such a course of action may be identical even when my behaviour is prompted by entirely different instincts.

It is because human behaviour is guided by generalized and not by specialized instincts that it gives superficially the appearance of being not guided by instinct at all. Man is regarded as 'the rational animal', and it has been maintained that he has no instincts.[4] But the function of reason is to show us how to obtain what we desire, and the driving force underlying our behaviour is still the desire. While the reasoning process guides us towards our goal, the goal must first exert some kind of instinctive attraction before this process can be brought into play. This was perfectly well understood by the philosophers of the so-called 'Enlightenment', so often accused of underestimating the efficacy of non-rational factors. Thus Locke says that, were it not for desires or fears, there would be nothing to direct thoughts or prevent them wandering in endless reverie;[5] and Hume noted that "reason, being cool and disengaged, is no motive to action, and directs only the impulse received from appetite or inclination by showing us the means of attaining happiness or avoiding misery".[6] Fear or hunger, for instance, stimulate to activity, but leave the choice of action mainly to reason. As a simple example: I find myself a visitor in an unfamiliar university and feel the need for some lunch. I could go to the staff common room, but have no entitlement to do so, and might be regarded as an intruder. I think next of the students' canteen, but regard it as too noisy and squalid. A restaurant, perhaps, but it would be too expensive, too crowded, and the service too slow, and I would lose time getting there. So I decide to buy sandwiches from a nearby snack bar and eat them on a bench in the sunshine. As I consider each of these possibilities, my mind envisages their attendant circumstances and consequences. The work of the intellect, says Trotter, put in the most general terms, is "to cause delay between stimulus and response, and under circumstances to modify the direction of the latter"; and so the "dominance of instinct" in man is "obscured by the kaleidoscopic variety of the reactions by which it is more or less effectually satisfied" (1953, pp. 105, 198). The evolutionist will surely argue that ability to reason was evolved as a means of directing behaviour, of informing us what we have to do to achieve our desires.

People commonly speak of a conflict between reason and passion—reason supposedly prompting to one course of action and passion to another—when in fact the conflict is between two different passions. This tends to be overlooked because, when someone feels an emotion such as fear, he may, in order to attain a rational (that is, deliberately considered) end, suppress any behaviour that might reveal his emotion. When, for instance, his bag is being scrutinized by the customs officer, he may, for the purpose of avoiding taxation, try to look completely at ease; and such behaviour has often been interpreted as accomplished by a faculty of reason, independent of any emotion. In fact, of course, it is prompted by some emotion antagonistic to the fear, such as the hope of successfully smuggling prohibited wares. The role of reason in the matter is simply to review the consequences of the different actions to which his opposed passions prompt. Reason tells him that, if only he can bluff his way through, he can enjoy some cheap drink; but it also informs him that he risks the humiliation of being exposed as a liar and a cheat. What he actually does in the given situation will depend on which of the opposed passions is the stronger. Thus it is absurd to say that reason directs man if this means that reason supplies the motive. Reason can supply only the method, and the motives of our actions must be sought in one or other of our instincts.

As a Professor of biology, David Ehrenfeld cannot be unaware of all this, yet he tends to obscure it when, in his book *The Arrogance of Humanism* (Oxford University Press, 1981), he writes (disparagingly) of "the advocacy of logic at the expense of emotion" and pleads for "a balance between reason and emotion" (pp. 146, 162), as if the two could function independently. It is certainly not true that non-religious persons must necessarily undervalue non-rational factors in human behaviour, such as instinct, emotion, impulse, or habit.

The 'humanism' Ehrenfeld is attacking he defines as "a supreme faith in human reason—its ability to confront and solve the many problems that humans face" (p. 5). I suppose there may be persons who embrace this "dangerous fallacy" of "absolute faith in our ability to control our own destiny" (pp. 9–10). But a modicum of reflection should suffice to convince us that, in trying to discover how to cure our ills, we also discover which are incurable; and the progress of all sciences from one crude theory to another which in time proves to be only slightly less crude shows clearly enough that all our reasonings are provisional. It is unwarranted to suppose that any superior alternative to such gropings is available to us.

Intellectual processes, then, mediate between instincts, which supply the driving force, and the actual behaviour. Thinking is a process which requires some motive, and unfortunately the motive is apt to affect the results. Psychologists have shown themselves well aware of the way in which instincts, and the emotions associated with them, can be played upon, and how powerful emotions can become attached to the flimsiest of ideas. The literature of pietism, for instance, reveals how intense the emotional reaction may be even to isolated Biblical phrases. Childhood experiences may give to the familiar texts an emotional significance all the greater for the obscurity of its sources. A bias is a preference or a series of preferences, derived from desires, fears or hopes, in brief from emotional attitudes. Our beliefs are not simply determined by our emotions. Hatred, love, vanity or ambition will not necessarily warp the reasoning process, but may merely make the mind work all the harder to produce results which will stand up to searching scrutiny. I may be conscious of my bias and at the same time desire sincerely not to be deceived, as the truth has virtues which recommend it even when it is disagreeable. But emotion is often left with considerable scope in processes of abstract reasoning, where ideas can become so attenuated as to consist of words, indeterminate in meaning, but with strong emotional colouring. The late Bishop Robinson's use of the word 'God' is, as we shall see, a good example of this.

iii. DEFIANCE AND RELIANCE

Many persons' beliefs, religious and other, depend upon submission to an authority which speaks with confidence; and so it is relevant to the present inquiry to understand how a tendency to believe arises from a willingness to follow, and to see what psychological factors are involved in the relation between leaders and followers.[7]

Both the aggressive type of gregariousness found in the wolf pack and the protective type, as in the sheep flock and deer herd, require a leader with a different personality from his followers. A pack could not hold together, either in the chase or in war, if each individual were to exercise his private judgment, and one tendency obviously requisite to its leader's performance is a certain ferocity or aggressiveness. With herds, on the other hand, it is, as Read observes, "sagacity and prudence" that makes one leader more eligible than another—sagacity that leads the herd to pasture or to water or helps it to elude enemies (1925 B, p. 64).

McDougall (1920, Chapter 3) writes of the emotions of positive and negative self-feeling, based on instincts of self-assertion in the one case and self-abasement in the other. The leader is strongly self-assertive, *self*-reliant and defiant of others (particularly of outsiders). Englefield has suggested the terms *defiance* and *reliance* to characterize the behaviour of leaders and followers respectively, and the appropriateness of these terms will become apparent.

Every community, then, must distinguish between leader and followers. Fabre (1912, Chapter 3) shows that even such lowly creatures as processionary caterpillars do so. During the day these animals shelter together in a large web, but at night they emerge in procession to feed on pine needles. The one that happens to emerge first determines the route taken, since each caterpillar, as it walks, leaves a thread of silk behind as the guide which the succeeding one follows. The perception of this thread seems to inhibit all tendencies to independent action. It is only the leader who is not subject to this special stimulus, and who in consequence is free to react to others and to exhibit some independence and self-reliance. But he is only the temporary leader, for if the chain is broken and reformed with another caterpillar at the fore, the other takes over the leadership. With camels and sheep, however, certain individuals seem to be by nature capable of assuming the rôle of leader, and the herd coheres because the others always follow them.

Breeders can tell whether an ox or bull will turn out to be ferocious or docile when the animal is still quite young, and this suggests that the tendencies are inherited. An aggressive animal may, however, be submissive in the presence of one who is even more strongly defiant, as is true also of human beings. Gustav Freytag noted, of the German knights of the thirteenth century: "He who was so imperious towards his underlings became a servile courtier when under a powerful master".[8] Where two defiant individuals are evenly matched, there will be not co-operation, but rivalry.

Galton noted, of the African cattle he observed, that the ox

> cannot endure even a momentary severance from his herd. If he be separated from it by stratagem or force, he exhibits every sign of mental agony; he strives with all his might to get back again, and

when he succeeds he plunges into its middle to bathe his whole body
with the comfort of closest companionship. (1951, p. 49)

Such a 'need to belong' is not unimportant in human
communities where isolation is felt as disagreeable and
warmth is found in companionship. But to keep to Galton's oxen, the advantages of keeping with the herd as a
defence against surprise are obvious. A solitary animal
may be taken off its guard, but in a herd there are hundreds
of eyes and ears to see or hear the warning signal and
spread the alarm. But if such an instinct of conformity
were equally developed in all the animals, the herd's
behaviour would depend on the chance movement of any
one individual, even of its most timid and foolish member,
and so if chaos is to be avoided, the herd must contain
individuals of a specially courageous and sagacious type,
endowed with a special influence, power, prestige and
self-reliance. They must be disinclined to imitate and less
prone to panic, and their behaviour must be more in
accord with the actual requirements of the situation. Their
instincts must approximate more closely to those of a
solitary animal. But these self-reliant individuals must not
be too numerous, or the uniform action of the herd will be
destroyed. Galton found in fact that a few of the individuals in each herd of oxen are of this independent nature.
They furnish the initiative; they follow their inclination,
the remainder follow them.

Ranking-order in various animal colonies, and the
dependence of the majority on the sagacity of high-ranking
members, has been extensively studied, by Lorenz among
others. He gives the following impressive examples of its
importance:

The expression movements of a high-ranking jackdaw, particularly
of an old male, are paid much more attention to by the colony
members than those of a lower-ranking, young bird. For example, if
a young bird shows fright at some meaningless stimulus, the others,
especially the older ones, pay almost no attention to his expressions
of fear. But if the same sort of alarm proceeds from one of the old
males all the jackdaws within sight and earshot immediately take
flight. Since, in jackdaws, recognition of predatory enemies is not
innate but is learned by every individual from the behaviour of
experienced old birds, it is probably of considerable importance

that great store is set by the 'opinion' of old, high-ranking and experienced birds. . . . Washburn and de Vore observed that among free-living baboons the band was led not by a single animal but by a 'senate' of several old males. . . . On one occasion when the band was in a treeless area and in danger of encountering a lion, the animals stopped and the young, strong males formed a defensive circle round the weaker animals. But the oldest male went forward alone, performed the dangerous task of finding out exactly where the lion was lying, without being seen by him, and then returned to the horde and led them, by a wide detour round the lion, to the safety of their sleeping trees. All followed him blindly, no one doubting his authority. (1966, pp. 36–38)

The essence of reliance is absence of panic in the presence of danger when protected by a defiant individual. Read notes that "several species of buffalo and other cattle, . . . at the approach of beasts of prey, form a phalanx with the adult bulls and cows outside and the calves within, which no carnivore dare attack" (1925 B, p. 64). In an isolated family of gorillas in the forest, the father can protect his offspring provided they keep together. But if they were to scatter, terrified of the imminent danger, his task would be impossible. Hence there must be obedience and reliance. Were it not for the father's protective tendency and its power of overcoming fear, the helpless young would be abandoned whenever fear prompted him to take flight, and this would be equally disastrous. It is this courage associated with the instinct of protection which makes the term 'defiance' appropriate. Courage is also required in the reliant young to inhibit flight, but not ferocity. Submission and confidence perhaps better express their attitude.

From this we see that, even at this relatively primitive stage of social organization (and hence still more so in complex human societies), something more than mere imitation is needed. The reliant individual must not always do what the leader does, but what the leader requires, and he must have the authority to enforce obedience. He sometimes does this by expressions of anger, which are apt to evoke the symptoms of submissiveness in weaker individuals. Anger or aggressiveness is particularly appropriate when the defiant person directs it not at his own followers, but at those who are felt to be hostile by them. Angry tones will sometimes cow an antagonist, and are often adopted with this intention. Conversely, the expression of fear by the enemy or reliance on the part of the leader's followers will increase his self-confidence. We seem to be faced here with two complementary instincts. The one implies pugnacity, self-will and sagacity, and it is stimulated by the expression of the other in other persons; the other implies submissiveness, obedience, and is stimulated by the expression of the former instinct in another individual. Jane van Lawick Goodall noted, among the chimpanzees she observed, "a strong desire for dominance" as "a characteristic marked in some individuals and almost entirely lacking in others" (1971, p. 123) some of whom seemed capable only of submissive behaviour (p. 77).

For the proper functioning of these two instincts it is essential that the reliant, submissive one should predominate in the great majority of individuals in a society, and the defiant, self-confident one be well developed in only a restricted number. Society could not cohere if all were rebels, and although educationalists are apt to stress the value of independence and originality, the great majority of people are far better equipped to do things in a traditional manner, to follow a clear lead rather than to take the initiative. There could be no born leaders if there were not a far greater number of born followers. Nevertheless the defiant, self-confident tendency is to a limited extent present in all and can be stimulated by special circumstances. The female mammal is twice as fierce and redoubtable when she has her young to defend; their weakness and reliance stimulates her to protection and defiance. A timid child, when put in charge of a younger one, seems to gain new courage and self-reliance at having somebody to look after. Many an officer in wartime finds himself filled with unexpected courage in the presence of the men who rely on him, and even the most reliant person may be brought to a momentary independence by the stimulus of someone more submissive and imitative than himself. Conversely, the submissive, humble individual is made more coura-

geous by the sight of the leader. Many men who are
cowardly and irresolute when left to their own resources
are capable of prodigies of valour and endurance when
stirred by devotion to a leader. Thus the two tendencies
work together to increase the courage of all members of the
group.

The defiant human individual forms his own opinions.
Their grounds may be anything, but a strong ingredient
will usually be non-conformity. To hold different views
from the vulgar is, for him, more important than to hold
just views, although having chosen them, he will defend
them as best he can. The reliant, however, asks only what
the prevailing views are in order that he may profess them.
There are in his world certain persons of importance, to
whose opinion he will refer when called upon for a
judgement or decision. His dependence on leadership
involves what Trotter calls deference to "custom and
tradition, a credulity towards the dogmas of the herd"
(1953, p. 85). The particular master or idol he chooses will
depend largely on circumstances. He may, according to the
accidents of his experience, become a follower of his
father, his teacher or his priest. But once a particular
attachment has been formed, it is not easily broken and
replaced by another. This is particularly striking in cases of
commitment to religious and political ideas. The same
thing occurs with other instinctive tendencies. Most young
persons have a strong need to form a relationship with a
member of the opposite sex, and with whom the bond is
actually formed depends on circumstances, but once
formed it is broken only with pain.

Anyone knows that, if he is respected, he may expect to
obtain more easily whatever he wants. Hence the defiant's
desire for respect is prompted by the will to power, perhaps
the strongest human drive after hunger and love. It covers
all kinds of display: exhibitions of learning, piety, valour,
chivalry, wit, cunning, or magnanimity. By the practice of
such 'virtues', power to influence the thought or actions of
others is acquired. The less scope a man has to satisfy his
defiance in accordance with established social usages and

institutions, the more likely is he to be driven to revolutionary activity. If his grievance against society is such that he cannot hope to win a large number of followers (or a small number of sufficiently esteemed followers), he will tend to become an ordinary criminal.

A teacher, preacher, or politician often owes his success to defiance in himself and reliance in his audience; and as a result he may be believed even if his doctrine is erroneous or unintelligible. There are other ways of establishing a reputation than by earning it. The crowds who hailed Hitler and Mussolini did not have to be motivated by rational evidence that they were great statesmen. Their obvious forcefulness (particularly in standing up to outsiders) was enough to win them a large number of followers. Carlyle too did not need cogent arguments in order to make a strong impression. He tells his mother of the audience at one of his lectures:

> I had bishops and all kinds of people among my hearers. I gave them to know . . . that . . . it was altogether a new kind of thing they were hearing today. The people seemed greatly astonished and greatly pleased. I vomited it forth on them (letter of 9 May, 1840).

Clearly, his astonished and admiring audience greatly strengthened his own sense of superiority to "bishops and all kinds of people". Under the influence of such an emotion of self-approval men are apt to say foolish things, but the very expression of this emotion excites submissiveness in listeners in whom the follower-tendency can be strongly stimulated. They are apt to judge of strength by superficial appearances, and especially by the outward display of a defiant emotion. Carlyle, Emerson, Matthew Arnold, and Ruskin are all familiar examples of men who, starting in a modest way, were led on by a gathering reputation to rely more and more on their intuition, which they regarded as inspiration. J.M. Robertson justly said that they "passed large judgements on relatively little knowledge, and have been much more prone to sum up the universe than to ascertain what it consists of" (1891, p. 212). The followers of such a leader may swear by him, as the communist may by Marx or Lenin and the Catholic by Aquinas, even without any serious attempt to judge his merits. They are glad to leave to him the task of demolishing the enemy, and will readily persuade themselves that he has already done so. They rejoice to feel that, in following him, they are in the front rank of the army of progress; they feel a thrill of pride in all his triumphs and are angered by every attack which is aimed at him.

Man is distinguished from other animals by his enhanced ability to react to imagined situations, instead of to what is immediately present to his senses. The actual presence of the leader of the herd is required if he is to elicit reliant behaviour from a cow, but with man memories and imaginings can take the place of external stimuli as guides to behaviour. A man can be a follower of Jesus or of Mohammed as easily as of someone personally known to him, and for some persons such religious ideas are much more powerful influences than are the stimuli of their environment, as is demonstrated by the history of religious martyrs. The reliant who believes he is supported by the creator and ruler of the universe naturally feels superior to one who is content to rely on a less powerful protector. Although he finds his support in humility, his humility is relative, and he may become defiant to all those who seem to him weaker than his own leader. Hence an attitude of reliance in religious matters can co-exist with the reverse attitude not only towards those who attack his religious beliefs, but also in matters where religion is not involved. Coleman, noting Pascal's refusal to defer, in physics, to anything except fact and experiment, says that "in his mathematical and scientific studies, Pascal always sought to dominate nature and to refute those who disagreed with him; but in his religious experiences he not only wanted but demanded to be dominated". "In Pascal's eyes the great evil of the epoch lay in espousing new ideas in religion that have no roots in authority, and rejecting new ideas in the sciences because they are incompatible with the dicta of the ancients" (1986, pp. 61, 63).[9] Newton likewise broke with tradition in his physical enquiries, but in his writings on the prophets he was much more faithful to tradition, holding, for instance that to reject the prophecies in Daniel "is to reject the Christian religion. For this religion is founded upon his Prophecy concerning the Messiah".[10]

J.S. Bezzant (the Cambridge theologian who died in 1967) mentions, as attitudes to God, "awe, veneration, worship, prayer, sacrifice, the sense of dependence, insignificance and guilt, instinctive obedience, need of purification, a sense of deliverance and joy". These, he says, are found in many religions, and "nothing but dogmatism can dismiss these activities and experiences of human nature as universal illusion" (1963, p. 105). The illusion, when it exists, concerns the object or occasions of such feelings, not the feelings themselves. Because we can sometimes recognize the psychological foundations of strong religious emotion, we are not obliged to be blind to its effectiveness. The reliant emotions which Bezzant specifies come naturally to the gregarious type who, as Trotter says, has as an individual a sense of incompleteness which "compels him to reach out towards some larger existence than his own, some encompassing being in whom his perplexities may find a solution and his longings peace" (pp. 87–88). William James quotes a religious writer as saying: "The compensation for the loss of that sense of personal independence which man so unwillingly gives up is the disappearance of all *fear* from one's life, the quite indescribable and inexplicable feeling of an inner *security*".[11] This feeling, far from being inexplicable, naturally arises from the identification of the whole power of the universe with that being on whom one relies.

It may be that in some cases the two great impulses of reliance and defiance have become assimilated. The ascetic who subjects himself utterly to the will of his god may simultaneously be seeking the power that derives from his omnipotent ally. If the same belief or delusion permits in this way the simultaneous resolution of both impulses, then the force of both will be combined. This may explain the tremendous strength of religious conviction. The will to power and the will to submission are perfectly combined in submission to omnipotence.

Experiences during this century have drawn attention to the dangers inherent in human readiness to submit to authority, while it is nonetheless recognized that development of such a tendency has been an inevitable result of natural selection. Milgram, for instance, says that "some system of authority is a requirement of all communal living" (1974, p. 1), that hierarchically organized groups have great advantages over undisciplined ones in coping with the dangers of the physical environment, with threats posed by competing species, and with potential disruption from within, and that in consequence a "potential for obedience" has been bred into the human organism "through the extended operation of evolutionary processes" (pp. 123–25). He nevertheless finds that these very virtues of loyalty, discipline, and self-sacrifice that are valued highly in the individual "create destructive organizational engines of war and bind men to malevolent systems of authority", leaving our species "in the long run only a modest chance of survival" (p. 188).

iv. FEAR AND THE NEED FOR PROTECTION

It may be that many human instincts and organic needs have played their part in forming the religious commitments of different individuals. Nevertheless, fear and the need for protection have been very common ingredients. A feeling of community, of solidarity with others, is important for the banishment of fear, and is of course often evident in non-religious contexts. Man's relations with his fellows are often dependent on mutual recognition as members of a particular class, sect or club, so that conversation is, in Trotter's phrase, "rich in the ritual of recognition" (p. 93), and then serves not to exchange ideas or information, but to confirm the participants in their sympathy with one another which they feel as members of the same group. There is a particular form of behaviour, a manner of speech, a specialty of topics peculiar to the sect;

and its members come together and flatter and admire one another in order to be flattered and admired in turn. The Austrian dramatist Grillparzer, in an essay where he reminisces on the political upheavals of 1848, notes how people like to vent their opinions "in phrases not their own", and how at that time so many were alert to catch the trend of popular feeling in order to show their allegiance.

There is thus a kind of reliance to which the stimulus is not one defiant individual or leader, but a general attitude common to the members of a group. One feels more confident in following a particular course of conduct if it is evidently being followed by the bulk of one's companions. Correlatively, individual creeds are despised. For T.S. Eliot, for instance, what one man believes as a result of his private inquiries and reflections is inferior to beliefs that have been held by millions for more than a thousand years. This is why he rates Dante above Lucretius and Goethe, neither of whom belonged to a powerful sect, but professed beliefs in many ways peculiar to themselves. He writes in this connection of "the advantage of a coherent traditional system of dogma and morals like the Catholic. . . . Goethe always arouses in me a strong sentiment of disbelief in what he believes: Dante does not" (1951, p. 258).

One way in which solidarity with others is often achieved is by sharing a sense of suffering. A story of misfortune brings home to the reader that he is not alone in his distress, thus banishing the insecurity felt in isolation. Literary writers are well aware of this basis of appeal. Goethe wrote his play *Torquato Tasso* about a young man in trouble, and said he understood very well why it was enjoyed by young people who know what it is to be in trouble. The reader can take even more pleasure if he believes the story to be true. The Catholic scholar Karl Rahner notes:

> How many sorrowful souls have been comforted and have seen through their tears the everlasting stars of love and peace because in their faith they know 'He, the eternal meaning of the world, the Word, has wept with me. He too has drunk of the chalice' (1961, p. 177).

He adds: how many have been comforted in dying by the thought that "He—really He himself—died".

The same comfort will be present even if the belief that the story is true is erroneous; just as the same confidence will be present even if the individual is deluded in thinking that views important to him are widely shared. The "cloud of witnesses" (Hebrews 12:1) may be quite imaginary, and yet as effective as a host of material supporters. In more general terms, some instincts, like hunger, can be satisfied only by some definite activity—an imaginary meal will not nourish the body—but others can be satisfied by some external situation, and in this case it suffices if the situation is believed to exist. The defiant human being wishes to be admired, respected, or feared; the reliant to be loved and protected. In either case the desire is met when the individual believes that what he craves is in fact the case. The reliant's doubt and fear can be silenced if only he can convince himself, with Caroline Franks Davis, that "there is a holy power beyond the world of the senses, which is perceptible as the ultimate, unitary ground of being, as an awesome, creature-consciousness inspiring power, as the 'something more' which shines through the world of nature, and as a personal loving presence" (1989, p. 239); or with William James, who says, of his own religious experiences, that "they all converge towards a kind of insight" the keynote of which "is invariably a reconciliation. It is as if the opposites of the world, whose contradictoriness and conflict make all our difficulties and troubles, were melted into unity".[12]

The simplest method of creating this harmony is to repress the disturbing elements by training one's mind to confine itself to a restricted number of ideas, and to ignore experiences which might disturb them. One possibility is to raise the whole reflective process into a realm of abstraction where the ideas are so attenuated that conflict between them becomes almost impossible. Words play an important part here. When the underlying ideas are thin, it is easy to find a comforting verbal formula. Of this the metaphysicians and the mystics provide plentiful examples.

All depends on the degree of conviction attained, the extent to which doubts and questionings are brushed aside. Sometimes this can be accomplished only by a partial splitting of the mind. One's idea of oneself is something only gradually built up, on the basis of experience, and may be fragmented, consisting of ideas of different selves, each one of which is appropriate to a particular setting. In his business environment, a man's self is perhaps a hard-headed unscrupulous egoist; at home it may be a benign and sympathetic pater familias; at the club a dissipated rake. Since the materials for each of these models have been gathered from different sets of experiences, they need not interfere with each other. But such immunity from interference involves some degree of mental segregation. In extreme cases there is complete isolation of the two or more selves, but in normal minds this does not occur, and the two personalities may struggle for dominion. James gives many examples: St. Augustine, for instance, enjoying what he called his "disease of lust", while his other self wanted to live a purely spiritual life. Conflict between different selves is familiarly experienced as remorse, felt when, having done the wrong thing, we are disappointed because it turns out that we had not after all the kind of self that we supposed, and would have liked to believe we had. In more general terms, conscience implies a recognized standard of conduct together with the consciousness of not always being able to sustain it.

Another way of resolving the conflict is to convince oneself that the different selves are not in fact opposed. The author of the epistle of Jude came across Christians who seem to have argued that, as body and soul are quite distinct, the one can be indulged without impairing the other. But the repression of the offending self is perhaps more common, and there are numerous cases of 'conversion' where the process of repression, having continued for some time, is finally consummated in some particular experience. Sargant noticed how often such conversion follows "long periods of accumulated anxiety, doubt, physical debilitation or a sudden overwhelming emotional crisis" (1967, p. 116). One may think of the thunderstorm which, interpreted as a sign of divine wrath, frightened Luther into promising St. Anne to enter a religious order if she would save his life. As with fear of the dark, fear of storms is not entirely irrational, yet its intensity bears as a rule no ratio to the danger, and this suggests an instinctive origin. The fear of divine wrath is, of course, rational—or, if the term be preferred, imaginative; but remnant instinctive fear would strongly reinforce it.[13]

By comparing the more hopeful creeds of later religions with the gloomy fears of more primitive times, we can see how much comfort religious beliefs may have afforded. According to early Egyptian ideas, all that the soul experienced after death was unceasing regret at the loss of the bright world it had left behind.[14] But later creeds have been mournful enough, and illustrate how religion flourishes in the rich soil of despair and affliction. Bunyan tells how, in his early years, he was greatly troubled with "thoughts of the fearful torments of hell-fire". As he grew up, this state of terror was mitigated by healthy youthful activities; but that he was still oppressed by fears of the future life appears from his concern to discover whether he could count himself one of the Israelites.[15] Ruskin was brought by illness to resolve that he would "at any rate act as if the Bible were true" and "believe in Christ".[16] One may ask how anybody can decide to change his beliefs because to do so might be profitable and can in any case not make him "worse off". Beliefs that rest on anything at all cannot be changed like that. But the importance of nagging fear in the process is, at least, obvious.

Preachers know how to play on such fears. In *The City of God,* Augustine represents the eternal fire of hell as real, literal fire, and the only mitigation he will allow is that it "will be proportioned to the deserts of the wicked, so that to some it will be more and to others less painful, whether this result be accomplished by a variation in the temperature of the fire itself, graduated according to everyone's merit, or whether it be that the heat remains the same, but that all do not feel it with equal intensity of torment" (Book 21, chapter 16). Wesley preached in such a way as "deliberately to induce states of terror-stricken awe, leading first to excitement and culminating in exhaustion; whereupon, as he put it, some sinners would be 'pierced to the heart', cry aloud for mercy and salvation and remain for a while highly suggestible to the implanting of new regenerative beliefs". Sargant, from whom I have quoted this comment, adds that "only with this basic technique in mind can we hope to understand such political upheavals as the Communist and Fascist and Nazi revolutions; a depressed and hungry people having been reduced by well-organised bursts of hysterical outcry and frenzy to states of increased suggestibility and emotional and intellectual chaos" (p. 135).

Fear is important not only apropos of the behaviour of individuals, but also of that of a whole community. It makes the individual members both less defiant and also less tolerant of unorthodox views. Crawshay-Williams has observed that "in times of danger to the community, the whole tendency to conformity is greatly strengthened; the herd huddles together and becomes more intolerant than ever of 'cranky' opinion" (1947, p. 28). Dodds notes that, in the history of ancient Greece, "the Age of Persecution coincides pretty closely with the longest and most disastrous war", and "the coincidence is hardly accidental" (1951, p. 190). Gilbert Murray points to modern parallels:

> To have found a 'spiritual home' in Germany was an innocent philosophical preference in 1911; in 1915 it was a criminal perversity, enough to drive Lord Haldane out of public life. To believe in the perfectibility of mankind in 1780 was an amiable fad; fifteen years later it was held to imply sympathy with the worst excesses of the French Revolution and to justify loyal citizens in burning Dr. Priestley's house down. (1933, p. 100)

"In an age of anxiety", says Dodds, "any 'totalist' creed exerts a powerful attraction: one has only to think of the appeal of communism to many bewildered minds in our own day". He argues that early Christianity grew strong in just such an age; when Marcus Aurelius began his rule, "the *pax Romana* was about to end and be succeeded by an age of barbarian invasions, bloody civil wars, recurrent epidemics, galloping inflation and extreme personal insecurity" (1965, pp. 3–4, 133–34).

When a society is menaced by an external foe, the occasion often seems to produce a competent leader because, where there is no danger, the rebellious, querulous tendencies of individuals are able to show themselves, and factional strife then obscures the competence of the superior mind. Hobbes says: "Man is then most troublesome when he is most at ease: for then it is that he loves to show his wisdom, and control the actions of them that govern the commonwealth" (*Leviathan,* Chapter 17). And Goethe writes of "the need for independence, which always arises in time of peace," whereas the compulsions and restraints which go with wartime are not felt to be moral affronts (*Dichtung und Wahrheit,* Book 12). How readily Britain made the considerable sacrifices demanded of it by its leaders during the two major wars of the present century! Yet today, when external danger is less obvious and less imminent, there is little response to appeals even for moderate sacrifices for the common good. In time of war, then, the majority become submissive, whereas in peace defiance is more generally distributed. A man may well have courage to face a trifling danger on his own resources, but when the situation seems more threatening, his self-reliance vanishes. He becomes loyal and orthodox, and looks to a leader.

National groupings, like religious ones, can thus owe much to the strength which comes from the readiness of individuals to subordinate their special interests to those of the group. But this happens only if the transfer of emotion from self to group has been adequate. There was but an incipient union of the Hellenic world under the influence of Persian invasion, as the threat and danger did not last long enough to produce an enduring sense of the Hellenic group.[17] Today, the conception of Europe is only beginning to acquire emotional flavour, because Europe has never figured in any great conflict with another group. Had the European nations found themselves struggling for a hundred years with those of Asia, the national sentiments of Englishman, Frenchman, Italian, German and Russian would have been swallowed up in the European sense, just as rivalry between Lancashire and Yorkshire vanishes in the face of conflict with France or Germany. 'Esprit de corps' may result from more peaceful forms of rivalry, but if the group feeling is to be strong, the idea of the group must become associated with powerful emotions, and these are not excited by trivial occurrences.

The group sense developed essentially as a means of defence, but the human mind readily substitutes one idea for another and can transfer to it the emotions attaching to the one replaced. During the French Revolution, the threat of attack from without unified the people. Napoleon represented the people, and the emotions associated with the idea of France became attached to him. But the original emotion of fear disappeared, and nevertheless Napoleon was enthusiastically supported in his wars of aggression.

Many have supposed that the cohesion of society depends on religious or quasi-religious delusions about the sanctity of authority, delusions which cannot be maintained in a free society, where dissent, criticism and unconventional opinions are encouraged, when everything can be put in question, so that the climate of opinion becomes unsettled, and certain acts are no longer universally approved or disapproved. In such a situation, the ordinary man's main motive for social behaviour (namely fear of censure from his fellows and desire for their approval) is very much weakened.[18] It is probably true that, in the past, some societies have been sustained by their delusions and have come to grief as a result of losing them. The Athenian authorities who wanted Socrates out of the way (before he in any case infuriated his judges by his behaviour at his trial) thought that if the young men ceased to believe in the gods—as they surely would if he went on encouraging them to question everything—then they would lose their respect for the ancient rites and customs, and with these their devotion to the state. But is there no alternative way of preserving and strengthening a society other than by keeping up certain delusions? If the young Athenians could have been brought to understand that the preservation of their country depended on their own actions, which was true, it might have been possible to persuade them to work for that end without the inducement of a false belief. It can, however, still be questioned whether rational insight into the needs of a situation, and into the long-term interests of those involved in it, can be relied upon to supply a motive that is strong enough to occasion effective action. Bonhoeffer's belief that he was inspired and supported by the ruler of the universe played a vital part in giving him both the strength to act as he did against Naziism and to endure the consequences—mere rational conviction that such action was appropriate would hardly, in his difficult situation, have sufficed.[19] Similarly, some religiously orientated persons are prepared to make personal sacrifices in caring for the needy to an extent which is less common among those who do not believe that such service is at the same time pleasing to a deity. I am not suggesting that the self-sacrifice which may go with strong religious commitment is always benign. The terrorist, religiously and/or politically motivated, is capable of considerable self-sacrifice. My point is that two or more motives working in concert produce much more forceful and sustained behaviour than does one, and that both the inadequacy of a single rational motive, and the ferocious behaviour sometimes occasioned by compound ones, are factors in human psychology which give ground for concern. The only reassurance is that awareness of their dangers may help to diminish these.

PART TWO

THE BIBLE AS A BASIS FOR RELIGIOUS BELIEF

INTRODUCTION

Included in R.L. Stevenson's *Fables* is a chilling story entitled 'The House of Eld'. A boy with an active inquiring mind lives in a country where by tradition iron fetters are riveted over the right ankles of children as soon as they begin to speak. From then on, they limp and nurse the ulcers on their legs. When he is ten years old, the boy notices travellers from other lands striding freely along the roads. He inquires of his uncle, the catechist, why this should be so.

> "My dear Boy", said his uncle, "do not complain about your fetter, for it is the only thing that makes life worth living. None are happy, none are good, none are respectable that are not gyved like us. And I must tell you besides, it is very dangerous talk. If you grumble of your iron, you will have no luck; if ever you take it off, you will be instantly smitten by a thunderbolt." "Are there no thunderbolts for these strangers?", asked Jack. "Jupiter is longsuffering to the benighted", returned the catechist.

One day, when he is 15 years old, Jack comes across a child from his village jumping and dancing in a wood, with his fetter lying on the grass beside him.

> "For God's sake, don't tell your uncle!" cried the lad. "If you fear my uncle", returned Jack, "why do you not fear the thunderbolt?" "That is only an old wives' tale", said the other. "It is only told to children. Scores of us come here among the woods and dance for nights together, and are none the worse."

After this he begins to waylay and question heathen travellers, who tell him things of weight.

> The wearing of gyves (they said) was no command of Jupiter's. It was the contrivance of a white-faced thing, a sorcerer, that dwelt in that country in the Wood of Eld. He was one like Glaucus that could change his shape, yet he could be always told; for when he was crossed, he gobbled like a turkey. He had three lives; but the third smiting would make an end of him indeed; and with that his house of sorcery would vanish, the gyves fall and the villagers take hands and dance like children.
> "And in your country?" Jack would ask. But at this the travellers, with one accord would put him off.

Finally, haunted by the sight of the limping children and the pain from their ulcers, Jack determines that he was

born to free them. He takes a sword and sets out to find the
sorcerer. He finds an empty house in the Wood of Eld, with
a fire burning and food set out on a table.

> As he was yet eating, there came into that room the appearance of
> his uncle, and Jack was afraid. . . . But his uncle was never more
> kind, and sat down to meat with him, and praised him. . . . Never
> had these two been more pleasantly together, and Jack was full of
> love to the man.
>
> "It was very well done", said his uncle, "to take the sword and
> come yourself into the House of Eld; a good thought and a brave
> deed. But now you are satisfied, and we may go home to dinner arm
> in arm".
>
> "Oh dear, no!" said Jack. "I am not satisfied yet".
>
> "How?" cried his uncle. "Are you not warmed by the fire? Does
> not this food sustain you?"
>
> "I see the food to be wholesome", said Jack; "and still it is no
> proof that man should wear a gyve on his right leg".
>
> Now at this the appearance of his uncle gobbled like a turkey.
>
> "Jupiter!" cried Jack, "is this the sorcerer?" His hand held back
> and his heart failed him for the love he bore his uncle; but he heaved
> up the sword and smote the appearance on the head; and it cried
> out aloud with the voice of his uncle; and fell to the ground; and a
> little bloodless white thing fled from the room.

Overcoming his horror, Jack goes after the bloodless thing.
In the way, he meets the appearance of his father, who
scolds him, and bids him to come home, when all will be
forgiven. Jack persists in his pursuit, at which the appearance gobbles like a turkey. Faced with his beloved father
Jack heaves up the sword and plunges it into the heart of
the appearance, which cries out with the voice of his father;
and a little bloodless thing escapes. Pursuing it, Jack meets
the appearance of his mother, who tearfully implores him
to come home before he does more harm,

> "for it is enough to smite my brother and your father".
>
> "Dear mother, it is not these that I have smitten", said Jack; "it
> was but the enchanter in their shape. And even if I had, it would not
> prove that a man should wear a gyve on his right leg". And at this
> the appearance gobbled like a turkey. He never knew how he did
> that; but he swung the sword on the one side, and clove the
> appearance through the midst; and it cried out with the voice of his
> mother; and fell to the ground; and with the fall of it the house was
> gone . . . and he stood alone in the woods, and the gyve was
> loosened from his leg.

The enchanter being disposed of, Jack returns to see the good effects of what he has achieved. On the way, he meets folk from his village. They wear no fetter on the right leg, but now have one on the left. On inquiry they say that this is the new wear, for the old has been found to be a superstition. There are now ulcers on their left ankles, and the ulcers on the right have not yet healed. And when he comes home there lie his uncle smitten on the head, his father pierced through the heart, and his mother cloven through the midst. And he sits in the lone house and weeps beside the bodies.

In the next two chapters, I shall be discussing the writings of a few catechists. They reveal a number of doctrinal differences; and they differ to a surprising extent in the candour with which they face the outstanding difficulties of traditional Christian theology. What they appear to have in common is that, however honest and straightforward their critical attitudes may be, sooner or later there comes the moment when they begin to gobble like a turkey. The reader will, I hope, be able to identify such moments when he comes to them. The second of these two chapters is focussed on the figure of Jesus and shows how little can be known of him. It is followed by a chapter on the Christian scheme of salvation, as stated principally in the oldest parts of the New Testament, namely the epistles. Here we shall find serious scholars of today very hard put to mount a defence of any kind.

3

THE BIBLE—WITH OR WITHOUT ILLUSIONS?

Professor A.T. Hanson and his brother Bishop R.P.C. Hanson, both recently deceased, have written *The Bible Without Illusions* (1989), where they note, as we shall see other apologists have done, that the present has not been the only period of uncertainty for Christians: past believers were perplexed successively by Gnosticism, Arianism, Aristotelianism, the Renaissance, and the rise of modern sciences; nonetheless "God brought his church through these periods of doubt" (p. 8). Today, they complain, clergy are apt to evade the equally serious problems that have arisen as a result of the critical study of the Bible that has developed since the nineteenth century. As Anglicans who have spent most of their lives studying and teaching theology, they presumably know of what they speak when they say that, although Anglican and other clergy will have been taught some biblical and historical criticism during their training, "many of them will never really have accepted it, and step easily into a sort of quasi-fundamentalism when it comes to preaching and teaching" (p. 5). Consequently, there is an "almost universal conspiracy to conceal the truth" about the Bible (p. 43). Against this, the Hansons' book is a strong and effective protest.

For our two authors, the Bible is neither inerrant, nor inspired, nor altogether consistent. It does not give an accurate account of the origin of the world, nor of mankind, and even its story of Israel's origin from Abraham till almost the time of Saul and David is legend (pp. 13–14). Samson is mere sun-myth and the historicity of Abraham, Joseph, Esther, and others precarious. "Balaam is a character in a folk tale and is no more historical than Robin Hood" (p. 75). The miracles recorded of Joshua, Jonah, and others are legendary. Moses did not write the Pentateuch, nor David the Psalms, nor Solomon the Proverbs or other Wisdom literature. The prophets were not primarily predictors and were granted no superhuman knowledge about future events. The Hansons do not, of course, represent any of this as startlingly new, but as what ought to be common knowledge by now.

As for the New Testament, the apostles referred to in the gospels as Matthew and John did not write the gospels attributed to them, nor Paul the epistle to the Hebrews or the Pastoral epistles. The second epistle of Peter (of course pseudonymous) "might well strike the unprejudiced reader as a blustering piece of crude propaganda" (p. 45). It is highly unlikely that Jesus was virgin-born; and the accounts of his resurrection are "in some places contradictory and confusing" (p. 114). The imminence of his return, so clearly promised by the earlier of the New Testament writers, is illusory and an embarrassment to intelligent Christians. An event that has been just round the corner for the best part of two thousand years is a non-event. As for his teaching, there is as yet no reliable criterion for determining which of his words are authentic. All that can be said with confidence is that they cannot all be authentic (p. 41).

The Hansons also note that epistles and gospels repeatedly appeal to totally inappropriate Old Testament passages which they represent as 'prophecies' of events or doctrines in early Christianity; and that this technique frequently involves considerable manipulation of the Hebrew scriptures—manipulation sometimes based on Greek mistranslations of the originals. The Fathers followed these leads and additionally used allegory to overcome difficulties such as contradictions or barbarities in the accounts. Although this preserved them from Fundamentalism, it precluded any proper study of the real meaning of the documents (p. 35). I think it would be juster to say that their real and obvious meaning was so often unacceptable that there was some danger that they would be rejected *in toto,* as they were by Marcion and his followers in the latter part of the second century. Hatch (1895, pp. 77, 79) said that the Old Testament was such a "stumbling block"—with "its anthropomorphisms, its improbabilities, the sanction which it seemed to give to immoralities, the dark picture which it sometimes paints both of God and of the servants of God"—that the allegorising method of interpreting it "largely helped to prevent it from being discarded" by Christians.[1] One might add that, even discarding it would not have freed them from all embarrassment, as the imminent and catastrophic end of the world, the activities of demons, and the existence of hell are New Testament rather than Old Testament positions.

The Hansons complain that few Christians are aware of any of the facts to which they are drawing attention because "intellectual courage is not . . . an outstanding quality of clergy in the twentieth century" (p. 42). Our two authors here perhaps underestimate the difficulties which outspokenness would bring upon the average clergyman, fearing as he surely does that many in his congregation have no wish to be told that what they believe, and what has been believed for hundreds of years, is untrue, and knowing that few of the faithful are intellectually and emotionally equipped to assimilate scholarly reappraisals. Our two authors perhaps also underestimate the extent to which the general knowledge of today is sufficient to make Christians who know the Bible at all—a surprising number, as we shall see, do not—query biblical statements on their own initiative. They know that the earth goes round the sun and is millions of years old, and that fossil and other evidence strongly suggests that the human species has been evolved like other animals from simpler forms.

They are also apt to ask whether Yahweh represented in so many passages as bloodthirsty and ferocious, is likely to be 'the one true God'. They perhaps have some difficulty in believing that Jesus could really still the tempest, walk on the water, and raise the dead to life. They will be aware that some of his miracles seem even to have no point, like the cursing of the fig tree and the incident of the Gadarene swine. And they surely cannot accept that damnation will befall anyone who does not believe in Jesus, although this is unequivocally stated in the New Testament (cf. below, p. 255). I suspect that there are many such parishioners, and that they keep their own counsel, perhaps because they do not wish to upset their vicar and their fellow worshippers by voicing reservations, perhaps alternatively because they have no strong theological beliefs and go to church to find warmth, companionship and a sense of belonging in a caring community. John Hick (1973, p. 20) has noted that the present-day public tends to regard the Protestant minister—approvingly—as someone who performs services of social welfare, and that the minister himself is apt to encourage this attitude which has "replaced the traditional conception that there are great and saving truths to be proclaimed and all-important transcendent realities to be witnessed to".

Whatever the motives for silence by clergy and laity alike, the Hansons believe that it is quite unnecessary, that the truth will not harm Christianity. Their persisting belief in some kind of divine dispensation colours their attitude to the ancient records and allows them, by means of broad generalizations, to construct a background for their faith. Some of these generalizations are advisedly very guarded, as, for instance: "It has been suggested that the Greek tradition of free enquiry and the appeal to reason combined with the Christian emphasis upon the importance and significance of the material world made the seed-bed for the rise of modern science" (p. 102). But when they speak more specifically of the Bible, they are less tentative. "There is more than one way of conveying truth. Legend, myth, story and poetry can all be used, and have been used, by the Holy Spirit to witness to God's dealings with men" (p. 60). For all their criticism, they feel entitled to hold to what they call "the main drift" of the Bible, "as understood by the Church down the ages"; and this, they say, "means in effect the doctrines of the incarnation, the atonement and the Trinity" (p. 27). From which it seems that they are not proposing to give up very much. The sequel confirms this impression.

First, they are insistent (and here they are surely right) that the Bible requires interpretation, and that there never has been an uninterpreted Bible. Those Christians who purport to be independent of interpretative traditions external to it ignore the fact that even what the New Testament itself says about Old Testament passages is sometimes based not on the sacred text, but on quite arbitrary Jewish interpretations of it current at the time of writing. One example the Hansons give in this connection is that Paul, having identified the rock from which Moses drew water with Christ, adds that the rock followed the Israelites, thus implying that it provided water during the whole period of the desert wanderings. There is nothing in scripture to this effect, but rabbinic writings include such a tradition and "Paul simply takes this piece of traditional interpretation for granted" (p. 19).

For the Hansons, the need for interpretation does not mean that the Christian must renounce private judgment and leave the whole matter for the Church; for to surrender all private judgment would itself be an act of private judgment, renewed every time submission is made to the Church (p. 99). What they believe is that "the way in which the church through the ages has interpreted the Bible is right" (pp. 24–25). The qualifying phrase "through the ages" implies assent only to what they claim to distinguish as common elements in varying interpretations over the centuries. These can be illustrated by what they say about prophecy. The Old Testament prophets looked forward to a time when God would fully manifest himself and sin be overcome, and this forward-looking element "was fulfilled in the coming of Jesus Christ". They concede that "this is a rather vague form of prophetic fulfilment", and they try to make it more specific by claiming that the prophets also revealed something of "God's character" (p. 82). Hosea shows that we are wrong to think that the Old Testament presents only a god of wrath (p. 76). He taught that "God loves those whom he has chosen", a love which "was to have profound echoes in the New Testament" (p. 83). As we shall see (below, pp. 157ff), some of these echoes embarrass liberal-minded Christians. Much later, Deutero-Isaiah (the anonymous prophet of the Babylonian exile responsible for Chapters 40–55) was "the first prophet to announce with absolute clarity that Yahweh is the only God", and "Israel had to achieve an understanding of God as one before, in the time of the church, men could begin to understand him as Three in One" (p. 84). This prophet also portrays God as saviour, so making it "easier for Christians six hundred years later to proclaim Jesus Christ as saviour of the world" (p. 84). The prophets, then, had these and other fragmentary insights into God's character, and Jesus brought its "full revelation" (p. 85).

All this implies that the Church has had knowledge of God's character independently of the Bible—a claim more common among Catholics than Protestants—and was therefore able to pick passages from both Testaments that illustrate it, while rejecting others that are equally well attested. Our two authors admit that their illustrations select what they consider "salient, significant, creative" (p. 121), and they speak of "the high spots of the Old Testament" (p. 138). Thus they will have no truck with "the practice of ritually massacring a whole community in order to dedicate them to a particular deity, which is to be found warmly approved of in the case of the people of Jericho, and of the Amalekites and several others in the Old Testament" (p. 100). Nor do they believe that God actually commanded that the man who gathered sticks on the Sabbath day should be stoned to death (p. 59, with

reference to Numbers 15:32–36). But when Nathan condemns David for abducting Uriah's wife and for having her
husband killed, this constitutes "an insight into God's
nature" (p. 93). Again, the Hansons, as we saw, greatly
admire the monotheism of Deutero-Isaiah, but fail to note
that it entails making God responsible for everything,
including evil. "I am the Lord, and there is none else . . . I
make peace and create evil" (Isaiah 45:7).

A similar process of selection underlies their treatment
of the New Testament, although here they do not go into as
much detail and are noticeably kinder towards it. They say
little about the miraculous element in the gospels, which
the ordinary educated reader finds all too prominent for
comfort, although they do concede that if Jesus believed
that the world is full of demons or devils bent on doing
human beings harm—and it is "difficult to avoid the
conclusion" that he did—then he was deluded (p. 100).
They do not discuss morally repellent elements in his
behaviour. These include his ruling that unbelief is a
cardinal crime (John 3:18 and 36) for which whole communities are to be frightfully punished (Matthew 10:14–15),
and that causing believers to doubt the truth of their
convictions is likewise culpable: "Whosoever shall cause
one of these little ones that believe on me to stumble, it
were better for him if a great millstone were hanged about
his neck, and he were cast into the sea" (Mark 9:42. If the
reference is to causing immoral behaviour rather than
unbelief, then the implication would be that immorality in
little ones who do not 'believe on me' is of less account. But
commentators agree that the 'stumbling' implies loss of
belief, and this embarrasses them[2]). Equally repellent is
Jesus's continuous vilification of the Pharisees in Matthew
23 ("ye serpents", "ye offspring of vipers, how shall ye
escape the judgement of hell?")—this from a preacher of
meekness and non-resistance ("resist not him that is evil",
Matthew 5:39)!—and his division (Matthew 25) of all
mankind at the final judgment into two groups—just
two—one of which will be consigned to "the eternal fire

prepared for the devil and his angels". The Hansons allude
more than once to Mark 4:11–12 without making clear
that Jesus here states that the purpose of his parables is to
conceal the truth from the generality of people and so to
prevent all but an elect from being saved. Perhaps it is such
passages that they have in mind when they say that in the
course of oral transmission his teaching may well have
been distorted (p. 101. On p. 21 they attribute Mark 4:12
to Mark rather than to Jesus). Even so, it is hard to see how
they can be so confident that the incarnation presents us
with "the perfection of human moral character" (p. 98).
This sort of thing has, however, been said so often[3] that
they are probably not conscious of any risk in repeating it.

The Hansons' way of dealing with such awkward passages as they mention at all is to apply their technique of
"balancing one part of the Bible against another" so as to
ascertain its "main impression" (p. 114), its "burden" or
"total effect" (p. 124). This involves, as with their exegesis
of the Old Testament, selecting 'high spots', particularly
among the later of the documents, so that the revelation of
God can be regarded as progressive. Instructive here is the
way they value the late fourth gospel for effecting "with
consummate skill the shift . . . from eschatology to christology" (p. 118), that is, for abandoning the doctrine of
Jesus's imminent return to earth, and emphasizing instead
that the Redeemer is present in the church now. They
concede that this fourth gospel "takes great liberties with
historical facts and does not hesitate on occasion to add to
and even invent new teachings of Jesus"; hence "it is on the
first three gospels that we rely for all that we know about
the historical Jesus" (p. 94). Yet we must not "discard" the
fourth (p. 120), but treat it as "a profound and authoritative interpretation" of Jesus's significance (p. 117), to be
"controlled and balanced" by what is said of him in the
others. The Hansons give numerous illustrations in this
context of incompatibility between it and them. But in
general our two authors underplay such incompatibility by
speaking of a general drift common to all the documents.

Revealing in this connection is what they say about the very different standpoints of Paul and John. The Bernese theologian Martin Werner argued that things went disastrously wrong between the writing of the genuine Pauline letters and the composition of the fourth gospel. For the Hansons, acceptance of such a thesis "would mean the end of Christianity. A New Testament that is so interpreted as to be fatally divided against itself cannot be used as the norm of doctrine. There must be some agreed interpretation of the Bible in the church, no matter how general and unconcerned with details it may be" (p. 17). It is, of course, omitting the details and sticking to generalities that suppresses the real discrepancies. The Hansons praise the Bible's honesty and give the frankness of Paul's epistle to the Galatians as an example (p. 133). But Paul's account here of his serious and extended quarrel with the Jerusalem apostles over the question of circumcision is incompatible with Acts' portrayal of complete harmony between all concerned on this issue.[4] The New Testament is, *pace* the Hansons, here as on other matters, divided against itself, as is the Old Testament, on their own detailed showing: God of wrath versus God of love; a God who punishes the son for sins of the father, and a God who does no such thing (pp. 83–84). The Hansons would clearly like the Bible to be regarded at least to some extent as a unitary, coherent book. But it is really a book only from the point of view of the publishers and the binders.

The *non plus ultra* of a defence in terms of broad generalities is reached when the Hansons declare that "the Bible's status and authority rest on its function as witness . . . Under this category we can unite virtually all its contents". This can mean no more than: each biblical book witnesses to the ideas expressed in it. Thus Genesis "witnesses to the ancient Jewish understanding of God in relation to creation", while the Law books "testify to the Jewish conception of God in relation to ethics" (we recall the stipulation about stoning the gatherer of sticks on the Sabbath!), and so on. From such enumeration of ancient tribal ideas the Hansons leap to the quite unwarranted conclusion that the Bible is "a book of witness to the character and activity of God unfolded over many centuries and culminating in the appearance of Jesus Christ" (p. 123).

We see, then, that our authors operate with two tools (which they do not always carefully distinguish): choosing the more edifying elements, particularly (though not exclusively) from later documents which can be held to cancel earlier views if these are less appealing; and alleging that there are common elements, or elements more heavily emphasized than others, in the disparate collection, and that these are to be accepted. The method of singling out what is common could be used to certificate what they would, in some cases at any rate, reject as unhistorical. There are common elements between stories about Robin Hood, but this does not authenticate them. The two quite incompatible nativity stories of Matthew and Luke agree that Jesus was virgin-born at Bethlehem in the reign of Herod the Great. The true inference is surely not that this, as a 'main drift', must be accepted as historical fact, but that this much reached both evangelists as tradition (the origin of which needs to be investigated) and formed the basis on which each of them built very differently.

The Hansons' final chapter, headed 'In Praise of the Bible', specifies first some of its literary merits, although earlier they concede that the style of both Testaments has often been criticized as "strange and inelegant", that it repelled pagans from Christianity and "repelled Augustine for long" (p. 32). But I must allow that literary merit is not purely a matter of style: the reader can respond to an emotionally charged situation or train of thought, even if it is conveyed to him inelegantly or in the "very simple Greek" (p. 131) of Mark's Passion narrative. Second, they praise the Bible's honesty which, I have argued, they overestimate, and thirdly its value for devotional use. They mention a Frenchman held hostage in Lebanon for almost a year who found that devotional reading of it kept him sane, and who was convinced that "it was God who set me free". Is, then, God responsible for failing to liberate others in a like plight?

Since the eighteenth century, many theologians have tried to eliminate from the Bible elements they found obnoxious. Their great difficulty has always been to leave enough to provide a plausible basis for their Christian faith. To my mind it is an insuperable difficulty, and some Christians have virtually conceded that this is so.[5] The Hansons think otherwise. Their standpoint—that when historical criticism has done its worst, there remains in the Bible an overall drift acceptable as a more than human revelation—is one that is today being pressed upon the faithful by other liberal theologians. John Hick, for instance, declares that, as a result of the last 150 years of critical study, "we have learned to distinguish between the central message of the gospel and its expression in the now obsolete thought forms of earlier ages" (1973, p. 104). But then one finds that, with Hick as with the Hansons, this 'central message' is not a mere residue, but comprises nearly all that traditional doctrine has prescribed; for the salient events of Jesus's career, as narrated in the gospels, are retained as historically true, while what is designated myth, symbol, or poetry is accepted as true in some other sense. Thus, regarding what is historically true, Hick says that "the life, death and resurrection of Jesus of Nazareth, his influence upon those who responded to him in faith, their memories of him and of his words . . . —all this is something that has happened and cannot unhappen. And it is this that forms the permanent basis of Christianity" (p. 111). The incarnation, however, is mythical because he did not claim to be God, nor did his disciples take him for God. Nevertheless the myth that identifies him as God is true if it serves "to evoke an attitude which is *appropriate* to the real character of that which is being identified" (p. 176). And the attitude evoked *is* appropriate, because Christians believe that salvation through Christ is a reality; countless of them have been "opened to the divine presence through their responses to the person of Jesus". Hence "in regarding the attitude as appropriate we are regarding the myth as true" (p. 179). This comes close to arguing that what is emotionally satisfying is thereby certificated as true—a not uncommon standpoint among apologists.[6] Hick sums up his position by saying that "(a) it is vitally important to maintain the genuinely factual character of the central affirmations of the Christian faith; and (b) given a basic structure of factual belief, there is ample scope for the non-factual language of myth, symbol and poetry to express the believer's awareness of the illimitable mysteries which surround that core of religious fact" (pp. 22–23).

The manner of defending a sacred text adopted by the Hansons and by Hick can be found among the stages of exegesis which are familiar to students of mythology and which are exemplified, for instance, in the history of interpretations of Homer (summarized by Hatch 1895, pp. 51–60). First, his verses were taken for inspired utterances of undying wisdom. But as some of them, if taken as they stood, were morally unacceptable, it began to be said (in the manner of the Hansons) that, on balance, what is good predominates over what is evil in them. When this defence proved insufficient, hidden meanings were found underlying their plain statements. It is only when a story seems incompatible with the ideas or principles of the commentators, and yet is part of a sacred or semi-sacred tradition which cannot be simply discarded, that there is any need of such interpretation. It is the last resource of those still interested in keeping alive the religious traditions.

All this shows how concerned are liberal theologians to neutralize supposed damaging effects of historical criticism. Perhaps their concern is unnecessary, for a surprising number of Christians are safely insulated from any such effects by an almost complete ignorance of even the plain statements in the Bible, let alone of what critical scholarship has made of them. The sociologists Stark and Glock record that a 1954 nationwide Gallup Poll showed that "more than two thirds of American Christians did not know who delivered the Sermon on the Mount", so that it seems pointless to ask samples of that population for their accounts or interpretations of what it is about. The same Poll revealed that "79 per cent of the Protestants and 86 per cent of the Catholics could not name a single Old Testament prophet, and more than a third did not know where Jesus was born."[7] A psychologist has commented that we find the same ignorance underlying political commitments: few people know the name of their Member of Parliament or are well-informed about the policies of each party: "Such 'general (trivial?) knowledge' has been shown to be independent of the confidence that is placed in either a religious or political system" (Brown 1988, p. 37). As we saw, leaders can attract large numbers of followers on a very flimsy intellectual basis; and so it is no surprise to learn that ignorance of the elements of the Christian faith is not confined to American Christians. The *Sunday Express* of 31 March 1991 reported the results of a MORI investigation conducted earlier that month in 55 constituencies throughout Great Britain. Eleven hundred adults were interviewed, 85 percent of them claiming to be Christians; yet 34 percent of all the interviewees did not know why Easter Day is celebrated, 39 percent could not say what happened on Good Friday, and more than 50 percent could not name the Roman governor who washed his hands after sentencing Jesus to death. The younger people interviewed knew far less than the older age groups, and a Member of Parliament attributed this to what he called "constant attacks on Christian education in our schools". In fact, however, the MORI findings revealed nothing new, and the Bishop of Peterborough said they did not surprise him. A report on religion in the British army during the first world war attested "widespread ignorance of the meaning even of Christmas and Easter, let alone other features of the Christian year" (Details in Wood 1955, Chapter 1).

In a book published by SCM in 1962, entitled *Tradition in the Early Church,* R.P.C. Hanson, who was then Professor of Divinity at Durham, declared that "nobody who has read the literature of the Christian Church of the first two centuries can avoid the conclusion that eminent Christian writers very readily attributed to apostolic tradition any custom or rite or tradition which they could not find directly referred to in the Bible and which they thought to be older than living memory" (p. 51). In my next chapter I shall give evidence that salient items in the gospels can be shown to be equally unreliably based if one bears in mind the dictum about tradition which Hanson himself endorses in this same book, namely that "an authentic tradition will become clearer and clearer the nearer it is traced to its source, whereas a spurious tradition may appear strongly and widely attested at a late stage in its history, but will appear more uncertain the further back it can be followed" (p. 35).

4

PORTRAITS OF JESUS, OLD AND NEW

i. JESUS AS UNKNOWABLE

Long ago, T.H. Huxley justly declared that "the question as to what Jesus really said and did is strictly a scientific problem, which is capable of solution by no other methods than those practised by the historian" (1894, p. 212). It is, he adds, "a problem of immense difficulty", and the gospels cannot be used uncritically to solve it. For instance, they include stories of Jesus feeding thousands with a few loaves and fishes (Chapters 6 and 8 of Mark, with some parallel material in the other gospels), to the complete satisfaction of their hunger, and with fragments left over amounting to much more than the original store. Before one could feel justified in believing such an event to have occurred, one would need, says Huxley, proof of the initial weight and quality of the food, of its distribution to the multitude without any additional supply, and of the weight of the fragments gathered up afterwards. But what the gospels offer is "two sets of discrepant stories, originating nobody knows how or when, among persons who could believe as firmly in devils which enter pigs", as in the story of the Gadarene swine in Chapter 5 of Mark and in the parallels in Matthew and Luke. With no more evidence for the feedings than this, Huxley confesses to feeling "astonishment that anyone should expect a reasonable man to take such testimony seriously" (pp. 203–04).

We can perhaps now better understand why some apologists, as we saw in Chapter 1, have been anxious to keep history and science apart. Science, we saw, is not fundamentally different from common sense, and Huxley reminds us that "the rule of common sense is *prima facie* to trust a witness in all matters in which neither his self-interest, his passions, his prejudices, nor that love of the marvellous, which is inherent to a greater or less degree in all mankind, are strongly concerned; and when they are involved, to require corroborative evidence in exact proportion to the contravention of probability by the thing testified" (p. 226). Huxley points out that there are many records of miracles much better attested than those narrated in the gospels, although everyone dismisses them as fables. But to reject these, while accepting the gospel accounts of similar occurrences, involves indefensible double standards. If, on the other hand, the evangelists' report on these matters to which they give such prominence is admitted to be unreliable, how can we be sure of its general trustworthiness?

Although it is convenient to go on using the traditional titles 'According to Matthew' and so forth, many theologians now concede that the four canonical gospels were originally anonymous and were composed not by eyewitnesses of the events described in them, but by unknown authors between the late 60s AD and the end of the first century—after the break in tradition occasioned by the Jewish War with Rome which began in AD 66 and culminated in the destruction of Jerusalem in AD 70. This break will have made it very difficult for evangelists to have accurate knowledge of earlier Palestinian Christianity which they purport to describe. Sanders and Davies illustrate what they themselves call the "difficulties" in this regard by envisaging the situation of Luke, who "was probably a Gentile":

> The Jews [had] rebelled, and the consequence was that parts of Galilee were ravaged, Jerusalem laid waste and the temple destroyed. Thousands had died, and more thousands had been sold as slaves. Whatever records there had been had vanished, as had

virtually all of the eyewitnesses of deeds done fifty years before. (1989, pp. 38–39)

In contrast to the authors of the gospels, Paul obviously wrote his letters before the Jewish War; for he refers to his dealings with an influential Christian community at Jerusalem that had clearly not then experienced the disruption and worse that the war would occasion.[1] Hence if even the outlines of the portraits of Jesus given in the gospels are to be accepted as accounts of someone who had been active in Galilee and in Jerusalem in the first three decades of the first century, one would expect some confirmation of them from Paul. It is, however, very striking that this is not forthcoming—neither from him, nor from the authors of other epistles written before about AD 90.

It is quite obvious that Paul did not believe Jesus to have been born of a virgin. He is not merely silent on the matter: the way he speaks about Jesus's birth excludes it.[2] More surprising, there is very little in his letters that can be construed even as suggesting that Jesus had lived recently, and what little there is need not be so interpreted, as I have tried to show elsewhere.[3] He represents Jesus as a supernatural personage whom God had sent in human form into the world to redeem it, and who had died there by crucifixion in unspecified circumstances. Paul never refers to a trial, let alone a trial before a Roman official, nor to Jerusalem (or any other locality) as the place of execution. He regards the resurrection, which he dates three days after the crucifixion, as an immediate ascent to heaven,[4] but does not suggest that either of these two events was a recent occurrence. It is the appearance of Jesus's ghost (from heaven) to himself and to others that he says occurred recently, and he thought that these appearances signalled that the general resurrection of the dead and the return of Jesus in a second coming could not be long delayed.

In a recent survey of Paul's letters, the theologian Nikolaus Walter agrees that Paul does not there mention any actions of Jesus prior to his giving himself up to death, "and certainly not his actions as a performer of miracles" (1989, p. 61). When Walter adds: "nor is his teaching activity emphasised", this is an understatement made to allow for the fact that Paul does, on three occasions, quote 'words of the Lord' resembling something that Jesus is made to say in the gospels. I discuss them below (pp. 184ff) and note that they have been regarded—I think justly—as words supposedly spoken by the risen Jesus either to Paul directly or through the voices of Christian prophets. Paul actually gives an example of a direct communication to him when he says that, in the course of his missionary activity, "I was given a sharp physical pain . . . Three times I begged the Lord to rid me of it, but his answer was: 'My grace is all you need; power comes to its full strength in weakness'" (2 Corinthians 12:7–9, NEB). Paul never says that the very few words of the Lord which he quotes or refers to were spoken by the 'earthly' Jesus and reached him via human tradition from that source. Walter is quite right to say (*loc. cit.*) that "nowhere in Paul's Christological or soteriological statements is there any other reference to the 'earthly Jesus' than to him as the one who suffered, died and was crucified." But more significant still is that even this is given no historical context, no setting in time and place—a fact which consistently passes unmentioned.

Any writer of course knows a great many things that he fails to record, and his silence is significant only if it extends to matters obviously relevant to what he has chosen to discuss. Commentators have repeatedly conceded that there is much in Jesus's teaching and behaviour, as recorded in the gospels, that would have been relevant to disputes in which Paul was embroiled.[5] His silence has sometimes been explained by appeal to 2 Corinthians 5:16, taken as implying that he was on principle averse to acquiring knowledge of, or showing an interest in, the earthly Jesus. There is, however, what Walter (p. 60) calls "widespread agreement" today that the passage cannot be taken in this sense.[6]

Although, then, there are no grounds for supposing Paul to have been uninterested on principle in the details of Jesus's life and behaviour, his silence about them could still perhaps be dismissed as amounting to no more than the attitude of an unhelpful mystic if it were an isolated phenomenon. But all extant Christian epistles that can be plausibly dated as among the earliest refer to Jesus in essentially the same manner as he does.[7] They may mention one or more of Jesus's supernatural aspects—his existence in heaven before his life on earth, his resurrection, or his second coming—but say nothing of the teachings or miracles ascribed to him in the gospels, and give no historical setting to the Crucifixion, which remains the one episode in his incarnate life unambiguously mentioned at least in some of them. On the other hand, those epistles that are widely agreed to have been written from AD 90 begin to show significant resemblances to the gospels' portraits of him—obviously because the traditions represented in the gospels were beginning to take shape.[8]

In sum, although Paul, like all the other earliest Christian writers, thought that Jesus came to earth as a man and was crucified, it is really very hard to believe from their accounts that they thought of these as recent events that had occurred in anything like the circumstances specified in the gospels. I have argued all this in detail elsewhere, and have tried to show on what the earliest ideas concerning Jesus were based, and how they became transmuted into the representations of him familiar to us from the gospels.[9] Few theologians allow the discrepancy between these layers of tradition the very great seriousness that it deserves.

The four gospels are not only unconfirmed by earlier literature, but also—as is well known to theologians but not to the average Christian—they also differ very widely from each other in their representations of Jesus.[10] This is what one would expect if their sources were traditions about a personage concerning whose life in human form nothing much was known, except that it was supposed to have ended in crucifixion. That such variegated material nevertheless continues to be used for constructing the authentic Jesus has the result that each theologian produces a different construct. That nothing like a coherent portrait can be extracted from the material has been shown clearly by Downing, who concluded his 1968 book with the regretful comment: "I can only suppose that this is what God intends and that he can make good use of it. An appropriate Christian theistic response is to accept a part in the debate, continue it, enjoy it, and expect love to be enhanced by it". But "there is no room for dogmatism, no room for claims to have arrived, claims to have found the one figure of Jesus on which all commitment should focus".[11] Because the earthly Jesus is so elusive, the suggestion has been made that Christological doctrines do not necessarily need to be based on "an 'historical Jesus' 'untainted' by the tradition and interpretation of the Church", and that the gospels have some kind of authority "as scripture, that is writings through whose medium the Church can bear witness to Jesus in a way that transcends his original historical context" (Moberly, 1990, p. 19n). This idea is by no means new (cf. below, p. 123); but a Church which frankly avowed that its 'witness to Jesus' was unsupported by historical fact would not recommend itself to the public.

ii. THE SIGNIFICANCE ORIGINALLY ASSIGNED TO THE CRUCIFIXION

If the author of the Pauline and other early letters in the canon betray no knowledge of a human teacher and miracle worker contemporary or near contemporary with themselves, there is nevertheless no doubt that they believed that Jesus the Christ was born and was crucified on earth; and 'Christ crucified' is central to their religious thinking. The reason for this is that they believed that his death had radically altered their relation to hostile supernatural beings.

Paul writes of the 'cosmos', sometimes meaning not

just the world in which man lives and the field of his activity, but rather, in Bultmann's formulation (1958, p. 257), "the sphere of anti-godly power, under whose sway the individual who is surrounded by it has fallen"—the sphere of "the god of this age" who has blinded the minds of unbelievers "to prevent them from seeing the light" (2 Corinthians 4:4), and of "the rulers (ἄρχοντες) of this age" (1 Corinthians 2:6, 8). Paul uses 'this cosmos' and 'this age' interchangeably (they are equated at 1 Corinthians 1:20 and 3:18–19), and Leivestad calls those whom he took to be its 'rulers' "some kind of mighty angelic powers" (1954, p. 94). They include "Satan" who "disguises himself as an angel of light" (2 Corinthians 11:14). Macgregor notes that Paul's wording resembles the title given in the fourth gospel to the supreme demonic being, "the ruler (ἄρχων) of this cosmos" or (RV) "prince of this world" (John 12:31; 16:11).[12]

'Angels' is not the term most frequently used in connection with these hostile powers. They are also designated with what Macgregor calls "a series of curiously abstract terms" (1954, p. 18), all meaning either the same entities or a cosmic totality in which individual differences are not regarded as important. These terms are particularly prominent in Colossians and Ephesians which, although ascribed to Paul, are probably of somewhat later date. They include (with the translations commonly used in English versions):

ἄρχαι, principalities, also used in the singular, ἀρχή when qualified by πᾶς (all), i.e. 'every rule'. Cognate is ἄρχων, ruler, plural ἄρχοντες.

{ ἐξουσίαι powers (or authorities).
{ δυνάμεις

κυριότητες, dominions, again also used in the singular, κυριότης, with πᾶς.

Θρόνοι, thrones. In the thinking of the ancient world, the empty throne, the seat of the godhead in the cosmos, often designated the god (Dibelius 1909, p. 128).[13]

An example of the use of these terms is the reference at Ephesians 2:2 to "the ruler of the power of the air". Many commentators have understood 'power' here as a collective term, making the meaning 'the ruler of the demonic powers of the air'. And Colossians says that worship of angels is to be deplored, since Christ is the head of "all rule and authority" (2:10, 18).

Another term is "the elements" ($\sigma\tau\omicron\iota\chi\epsilon\iota\alpha$) (Galatians 4:3). Paul tells his audience that, before they became Christians, they were enslaved to them, "in bondage" to beings "which by nature are no gods", to "the weak and wretched elements" (verses 8–9). True Christians, it is said elsewhere, have died to these "elements of the cosmos" (Colossians 2:20). Macgregor (pp. 21–22) adduces a number of pagan and Jewish parallels to this usage.

The idea that various forces within the cosmos also have their proper angels is represented in Revelation, where we learn that an angel stands in the sun (19:17), that four angels control the four winds (7:1), and that there exists "an angel who has power over fire" (14:18). Such ideas are met in the Jewish background. Jubilees (from the apocryphal Old Testament and dated by most scholars at about 100 BC) speaks (2:2) of the angels of the spirit of fire, of the winds, clouds, darkness, and so forth; and 1 Enoch 60:17 has it that "the spirit of the hoar frost is its own angel". That each nation has its own angelic ruler or guardian, except Israel, which is under the direct sovereignty of God, was also a widespread belief in Judaism.[14]

A number of New Testament passages declare that the invisible cosmic forces have been put into subjection by Jesus:

> Christ sits in heaven "far above all rule and authority and power and dominion" and God "put all things. . . . under his feet." (Ephesians 1:21)
> Jesus Christ, "who is on the right hand of God, having gone into heaven; angels and authorities and powers being made subject unto him". (1 Peter 3:22)

Cullmann notes that, since such statements are included "in all the ancient confessions of faith, from the first and the opening of the second century", belief in the existence

of invisible cosmic powers is a central tenet of early
Christianity, however unappealing today, and not merely a
"concession to Jewish contemporary thought", where they
are well represented (1962, p. 103).

Spirit forces which control the course of the universe
are prominent also in the astrological ideas of this period.
The planets were held to be astral deities, "kosmokratores
or 'potentates of this world' ", and man's fate was believed
to depend on them (Macgregor, p. 20). "Following the
example of the Babylonians, the Greeks had identified the
planets with the five principal gods in the pantheon—
Hermes, Aphrodite, Ares, Zeus and Kronos—and these
are the names which in their Roman guise [Mercury,
Venus, Mars, Jupiter, and Saturn] the planets bear among
us to this day. These astral gods were known to their
worshippers as ἄρχοντες" (Caird 1956, p. 14). Such was the
background of the religious experience of many pagan
converts to Christianity, and Ephesians 6:12 alludes to it in
speaking of "the world rulers (κοσμοκράτορες) of this
(present) darkness". The statement there is that "our
wrestling is not against flesh and blood", but against these
"world rulers" and against "the principalities, the powers
and the spiritual hosts of wickedness in the heavenly
places".

If Ephesians is not from Paul, Romans certainly is, and
in it he declares:

> I am persuaded that neither death nor life, nor angels, nor
> principalities,. . . . nor powers, nor height, nor depth, nor any other
> creature (κτίσις), shall be able to separate us from the love of God,
> which is in Christ Jesus our Lord (8:38).

'Height' and 'depth' are, as Macgregor notes (p. 23),
astrological terms—"the ascension and declination of the
stars".

The relevance of all this to the Crucifixion is that Paul
holds these supernatural powers ultimately responsible for
it. He speaks in this connection of "the rulers of this age", a
phrase which we have seen to have cosmic emphasis; and
he implies that these rulers, failing to recognize Jesus's true

identity, incited human authorities to kill him.[15] Had they known God's mysterious wisdom, they "would not have crucified the Lord of glory" (1 Corinthians 2:7–8). The idea is that, behind the human authorities responsible, there stand "invisible powers infinitely more dangerous, of whom the visible human 'rulers' are the mere agents" (Macgregor, pp. 22–23).

That more than mere human rulers were involved is indicated also in Colossians, which states that the result of the rulers' action was their own discomfiture: in dying, Christ "put off from himself the principalities and the powers; he made a show of them openly, triumphing over them in it" (2:15).[16] The phrase 'put' or 'stripped off from himself' can be understood if we bear in mind that Paul consistently argues that Christ must first subject himself to that from which he is to save others. Thus he was born as a Jew, subject to the Jewish law, to redeem those who were under this law, to free them from its "curse" (Galatians 3:13 and 4:4). Similarly, in entering the world he emptied himself of his supernatural form (Philippians 2:7) and assumed "the likeness of sinful flesh" (Romans 8:3)—flesh being that part of mankind in which the evil spirit powers can lodge; and so, in dying, he not only divested himself of his flesh, but also 'stripped off the principalities and powers' with it, thus—I quote Macgregor—"breaking their dominion and carrying with himself in his victory all those who through faith had come to be 'in him' and thus shared his experience" (p. 23).[17] Hence Paul is able to assure his audience that "ye are not in the flesh but in the spirit" (Romans 8:9).

The idea that evil spirits instigated the Crucifixion because they were ignorant of Jesus's true identity was more widespread than readers of the New Testament realize. It is clearly stated in an early Christian apocalypse known as 'The Ascension of Isaiah'[18] which purports to foretell that when "the Lord, who will be called Christ, will descend into the world, ... the God of that world will stretch forth his hand against the Son, and they will lay hands on him and crucify him on a tree, without knowing who he is" (9:14). By "the God of that world", Satan is meant, for a later passage states that the instigator of Christ's Crucifixion was "the adversary", who "roused the children of Israel against him, not knowing who he was" (11:19). Dibelius, in a pioneer work on the role of the world of spirits in Paul's thinking, gives evidence that the fundamental theme of this apocalypse—the failure of supernatural forces hostile to Christ to recognize him in his human guise—appears in a number of other ancient works, and so may be accepted as current in early Christianity (1909, pp. 97–99).

Such an assessment of Jesus's relation to the spirit world is incompatible with stories in the gospels where he is recognized by demons when he works prodigious miracles. At Mark 1:34, for instance, he "cast out many devils" (RSV "demons"), but would not let them speak "because they knew him". Leivestad notes (p. 107) that the fact that these demons are relatively minor powers does not remove the inconsistency; for if the small fry of the supernatural world recognized Jesus's true status, it is not credible that the angels ruling the world should fail to do so. Werner records that some ancient apologists tried to harmonize the data by denying that "the rulers of this age" of 1 Corinthians 2:8 refers to supernatural forces (1941, p. 246); and there are, of course, modern apologists who take it to mean Pilate and Caiaphas (of whom Paul makes no mention anywhere). For Caird, the 'powers' of which Paul speaks are merely "the political, social, economic and religious structures of power, Jewish and pagan, of the old world order which he believed to be obsolescent"; and the "fight against the superhuman forces of evil in the heavens" (Ephesians 6:12) is "metaphorical" (1980, pp. 18, 242). Caird's arguments in this regard are set in a context of determined effort to interpret the whole Bible so as to avoid ascribing unacceptable ideas to its authors: "There are always some naive people in any age. . . . But the writers of the Bible and its leading figures were not among them". They were not subject to the almost universal delusions of their age. "They might imagine the stars as angels and the host of heaven as a privy council around the throne of God (1 Kings 22:19). But they knew that this was only a picture" (p. 43).

My argument has been that, according to the epistles I have quoted, Jesus did not subject supernatural forces to his power until the moment of his death. Hebrews 2:7–9 has it that it was because of his "suffering and death" that he had everything "put in subjection under his feet". And it was "by the blood of his cross" that he "reconciled to himself all things, whether on earth or in heaven" (Colossians 1:20). Best has argued, I think plausibly, that the defeat of Satan, assigned in such passages to Jesus's death, is brought forward by Mark to his Temptation, at the very outset of his public ministry.[19] It really is not possible to reconcile the obscure and unrecognized earthly Jesus of the earliest Christian documents with the influential teacher and miracle worker of the gospels. And it will not do to accept the latter and ignore the former. The later, gospel modifications of the earliest ideas of Jesus on record are no more likely to represent any reality than are those ideas themselves. In the earliest documents the Crucifixion is an event, at an unspecified time and place, carried out by unnamed human personages at the instigation of supernatural forces, which ensures the salvation of believers because in the upshot it thwarted these forces which stood between them and God. This gives no basis of plausibility to the later idea that the event had occurred in Jerusalem, involving well-known Jewish and Roman officials, as recently as a few decades before the earliest documents were written.

Colossians speaks of the "fulness (pleroma) of the godhead" which is said to "dwell bodily" in Christ, so that it is no longer necessary to defer to "the elements of the cosmos" (2:8–9). This "fulness" seems to be a collective term for all the supernatural powers, "as if the ineffable divine essence were unfolded through them" (Beare 1962,

p. 107).[20] The previous chapter in Colossians has already stressed that this "fulness" is completely represented in the one person of Jesus:

> He is the image of the invisible God, the firstborn of all creation; for in him were all things created, in the heavens and upon the earth, things visible and things invisible, whether thrones or dominions or principalities or powers; all things have been created through him, and unto him; and he is before all things, and in him all things consist. And he is the head of the body, the church, who is the beginning, the first-born from the dead; that in all things he might have the pre-eminence. For it was the good pleasure of the Father that in him should all the fulness dwell; and through him to reconcile all things unto himself, having made peace through the blood of his cross; through him, I say, whether things upon the earth, or things in the heavens. (1:15–20)

The claim here is that, as a result of the Crucifixion, man can now commune with God without intermediaries other than Jesus. This is why Paul can, as we saw, maintain that we need no longer be slaves to the "elements", and that no spirits need now separate us from the love of God.

Paul's statement that the rulers of this age are "coming to nought", are being put out of action (1 Corinthians 2:6), leaves their final fate to Jesus's second coming. As we saw from Ephesians 6:12, it is still necessary for Christians to "wrestle against" them. But we must not expect complete consistency in time-tables of eschatological events, and the epistles give no uniform answer to such questions as: to what extent have the 'rulers' already been disposed of, and will they finally be destroyed or reconciled to proper subordination? The general picture is: first Christ's triumph over them at his Crucifixion, followed by his glorious ascent to heaven; then, at his second coming, the resurrection of the dead and the transformation of the bodies of those Christians still living (cf. below, p. 156); and finally his abolition of "every kind of rule, authority and power" (1 Corinthians 15:23–24). Paul expects Jesus to return to earth in the lifetime of his addressees, indeed in his own lifetime;[21] he distinguishes those who have "fallen asleep", meaning died, from those of us "who are alive, who are left" when Christ comes again (1 Thessalonians 4:15), and adds that when this occurs, "the dead in Christ shall rise first; then we that are alive, that are left, shall together with them be caught up in the clouds to meet the Lord in the air". Elsewhere he declares that, because "the appointed time has grown very short", those who have wives should "from now on live as though they had none; for the form of this world is passing away" (1 Corinthians 7:29–31, RSV). Attempts are still made to interpret this as meaning no more than: the present state of affairs will not last—with no implication of anything supernatural (for example Caird 1980, pp. 42, 103). But the idea that the second coming will shortly bring the world to an end is far too common in the epistles for this to be the case. Representative passages include:

> We, upon whom the ends of the ages are come (1 Corinthians 10:11).
> The night is far spent, and the day is at hand (Romans 13:12).
> The coming of the Lord is at hand (James 5:8).
> The end of all things is at hand (1 Peter 4:7).
> It is the last hour (1 John 2:18).

As we shall see (below, p. 112), the imminence of the second coming is also stated in some gospel passages. So long as this belief persisted, a general judgement of all the dead collectively could be linked with it. The few Christians who died before it occurred could be supposed, as Paul indicates, to be 'sleeping' for a brief period prior to their resurrection. But when centuries passed, it was felt desirable not to leave so many Christian deceased with their ultimate fate undecided, and so Catholic theology came forward with the doctrine of 'Particular Judgement', that is of each soul on its separation from the body at death. As, however, the second coming was still expected to occur, the Last Judgement remained, although it was hard still to regard it as a general judgement and not as greatly reduced in scale by pertaining only to the tiny minority still alive at the end. To resolve this difficulty, it has been supposed that at the second coming all souls will be reunited with their bodies. Thus the *Oxford Dictionary of the Christian Church* says, in its article 'The General Judgement', that this "is held to be the occasion of God's final sentence on humanity as a whole, as well as His verdict on both the soul and body of each individual", whereas "the so-called Particular Judgement" is "on souls only".

The passages I have been discussing, stressing as they do Jesus's supernatural status, are among those which have led to credal formulations such as 'Jesus is the Son of God', 'begotten not made, one in Being with the Father, Through him all things are made'. Bowden asks what such words in fact mean, and says there is no point in people "repeating them ever more loudly, certain like the proverbial Englishman abroad that if they shout the natives are certain to understand" (1977, p. 53). But do they really mean anything at all? And if they do stand for any intelligible ideas, do these correspond to anything real? Although Paul condemns any doctrine at variance with his own, even if it were to be preached by 'an angel from heaven" (Galatians 1:8), the epistolary doctrines discussed in this section contain nothing but fantasy and delusion, of a kind found equally well in other religious movements of the time which no one today would dream of making the basis of any serious commitment. Jewish apocalypses of the intertestamental period present a heavenly hierarchy of stupendous proportions, with whole classes of angels. The Qumran scrolls refer to angels at every turn, and the sectaries there expected them to join in an imminent eschatological war between themselves and all the heathen nations, good and evil angels being ranged on opposite sides in the conflict (Dupont-Sommer 1961, p. 165).

Whiteley, an eminent expositor of Paul's thinking, allows that such non-Biblical evidence must be considered, that 'the framework of thought of the Biblical writers, like our own, may well be wrong", and that we "probably" do not believe in demonic powers "quite as Paul did" (1974, pp. 281, 291). But, like most theologians, he contrives to avoid completely rejecting what Paul says about them, adding that "we can recognise in our own experience forces just as evil and just as powerful". As examples he mentions "the fact that things do not work together for good for those who love God in an obvious manner which all can see", and that "along the Russo-Chinese border there are millions for whom Christianity has never been a live option". He suggests "in all seriousness", that it is "realities such as these" which "correspond to" the 'powers', 'height' and 'depth', and so forth, of Romans 8 (p. 288). Macgregor likewise concludes his otherwise excellent article with a little demythologising, interpreting Paul's thought "existentially", "in terms of man's own personal existence and experience":

> We have only to look into our own hearts to be confronted by the 'principalities and powers'. We are still conscious that, apart from the victory of Christ, man is a helpless victim in a hostile cosmos . . . We still ask how a man is to triumph over an evil heredity. . . . We still suffer from . . . terror at the insignificance of man. . . . And can we ever conquer such fears except in the faith that Christ is Lord not only of the individual life but of the material universe . . . ? (p. 27)

First, then, New Testament scholars have to work hard and study much more than just the Bible to discover what Paul really meant. Then, because this meaning is obviously ridiculous, it has, by means of various contortions, to be given some other significance. What the work of most of the scholars I have quoted in this section shows quite clearly is: how untenable is the view of the Bible established at the Reformation—the view namely that, unlike other ancient documents, it can, as God's word, be understood by any literate person without scholarly help, and its various claims assented to. "Evangelical Christianity", says Van Harvey, "rests on this basic assumption" and "presupposes that just such reading and understanding is the basis of conversion". New Testament scholarship, in rejecting that claim, "threatens to alienate the Western consciousness from one of its most cherished assumptions" (1986, p. 198).

iii.   THE KORAN ON THE CRUCIFIXION

According to Sura 4 of the Koran, Jesus was not crucified. Neill (1984, p. 81) quotes the following English translation of the relevant passage:

> They [the Jews] said, See, we have killed the Messiah Jesus the Son of Mary, the sent one of God—they killed him not, they did not crucify him, but it was made to appear that way to them.

Rodwell's English translation of the Koran published in the Everyman's Library Series (detailed in Note 10 of Chapter 5 above) has a note saying that the literal rendering of the last clause quoted is: "one was made to appear to them like (Jesus)". Rodwell himself renders it as: "but they had only his likeness" (p. 427). Neill's version (the same in substance with Rodwell's) continues, after some few verses:

> They did not kill him in reality,
> but God exalted him to himself.

Some scholars have argued, in the interests of Islamic-Christian harmony, that the passage does not deny that Jesus died on the cross. Watt mentions a Muslim scholar who takes the implication to be that, not the Jews but God himself slew Jesus, and that the Jews took the credit for what was really God's own initiative (1987, p. 240). Neill is sympathetic towards such exegesis but allows that "it is, however, clear that the vast majority of Muslims believe, and have been taught, that Jesus was not crucified, but that God rescued him and carried him away to a safe place in the heavens". (He adds that "traditions tell that some other was substituted for him and was crucified in his place", although "there is no support in the Koran itself for this view". pp. 81–82 and note). And he stresses the implications of the text as it is thus normally understood: "If there was no death, there was no redemption through the death of the Messiah; thus one central article of the Christian creed is found to be baseless, and to rest on nothing other than a misunderstanding propagated by the Christian" (p. 82).

Christian hostility to Islam was never so bitter as it was to the Jews, or at least it was not so long lasting. There was personal contact with the Jews who lived in Christian towns, whereas the great majority of Europeans had no dealings at all with Islam and so no personal ground for quarrel. Also, Mohammed spoke respectfully of Jesus, and this the Jews could not do. They claimed what Christians call the Old Testament as their own sacred book, and denied that it foretold the coming of Christ. Islam had its own sacred book, and did not need to pay much attention to the Jewish scriptures, on which the Christians relied in their controversies with sceptics and heretics. Muslims soon came to regard both Old and New Testaments as 'corrupted' and therefore of no interest to them (Watt 1988, pp. 8, 11). In so far as strong aversion to Islam now exists in the West, it is due to recent mass immigration and to political developments in the Middle East rather than to any long-standing hostility. Watt is among the foremost spokesmen for reconciliation, but Muslims are unlikely to countenance his suggestion that they could make their views "much more credible to the modern Western outlook" by holding that Mohammed received his "messages" not directly from God, but "from his unconscious (in a Jungian sense)"—the unconscious being something vague enough ("a somewhat fluid conception") to accommodate this possibility (1988, p. 83).

The passage I have quoted from the Koran does not represent original thinking on Mohammed's part, but derives from aberrant Christian teaching which had reached him. Basilides had taught something similar in Alexandria in the second century. Irenaeus says, in his *Against all Heresies,* that Basilides posited a series of 'emanations' from God the Father which included various angelic 'powers' (we have met allusions to such beings in New Testament epistles); the 'firstborn' of the emanations was Christ, alias 'Mind', who, by his very nature as mind, was not susceptible to physical pain. Hence

He did not suffer, but a certain Simon of Cyrene was impressed to carry his cross for him and because of ignorance and error was crucified, transformed by him so that he might be thought to be Jesus. Jesus himself took on the form of Simon and stood there deriding them. [cf. Psalm 2:4, 'The Lord shall have them in derision'.] Since he was the incorporeal Power and Mind of the ungenerated Father, he was transformed as he wished and thus ascended to him who had sent him, deriding them, since he could not be held and was invisible to all.

Grant, who quotes this from Irenaeus, observes (1990, p. 49) that, in the account of the Crucifixion in the dozen verses following the point in Mark's Passion narrative where Simon of Cyrene is named as the person made to carry the cross (15:21), the pronoun 'he' is used instead of the name 'Jesus', so that it is possible for an interpreter convinced that Jesus did not suffer to argue that it was Simon who was crucified. (Jesus is not named until verse 34, and then not in all manuscripts.)

Basilides was but one of a number of second-century Christians who regarded suffering (which implies change and imperfection) as foreign to the divine nature. Such views had to be obliterated, and, until the discovery of gnostic tractates in Upper Egypt (Nag Hammadi) in 1945, they survived in Christian literature only in so far as 'orthodox' apologists refer to them. But the Koran was not subject to Christian censorship.

iv. SCHWEITZER

Albert Schweitzer (1875–1965) was well-known as theologian, physician, and organist. In his famous *Von Reimarus zu Wrede* (1906), he outlines the various reconstructions of Jesus's biography that have been made since the late eighteenth century, and gives his own theory as to what kind of person he was. Schweitzer took a medical degree in 1911, and in 1913 he gave up his academic career to care for the natives of French Equatorial Africa at the hospital of Lambaréné. He was awarded the Nobel Peace Prize in 1952.

The English translation of *Von Reimarus zu Wrede* was published in 1910, under the title *The Quest of the Historical Jesus,* and A. and C. Black issued a third edition of it in 1954. All three are based on the original German edition, even though in 1913 Schweitzer had published a second edition, entitled *Geschichte der Leben-Jesu Forschung,* with added chapters on the historicity of Jesus, which a number of scholars had called in question in the previous decade, and with new concluding remarks.

Schweitzer contributed a new introduction, dated 1950, to the third English edition of *The Quest,* and he there gives a summary of the views argued in the book. First, he sets aside Luke, as later than Mark and Matthew, and also John, as incompatible with the other three gospels (p. v). Whereas Matthew is generally regarded as an adaptation of Mark, supplemented with non-Marcan material, he accepts the portrayal of Jesus's ministry in both these gospels as basically reliable (p. vi) and thinks it of little account which of the two is "a trifle older" than the other, although "Matthew's fulness gives it greater importance" (p. xi). In fact he relies heavily on material available only in Matthew.

Schweitzer focusses on Jesus's teaching about the kingdom of God that is to be finally established. (It is sometimes called the kingdom of heaven, this nomenclature reflecting Jewish reluctance to use the name God). He holds that Jesus, and many of his Jewish contemporaries, believed that this kingdom would come soon, but only after a period of cosmic tribulation which would bring the world to an end. From Matthew's tenth chapter Schweitzer infers that Jesus believed all this would happen during his ministry in Galilee; for he there sends his disciples out to preach that "the kingdom of heaven is at hand" (verse 7), and tells them: "Ye shall not have gone through the cities of Israel till the Son of man be come" (verse 23—a saying represented only in Matthew). The Messiah-Son-of-man is a supernatural personage who is to come down from the clouds at the end of time (Matthew 24:29–31); and as Jesus

repeatedly refers to himself as the Son of man, he obviously, says Schweitzer, expected to be changed into this
personage and "to be recognised as such when the Kingdom of God arrives" (p. viii). That this will happen before
all the existing generation has died is the doctrine of Jesus
in a number of passages in both Mark and Matthew; but
only from the tenth chapter of Matthew can Schweitzer
infer that the kingdom will come in a matter of weeks.

When Jesus sends the disciples out to preach the
imminence of the kingdom he prophesies that they will
suffer persecution—as part, says Schweitzer, of the final
cosmic tribulation—yet in the sequel they return to him
from their mission without mishap (cf. Mark 6:30). Nor
had the Son of man appeared. Schweitzer claims that Jesus
must have said the words attributed to him by Matthew
when he sent them out; for no evangelist would invent a
speech containing such prophecies and then go on to
provide the evidence that they were not fulfilled and that
Jesus had been mistaken.

Schweitzer believes that Jesus's disappointment at this
non-fulfilment led him to revise his view of the tribulation
which he thought must precede the end; that he reflected
on Chapter 53 of Isaiah, which speaks of the servant of
God who gives his life for others; and on this basis he came
to think that, if he alone suffered and died, God would
spare mankind the final tribulation and would inaugurate
the kingdom (p. ix.)

One obvious criticism of all this is that uniform teaching about the kingdom of God can be extracted from
statements attributed to Jesus in the gospels only by setting
much of the material aside. According to the article
'Kingdom of God' in Grant and Rowley's 1963 *Dictionary
of the Bible,* "something over half of the passages" in the
first three gospels appear to regard this kingdom as future,
while others suggest that it is present already if only in
rudimentary form, in that it has been inaugurated by
Jesus's ministry. In this latter case, it can be regarded as
having come to fruition in the rise of the church, and

nothing catastrophic need be posited as a necessary antecedent. The author of this article is a little embarrassed by
this conflict of evidence, and concedes that "it may seem
ironical that so much uncertainty should attach to the
teaching of Jesus on a subject which must have been so
prominent in His message, and is so often mentioned in
the gospels". He explains this ambiguity by pointing to
"the variety of Jewish ideas on the subject"—a variety
represented among early Christians which led to different
standpoints being put into Jesus's mouth.[22]

The kind of passages on which Schweitzer relies are
exemplified in the following:

> "Verily I say unto you, there be some here of them that stand by,
> which shall in no wise taste of death till they see the kingdom of
> God come with power." (Mark 9:1)
>
> There "shall be tribulation", after which "the sun shall be
> darkened and the moon shall not give her light and the stars shall be
> falling from heaven, and the powers that are in the heavens shall be
> shaken. And then they shall see the Son of man coming in clouds
> with great power and glory. And then shall he send forth his angels,
> and shall gather together his elect . . . from the uttermost part of
> the earth. . . . Verily I say unto you, this generation shall not pass
> away, until all these things be accomplished." (Mark 13:19–30)

As we saw (above, p. 104), the epistles express similar
convictions.

Attempts have been made to harmonise conflicting
statements of Jesus on these matters by interpreting such
words of his as I have quoted as merely figurative. Thus
Glasson, anxious to support what he regards as the traditional view of the kingdom, namely that it is "the era of
redemption inaugurated by the life, death and resurrection
of Jesus" (1980, p. 5) and does not involve cosmic catastro-
phe of any kind, quotes, with approval (p. 14), the following passage from Hoskyns's *Cambridge Sermons:*

> Our Lord's eschatological language, as indeed all His teaching and
> actions, was mainly symbolical . . . He felt Himself standing on the
> brink of a new spiritual order which was to come into being as a
> direct result of His life and death. . . . To express this Gospel, He
> used the traditional language of Jewish expectation of the End,
> since it provided Him with a vehicle to express the significance of
> His life and death.

Caird (1980, p. 43) has taken the same view and complains that "the idea that the kingdom of heaven is an otherworldly sphere of existence is still prevalent, notwithstanding the central affirmation of the teaching of Jesus that the kingdom of God had arrived (Matthew 12:28) and was already being entered by the most unexpected people (Matthew 21:31)". He argues that "the biblical writers . . . regularly used end-of-the-world language metaphorically to refer to that which they well knew was not the end of the world. . . . And as with all other uses of metaphor, we have to allow for the likelihood of some literalist misinterpretation on the part of the hearer, and for the possibility of some blurring the edges between vehicle and tenor on the part of the speaker" (p. 256). We saw (above, p. 101) how concerned Caird is to avoid ascribing unreasonable views to Biblical authors. This concern is very apparent in his comments on incidents in the gospels that seem discreditable. He thinks that Jesus's words to the Syro-Phoenician woman which imply that the gentiles are "dogs" (Mark 7:27) "must have been spoken with a smile and in a tone of voice which invited the woman's witty reply" (p. 54);[23] and that by promising frightful punishment "on that day" (Luke 10:12), or "on the day of judgement" (Matthew 10:15), to communities who do not accept his disciples and their teaching that "the kingdom of God has come near", he means merely that if the Jews do not follow his advice and "abandon the road of aggressive nationalism", the Romans will destroy them (p. 265).

This is the merest special pleading, and there can really be little doubt that Schweitzer was right to suppose that the authors of many New Testament passages believed that the world would end within a generation. But as we saw, he thinks he can infer from Chapter 10 of Matthew that Jesus believed the end would come within weeks. Schweitzer envisages the disciples making a hasty tour of cities, rushing from one to another with their brief proclamation that the kingdom is at hand. He thinks that Jesus himself urged such haste upon them by telling them to take only a minimum of money and equipment: "Get you no gold, nor silver, nor brass in your purses; no wallet for your journey, neither two coats, nor shoes nor staff" (Matthew 10:9–10). The underlying idea is, Schweitzer says, that they will not need provisions and changes of clothing because the end of the world is so near. But in the text Jesus gives a quite different reason for his injunction: they are to travel light because "the labourer is worthy of his food", in other words, because they have the right to claim financial support from those they convert. The conversion is obviously going to be a long business, for Jesus warns them that they will be delivered up to councils, scourged in synagogues, and brought before governors. When they are thus persecuted in one city, they are to flee into the next. The statement that the end will come before they have 'gone through' all the cities of Israel could quite well presuppose a lengthy missionary activity in each.

Jesus's whole speech in Matthew Chapter 10 cannot be accepted as a discourse actually delivered by him, as it has been shown to be a compilation of units of different provenance, and includes sayings which are set in quite different contexts by Mark and Luke.[24] Glasson has pertinently asked (p. 18): "Is it credible that Jesus on one and the same occasion told his disciples not to go to Gentiles and Samaritans (Verse 5) and yet said they would be brought before governors and kings, 'for a testimony to them and the Gentiles' (Verse 18)?" The whole discourse can be understood as a compilation of rulings on matters of importance to Christian missionaries at the end of the first century, put into Jesus's mouth as an address to the missionaries he dispatched and thereby made into a paradigm of missionary behaviour. If Verse 23 means merely that the end will come before the new faith has gained a hold in all the Jewish cities, Jesus is not there being made to say anything that a Jewish-Christian writer of the late first century would have felt as inappropriate; and Matthew, in his usual way, has combined this material of Jewish outlook with material of more universalist tenor.[25]

I have tried to show elsewhere that Schweitzer attempted to make his view of Jesus as a deluded visionary
more acceptable by cloaking it in vague and mystical
language.[26] What he says about the gospel miracles is
similarly ambiguous. Strauss's critics, he says—I quote
from the third English edition of *The Quest*—could do
nothing to shake that writer's "conclusion that it was all
over with supernaturalism as a factor to be reckoned with
in the historical study of the life of Jesus" (p. 111). If we
accept the view of Strauss, we must say that belief in Jesus's
miracles arose at some time before the gospels were written
and was due to the feeling among some early Christians
that there must have been miracles. In other words, they
were merely myths. However, Schweitzer adds: "That does
not mean that the problem of miracle is solved. From the
historical point of view it is really impossible to solve it,
since we are not able to reconstruct the process by which a
series of miracle stories arose". But surely it is no insoluble
problem to explain how people could come to believe such
things, since history is filled with evidence that they do
believe very readily in just these things. If, however, he
means: in whose mind did a given miracle story first take
shape and why?, then the question is indeed insoluble, and
if such questions are asked of the historian of no matter
what period, of no matter what events, they will always be
unanswerable, as we cannot reconstruct the minute biography, external and internal, of every person that lived. If
Schweitzer means no more than this, he is not being
entirely candid. On the one hand he feels he has to concede
that it is 'all over with supernaturalism', yet on the other he
wants to put in the reservation that the gospel miracle
narratives "must simply be left with a question mark
standing against them".

Schweitzer also defends his own unorthodox view of
Jesus by repeatedly complaining that theologians' attempts
at reconstructing him have so often been guided by modern
notions of what he ought to be. They try to bring him up to
date. If what he is reported to have said or done does not

square with their ideas of what he should have said and done, then they exclude that from the record; and if he is inadequately reported by the evangelists, then they supply what is missing according to their own notions of what is required. Schweitzer might have noted in this context that such commentators are merely continuing what the evangelists themselves had done: they had put various doctrines into Jesus's mouth because they thought he must have had views which provided for the needs and controversies of their own day (cf. below, p. 135). Similar pressures underlie the so-called 'hadith', traditions about Mohammed's teaching which "originated in the first centuries of Islam in order to give the prophet's authority to decisions in judicial or doctrinal questions that had arisen in various circumstances" (Ringgren 1967, p. 58).

Schweitzer's protest against the tendency to regard as genuine only those elements which can be approved by the enlightened and humanitarian commentator has done little to stop this kind of writing. John Bowden complained (1970, p. 82) of a proclivity to ascribe to Jesus those qualities which a particular believer happens to regard as supremely good. This, he said, "can be used to harness all the emotional force behind the word 'Jesus' to endorse a particular view of life". The tendency is a general one: other heroes of the past are made more acceptable by being brought up to date. David Brown notes (1989, p. 47) that "the Methodist peer Lord Soper, speaking on the 250th anniversary of Wesley's conversion in 1988, claimed that Wesley would have been a socialist had he been living today, despite the fact that he had in actual life been a High Tory".

Schweitzer also objects, with much less justification from his premisses, to another way in which commentators' own notions can be introduced, namely when they try to understand Jesus and the records about him from what is known about human nature. In reconstructing the past, we can do no better than weigh the possibilities according to our notions of man's nature and of the sequence of cause and effect: we can apply no criterion except our own judgment of what is possible or likely, and in criticizing the authorities we can but try to assess their knowledge, motives, and opportunities, and the ways in which their statements have been transmitted. The trouble about the reconstruction of the historical Jesus is that, as Schweitzer intimates, there are other considerations besides that of simple probability, as the inquirer is seldom quite indifferent to the results of his inquiry.

Of course, if Jesus was truly a superhuman being, it is not possible that ordinary humans should portray him accurately if they did so in ordinary terms: if he was (is) God, then it seems foolish to explain him in terms of human psychology. If he, being God, took on the nature of man, the situation is rather different, for in that case we must ask whether, in assuming human form, he also assumed human psychology. If so, then—provided we have adequate records of his life—we can apply the usual criteria. Schweitzer, however, resents the application to him of what he calls "the petty standards of inquisitive modern psychology" (p. 309)—overlooking the fact that, if we cannot apply these, we cannot investigate history at all. He gives more praise to the sceptics than to the apologists, but he manages to preserve a mysterious figure, and even makes a virtue of the incredibilities and inconsistencies of the gospel portraits by saying that they depict a supreme personality whom we cannot expect to understand—a man, yet more than a man. Furthermore, in spite of his veto on psychology, he himself claims to trace the development in Jesus's thinking which led him to suppose that he alone needed to suffer and die in the final tribulation. Nineham has justly observed (1977, pp. 126–27) that this "detailed reconstruction of the development of Jesus' outlook and expectations . . . goes far beyond the evidence, and it is ironic that the very scholar who repeatedly pricked the bubble of the allegedly 'assured results' claimed by his predecessors, and whose survey showed the impossibility of writing a life of Jesus or tracing his 'development', should have thought himself able to trace that development in some detail, and should have claimed that the view he championed rested on a 'scientifically unassailable basis' ".

Psychological standards concerning the possible nature of a given human individual are inapplicable to Jesus, not because their application would degrade him, but because of the nature of the records about him. Since Schweitzer wrote, it has been established that Mark's gospel—the oldest of the four and one basis of both Matthew's and Luke's—is a stringing together of independent units of tradition, many of which had been used in the teaching and preaching of the church, handed on from preacher to preacher, and consisting of stories about Jesus deemed of doctrinal importance (cf. below, p. 134). Some of these will have been based on mere gossip, and they certainly cannot be put together as witnessing to the psychology of a single personage.

In the chapters added to the second edition of his book—there is no English translation of it published—Schweitzer tries to come to terms with the strange silence of Paul (1913, pp. 543–45) and says that, if we had only his testimony, we should never know that Jesus delivered a Sermon on the Mount and taught in parables. In his struggle against the powerful Christian group that wanted to subject gentile converts to the constraints of the Jewish law, Paul "could have appealed to this or that liberal-sounding saying of Jesus, but does not do so", even though he would thereby have "supported his opinion in an authoritative manner". Schweitzer's explanation of this silence depends on his theory that Jesus's consciousness that he was the Messiah was a secret he tried to keep to himself. I need not repeat here my criticism of this view: the so-called 'Messianic secret' can be shown to be an artificial element imposed on his material by Mark.[27] But if it is accepted as a factor in Jesus's biography, then Schweitzer can justly infer that "he left no detailed teaching about the significance of the death he expected to suffer", so that

Paul had to base his faith on the Resurrection that followed the Crucifixion, and "it was only the spirit of the risen one"—not the preacher of Galilee—who could "indicate the significance of these events". In any case, Paul's basic religious idea is "the belief in the coming events", and he did not need Jesus the preacher to tell him about these, as the conviction that the world was coming to an end permeated the Jewish background of earliest Christianity.

Schweitzer admits that this is not a totally satisfactory explanation of Paul's "remarkable one-sided emphasis on the authority of the exalted [the risen] Jesus"—quite apart from the fact that he is not the only early Christian writer whose strange silence has to be explained. "The fact remains", says Schweitzer, "that early Christianity does not take up Jesus's teachings into its religion in the way we should expect".

This was written when J.M. Robertson in England and Drews and others in Germany were questioning Jesus's very historicity.[28] Schweitzer admits that Paul's evidence does not settle this matter either way. "He is as enigmatic in what he says as in what he does not say" about it. But Schweitzer counter-attacks, saying: if theologians are hard put to explain why Jesus, as portrayed in the first three gospels, is ignored by Paul, Robertson and Drews have equal difficulty in explaining why the Jesus of these gospels does not resemble Paul's Jesus, from whom he has nevertheless arisen (p. 550). One might reply by asking why the Johannine Jesus is so different from the Jesus of the first three gospels, even though John used source material that was similar to theirs. There were many views of Jesus in early (as in later) Christianity, and already Paul complains of those who preach "another Jesus" and "another gospel" (2 Corinthians 11:4). Admittedly, it is reasonable to ask how the Pauline figure came to be made into the teacher who suffered under Pilate. I have tried to answer that question in Wells 1971, 1982, and 1986A.

Schweitzer argues further that it will not do to set aside "Peter and the others" as mythical figures (p. 548). But there is in fact no need to question the existence of the Peter and the James with whom Paul says he quarrelled. What is in question is whether they were companions of the historical Jesus, as alleged in the gospels. When Schweitzer declares that even "Paul's existence is not better attested than that of Jesus", he invites the reply that Jesus wrote nothing, while the principal letters ascribed to Paul were written in an identifiable (pre-AD 70) situation (cf. above, p. 93) and deal with problems relevant to that situation. How, for instance, can the arguments about circumcision in his letter to the Galatians be anything but early, when the whole question had ceased to excite interest in the documents of the next generation? And what later Christian would have invented the quarrel between him and Peter (and even represented it as unresolved) which in this same epistle gives him occasion to state his theological position? Schweitzer's statement that Paul's letters are not well attested in later literature—so that, if one were sufficiently perverse, one might doubt his author-ship of them—overstates the case, as quite a number of later epistles have been shown to be dependent on one or more of the Paulines.[29]

In these chapters added to the second edition Schweit-zer elaborates on his belief that consciousness can furnish what he calls "unmediated" or "immediate" (unmittelbar) certainties, whereas propositions concerning past events rest on testimony that is no longer directly available and so are no more than hypotheses (pp. 509ff). He began his whole book with the boast that "the German tempera-ment" is uniquely qualified to achieve "deep theology", as nowhere else is there to be found anything like the neces-sary complex of "philosophic thought, critical acumen, historical insight, and religious feeling" necessary to the task. And now, in this second edition, he censures the theologians of the late nineteenth century for having broken with the great German metaphysical tradition, so that they have come to neglect "unmediated thinking about being and life, finitude and infinity, God and ultimate causation", and have foolishly based their religion on what they took for the "assured results" of historical investigation. In this intellectual climate, "the mindless proposition that without Jesus we should all have to be atheists was accepted as the pinnacle of wisdom". But at this very time, theologians were themselves undermining this position by refusing to accept even the earliest gospel, Mark, as reliable in its entirety, and seeing it rather as but a statement of what an early Christian community believed. This, says Schweitzer, made it all the easier to argue that it is wholly unreliable, thus playing into the hands of those who were denying Jesus's very historicity.

Instead of responding to such scepticism with purely historical arguments, the theologians should, in Schweitzer's view, have insisted that to give up Jesus altogether would mean losing much, but by no means all, as liberal Christianity could still be sustained by "the insights and forces of unmediated religion independent of any historical foundation". The need for such independence of course arises because the evidence concerning Jesus is so unsatisfactory. If his career were as well attested as that of Julius Caesar, Mohammed, or Queen Anne, no one would need to denigrate the relevant evidence as establishing mere probability and to look elsewhere for certainty. Schweitzer really admits as much when he says that "theoretical considerations" are all the more important in the case of Jesus, as all information about him derives from Christian sources, and there are no confirmatory notices of any value from Jewish or pagan ones (p. 512).[30]

Schweitzer, then, advocates grounding religion "on mind, not on history" (p. 514) and even says that the great advantages of a metaphysic that is ready to hand can be observed in the quite unflurried reaction of theosophists to the questioning of Jesus's historicity (p. 512n). Furthermore, the theologians who have replied to such questioning are, he says, defending not Jesus as he really was, but a Jesus of a nature acceptable to them; they do not seem to realize that his standpoint was in fact too alien to be religiously acceptable today, that, for instance, his ethics either leave unmentioned or even positively devalue labour and acquisitiveness—intelligibly enough in someone expecting an immediate end to the world, but no model for us—and are also compromised by crass expectations of reward for good behaviour, by Jewish particularisms, and by the view that God is the father only of those who are predestined to be saved (p. 516). This, the real historical Jesus, is, he says, very different from the Christological constructions of the nineteenth century, not to mention the traditional ecclesiastical doctrines of "the person of Christ". Nor can these facts be evaded by recourse to the doctrine that the Jesus who matters is the "historic" rather than the historical Jesus—the figure who was effective over the centuries: for the record of this effectiveness is often a deeply shameful one (p. 521). Schweitzer also rejects the standpoint of those who declare Jesus to be an important "symbol", however little historical reality he may have had. A religious community, it was said, needs the support of something that can be clearly envisaged, not something general or abstract, as the focus of its religious life. A general term, such as "religion" has so many associations that it may excite no particular feeling; but thoughts of a child in a manger, of a teacher haranguing his audience on a mountain, or of a tortured figure on the cross consist of particular images to which emotions are more readily attached. But this gives too sensuous a basis to religion to be acceptable to Schweitzer the metaphysician; and so he concludes that neither the radical theologians who say very little can be known of Jesus, nor the Fathers with their Christologies, nor those who allow him mere symbolic status come to grips with the Jesus of history. And this is the situation in which Christians are trying to defend his historicity! "It is almost as if they were defending something they have never possessed" (p. 525).

For Schweitzer the real alternatives are: either there was no Jesus at all, or else there was the deluded visionary who is "all too historical". "Either he did not exist, or he was as Matthew and Mark quite literally depicted him" (p. 518). Later, however (p. 553n), he admits to having to set aside a good deal of the material in these two gospels, and concedes that their accounts are admixed with so much that is "miraculous, disconcerting, and inexplicable" that no clear division can be made between what is historical in them, and what is due to misunderstanding, imaginative construction, and elaboration.

Schweitzer's view that religion needs to be in essence independent of all history has been taken up by Bultmann, Tillich, and Van Harvey, among others, who are well aware that otherwise religious faith will be vulnerable, as the results of even the best historical scholarship may in time have to be revised. Harvey (1967, pp. 280–81) says that "faith has to do with one's confidence in God", and its "content can as well be mediated through a historically false story *of a certain kind* as through a true one." The italicised proviso is meant to allow for the fact that "the conditions of belief change from age to age. What may have been intelligible and valid for Augustine and Francis may not be so for those of us who live after the advent of Biblical criticism."

Schweitzer nevertheless thinks that, if Jesus is alloted a place as merely one element in religion, then all reservations about his function cease to be relevant, however much importance he claims, because under these circumstances the danger of narrowing down religion to a purely historical basis is no longer present (p. 519). And so in the conclusion (also new) to this second edition, he tries to argue some relevance of Jesus for modern man, and does so by means of strange doctrines about "the will". Here he is indebted in particular to Schopenhauer in the German metaphysical tradition. Schopenhauer held that "only internal occurrences, in so far as they concern the will, have true reality . . . Outer occurrences are mere configurations of the world of appearance, and so have neither reality nor significance that is immediate".[31] What Schweitzer has been saying about the "immediate" knowledge furnished by consciousness is in line with this. He further holds that "the ultimate and deepest knowledge of things comes from the will" (p. 636), which is "timeless" and reveals "the unfathomable and primary essence of a personality".

Before I try to explain how all this is made to appear relevant to our estimate of Jesus, I would note that there is really no reason to distinguish experiences attributable to the will as fundamentally different from other kinds of experience. The practical distinction is that they arise on the internal sensorium. Schopenhauer believed that there is an experiencing ego or soul that receives impressions from the external sense organs (eyes, ears, and so on), and that this soul has immediate consciousness of the volitions, but only mediate consciousness of the external world. Such a claim can be made only because the external sense organs are obvious, while the internal sensorium is concealed. The receptors in muscle and viscera are inaccessible; hence the assumption that internal experiences are direct, immediate, undisturbed by any recording apparatus. If it were as easy to demonstrate the relation of the brain to the emotional disturbances within the body as it is to trace its connection with the external stimuli that fall upon the skin, eyes, and ears, then this dualism could hardly have suggested itself. There is no other kind of knowledge except what can be had of the environment, and this knowledge is possible only if the sensory apparatus is intact or partly intact. If this is indirect knowledge, then there is none that is direct.

For Schweitzer the will is unchanging. The material which goes to form the ideas on which a world view is based has changed considerably over the centuries, but divergencies between ancient and modern world views are, for him, due primarily to divergencies in the directions taken by the will that shapes them. Hence to discover Jesus's relevance today, we must ask: "How can his will, comprehended in its immediacy and precise orientation, and in its whole compass, express itself in the material of our ideas, and form from this material a world view so moral and so powerful in its nature that it could serve as the modern equivalent of the one he created within the framework of late Jewish metaphysics and eschatology?" His function can thus lie "only in this, that as a powerful spirit he can bring motifs of willing and hoping, which we and those around us carry in ourselves, to such a height and to such a clarification which we would not achieve if we were restricted to our own resources and did not lie under the influence of his personality" (pp. 635–36). Modern people seem to "lack the strongly developed willing and hoping for the final moral perfection of the world which are of decisive importance for Jesus and for his world view". The limitations of his outlook fall away "once his will as such is transposed into the world as we see it" (pp. 639–640). The phrase 'a so-and-so as such' can really only mean that the thing in question is necessarily many things besides what its name especially signifies. Thus we may say: Jones is a policeman, and as such he has certain duties. But by "Jesus's will as such" Schweitzer means no more than a will that was particularly strong and assertive.

Schweitzer is pleading for what he calls an "ethical eschatology" as the "equivalent" of Jesus's late-Jewish eschatology (p. 638). He concludes, appropriately enough, by conceding that "in the last analysis our relation to Jesus is mystical in nature" (p. 641). We are to establish community with him by sharing his will to "put the kingdom of God above all else"—although what this phrase means to us (if anything at all) is not what it meant for him.

v. HOSKYNS AND DAVEY

Sir Edwyn Hoskyns's and Noel Davey's *The Riddle of the New Testament* was published in 1931 and, like Schweitzer's book, was immensely successful, and has even been translated into 18 languages. I shall quote from the 1958 edition.

Like Schweitzer, Hoskyns and Davey present themselves not as apologists, but as historians concerned only to ascertain the truth. Admittedly, they "suggest" that, to understand Jesus and the emergence of the church, it is necessary "to pass beyond that which is most characteristic in modern thought, to think of God as the living and active God, and to move freely in terms not only of revelation in general, but of the revelation of the power of the living God in a particular history" (p. 34). But the wording is non-committal: it is not said that, in 'thinking of God' in this manner, one need suppose such thoughts to be true.

To 'move freely' in 'terms' would seem to mean 'to be fluent in the use of a particular terminology'. This, perhaps, fairly describes their own expertise. An example is their use of the terms 'history' and 'historical'. They are aware that it has been maintained that "the original Christian gospel was a Christ-myth, which was subsequently clothed with flesh and blood". But they hold that "this possibility cannot be considered in an historical study, since on this assumption the Jesus of history would become a proper subject for historical investigation only at the Last Judgement" (p. 81n). The meaning appears to be that a historical study cannot be concerned with a non-historical character. Yet when we approach the question of the origin of any religion, one of the first questions we ask is whether the persons associated by tradition with that origin had a historical existence or were merely mythical. Whether such an inquiry can be called "a historical study" or not seems a rather subtle question. One can, however, understand why they prefer to postpone it till the Last Judgement.

Hoskyns and Davey are—again like Schweitzer—concerned to counter the view that Jesus was no more than a man of exceptional character who preached a doctrine of non-resistance and self-denial, but was innocent of all supernatural pretensions. Many who were unable to accept the miraculous element in the gospel story supposed that, if they idealized him and emphasized his supposedly revolutionary moral teaching, they could continue to call themselves Christians with a clear conscience. But the evidence which led them to discount so large a part of the gospel story was held by some to establish the unreliable character of the remainder. And, as Hoskyns and Davey point out, his moral teaching was in fact not at all new: "There is no single moral aphorism recorded as spoken by Jesus which cannot be paralleled, and often verbally paralleled, in rabbinic literature" (p. 135).

One of the most disturbing facts was the frequency with which the evangelists suggest, or even claim, that Jesus's behaviour can be related to Old Testament prophecy. This happens so frequently as to give rise to the suspicion that such incidents were not actually part of his life, but had been invented so as to give the appearance that he was the Messiah. Orthodox belief until fairly recent times always claimed such parallels as proofs of the fundamental tenets of Christianity. But if he was not the Messiah, the relevant details may have been subsequently foisted onto his career for the edification of believers. Both Schweitzer and Hoskyns and Davey wish to give a plausible explanation of the parallels without conceding this. They hold that Jesus was well-read in the Hebrew Scriptures and somehow came to suppose that he was destined to be the scapegoat for the salvation of mankind. He therefore arranged his life as closely as he could in conformity with prophecy. So if we find that incidents in his recorded life appear to have been accurately foretold by the Hebrew prophets, this is not because the New Testament writers have reported inaccurately, but because he managed to arrange things so that they agreed with the predictions.

Hoskyns and Davey admit that the evangelists exaggerate the extent to which Jesus's behaviour accorded with prophecy, and sometimes do so in a grotesque manner, as when he is made to sit astride two animals at his triumphal ride into Jerusalem because Matthew mistakenly thought that this was what a prophecy in the book of Zechariah required (p. 64). But they insist that all such distortion is no more than a "drawing out the implications" of what his behaviour had actually been (p. 62), not an attempt to pretend that a man who had been no more than an ordinary teacher was the Messiah.

Our two authors show that all four blocks of tradition which they distinguish as constituting the material of the first three gospels agree in representing Jesus as God's emissary. Hence, they say, this element must have been present in the material as it reached these evangelists, and could not have been imposed on it by their editorial handling. That he was not represented as a mere teacher in this material need in fact cause no surprise, and is less significant than Hoskyns and Davey suppose, since the pre-gospel traditions about him, extant in the Pauline and other early epistles, quite unambiguously make him a supernatural personage who assumed human form during his sojourn on earth, and do not suggest that he had been an ethical teacher at all. What needs to be ascertained is whether this, the oldest extant layer of Christian tradition, is truth or legend. It is quite unwarranted for Hoskyns and Davey to infer, as they do, that the uniformity of the four secondary layers shows that the ideas there represented originated not in "the creative faith of the primitive church", but in "the teaching and actions of Jesus of Nazareth" (p. 81). All that can really be justly inferred is that the evangelists did not impose a Messianic interpretation on what reached them as *tradition*. Whether, as Hoskyns and Davey imply (p. 172), this tradition accurately represented *history* is still questionable; and in more than one passage our two authors put their point in wording that really concedes this, saying for instance that the evangelists "extracted their purpose from the traditions they received: they did not impose it roughly upon a material unable to bear it" (p. 114; cf. pp. 111–12).

A typical example of what is said about Jesus in

Christian tradition earlier than the gospels—or at any rate before knowledge of them (or of the ideas represented in them) was available to the relevant Christian communities —can be found in the first epistle of Peter, today widely admitted to be pseudonymous. The author knows not of Jesus's manner of life, but only of his death as exemplary behaviour, and, as Hoskyns and Davey themselves show (p. 57), what is said about it in this epistle is taken directly from the Old Testament, from the story of the suffering servant of Yahweh in Chapter 53 of the book of Isaiah, not from historical reminiscence about 'Jesus of Nazareth'. The Jews regarded this chapter as containing Messianic prophecies, so it is quite intelligible that Christians, who believed that Jesus was the Messiah, should draw on it for details of his biography.

At the end of their book, Hoskyns and Davey claim to have "solved the historical problem" (p. 179) which at the outset they specified as "the riddle of the New Testament", namely: "What was the relation between Jesus of Nazareth and the primitive Christian church?" (p. 12). Their answer is: this church did not foist a messianic interpretation onto his behaviour. The messianic element was already there in it. "The future order, which it was the purpose of Jesus to bring into being, depended upon what he said and did, and finally upon his death" (p. 172). We are left asking what this future order was, why it depended on his death, whether it was in fact brought into being, and, if so, when and where. In sum, we wish to know whether he was deluded, or whether he was justified in regarding himself as a special emissary of God. Hoskyns and Davey decline to answer, although they stress that it is a question "of the highest possible urgency for all men and women" (p. 181). They are mere historians, whose task is not "to judge whether the significance which Jesus assigned to his actions and to his person was in the end true, but only to make clear what significance he did in fact give to his work" (p. 170).

When they write of the credibility of the gospels, they have some difficulty in sustaining this attitude of neutrality. Admittedly, they allow that some of the miracles recorded there may be dramatizations of what were originally mere parables (p. 124); and that we should not be confident that "the framework in which the evangelists have set the miracles, parables and aphorisms of Jesus is necessarily historical", nor that "even the miracles, parables and aphorisms themselves, when isolated from the framework, are straight historical records". And when they maintain that both the framework and the miracles, parables, and aphorisms set in it "emerge from, lie upon, and rightly interpret the general matter of the tradition" (p. 145), this 'right interpretation' means, in this context, no more than acceptance of tradition without distorting it, not a radical sifting of it so as to extract the truth, if any, from it. Again, our two authors concede that it is not possible "to pronounce a final judgement as to whether isolated events happened or did not happen as they are recorded in the gospels" (p. 11). But the word 'isolated' turns out to be important here; for although they admit that "a biography of Jesus cannot be provided", they hold that "a historical reconstruction" is nevertheless possible

> when the uniform nature of the whole material at our disposal is perceived, so that each fragment is seen not only to be part of the whole, but to contain the whole; or, to put it differently, so that each fragment of it not only rests upon a common background, but expresses it. To lay bare this uniform nature, this background, is to discover the Jesus of history (pp. 171–72).

The historian's results, they say, "forbid him to detach portions of the New Testament as good and true, and to discard the rest as of little or no value. The critical method has itself revealed most clearly the living unity of the documents. To praise this element, and to blame that one, would be to destroy this very delicate unity" (pp. 179–180). By describing this 'unity' as 'very delicate', they suggest that it could all too easily be dissolved by a critical method of the wrong kind. What they mean to assert is that their theory squares with the whole of the documentary evidence. But in saying this, they seem to imply that, although many items in the gospel story may be false, if we take the story as a whole and don't pick and choose, then it is all true. Even this, however, means only that it truly represents Jesus's actions and his own estimate of himself on which they were based, and leaves open the possibility that his pretensions were delusions.

The method of defending a text by insisting that it must be 'taken as a whole' is a familiar argument in literary criticism. Commentators often claim that a work recognized as a classic contains no details irrelevant to the artist's principal aim. But few works of art, except in sculpture, have satisfied this claim, although it is always possible to invent some relevance or to interpret the principal aim in such a way as to justify every detail. More often it is simply asserted that any apparently objectionable detail is somehow transformed in the whole, with no indication how. It is in this manner that T.S. Eliot defends Dante's account of hell and purgatory: "The vital matter is that Dante's poem is a whole" and one "must in the end come to understand every part in order to understand any part" (1951, p. 258). There are few who have the perseverance to read this particular whole, and they will be so proud of having achieved the feat that they are unlikely to admit that their efforts have not resolved all perplexities.[32]

Hoskyns's and Davey's very brief discussion of the Resurrection presumably follows the same lines as their previous arguments. They must be aware that the belief that he rose from the dead is attested in all layers of the tradition, and so they must surely hold that the evangelists were not foisting the idea onto recalcitrant material. But this means no more than that "St. Peter and St. Paul and others were convinced that they had seen him risen", not that he actually rose. Hoskyns and Davey want to brush the whole matter aside as "properly outside the sphere of the historian", because "the Omega as well as the Alpha, the

Ending as well as the Beginning, belongs only to God" (p. 177). One can understand their embarrassment here, if not their reasoning.

vi.   SANDERS AND DAVIES

Against the view that I have put in the first section of this chapter, two theologians have recently claimed that the application of critical criteria to records about Jesus has now at last yielded trustworthy results. They are E.P. Sanders and Margaret Davies, joint authors of *Studying the Synoptic Gospels* (1989). Sanders is particularly well-known, not only because of his professional eminence as Dean Ireland's Professor of the Exegesis of Holy Scripture in the University of Oxford, but also because his books on Paul have done so much to show that the conventional Christian picture of a Judaism totally inferior to early Christianity is a fantastic distortion.

In their present book, the two authors concentrate on the gospels of Matthew, Mark, and Luke (it is these that are known as 'the synoptics') and reach many conclusions which run counter to traditional Christianity. These are not new, and do not purport to be, but are very lucidly stated and argued. What they claim to be able to show is that "some aspects of Jesus's teaching and career" can be "firmly established, some things attributed to him are disproved, and most of the material is placed somewhere in between" (p. 304). They allow that the evangelists were not eyewitnesses of the events they describe and are unlikely to have had eyewitnesses as their informants. Minor and colourful details in Mark, for instance, "which were once regarded as stemming from Peter, are now regarded as indications not of eyewitness testimony but of stylistic preference. Details give life to the narrative, but they need not come directly from observation. They can be employed by a later author to imitate life" (pp. 19–20).

The relation of the synoptic gospels to each other is searchingly discussed in a chapter on 'the synoptic problem.' They have extended passages that are verbally so close to each other that one or more of their authors must have drawn from one or more of the others. Mark is almost universally accepted as the earliest. If he is not, he must have conflated and abbreviated the other two, leaving out much that could not have been unimportant for the faith (such as the Lord's prayer and the beatitudes) and adding only trivial detail, for example, that the paralytic brought to Jesus for cure was "carried by four" (2:3). Even if someone had written a gospel in this way, it is hard to see why the church would have preserved it (p. 92); and so Matthew and Luke are normally regarded as dependent on Mark. They are also widely believed to have been ignorant of each other, for agreement between them "begins [only] where Mark begins and ends where Mark ends" (p. 54). (Mark introduces Jesus as an adult and ends with the discovery that his body is no longer in his tomb. Matthew and Luke have birth and infancy narratives which are mutually incompatible, and equally incompatible post-Resurrection appearances of Jesus). Sanders and Davies, however, think that Luke must have known Matthew (or an earlier version of his gospel) as there are a large number of minor agreements between the two of them against Mark in the material they share with Mark—more than can be explained by coincidence or by supposing that they independently followed the same editorial policy in adapting Mark (p. 96). If this is correct, then it is no longer necessary to posit the existence of Q (a supposed second source, no longer extant, used by Matthew and Luke additionally to their use of Mark). Our authors do not pretend to have fully accounted for the relationship between the three, and conclude that there is "a general argument for a complicated solution, but one that cannot be precisely described" (p. 112).

Sanders and Davies think that "the birth narratives are not typical gospel material" and that "the stories about Jesus's activities", meaning his pre-Crucifixion ministry, "are much more reliable" (p. 36). The material on which the synoptics are based was, they say, "subject to alteration but was not treated with reckless abandon" (p. 131). "Reckless abandon" would, in my view, adequately characterize the flood of local traditions underlying birth and infancy stories and also the tales of Resurrection appearances in both canonical and apocryphal gospels, and it is difficult to share this confidence that the material which went to form the synoptics' account of the ministry is so radically different in quality. It was probably in large measure folk tradition which as such could be manipulated and adapted arbitrarily. As our authors themselves note, "students of folk literature know no rules of change" (p. 128). They allow that this synoptic material was put together from individual and unconnected units of tradition, "pericopes with no apparent causal links" (p. 135), and that in this way supposed sayings of Jesus were supplied with narrative settings. That this is how the evangelists went to work can in some cases be demonstrated, as different evangelists sometimes give different settings to the same sayings. Thus "the parable of the lost sheep in Matthew is addressed to the disciples, as admonition, but in Luke to the Pharisees as rebuke" (Matthew 18:10–14; Luke 15:2–7), and "there is no more reason to accept [the] one [setting] than the other." Again, "in Luke the saying 'You will not see me until you say "Blessed is he who comes in the name of the Lord!" ' " is fulfilled when Jesus enters Jerusalem (Luke 13:35; 19:38), while in Matthew it comes later and is still unfulfilled at the close of the gospel—thus pointing to the return of the Lord (Matthew 23:39). Even if we knew beyond doubt that Jesus said it, we could not know what it meant unless we could reconstruct the context" (p. 339). That the evangelists had only isolated stories at their disposal, not a connected account, can be seen also from what they say about Jesus's women followers: "It is remarkable that Mark and Matthew show that Mary [Magdalene] and other women followed Jesus from Galilee to Jerusalem, but give them no role in the Galilean ministry." Luke recognized that this was unsatisfactory, and so "retrojected Mary and other women into the stories of Jesus's own ministry" (p. 135). Another way in which Luke adapted or supplemented his material so as to make it accord with his own view of what must have been the case is that he portrays the disciples more favourably than do Matthew or Mark. It is clear from the Acts of the Apostles, written by Luke as a supplement to his gospel, that he regarded the apostolic age as free from the kind of discord which in fact characterized it (as we know from ample documentation in New Testament epistles of which Luke was ignorant); and so he is careful in his gospel to prepare the way for the "exemplary portraits" of the disciples given in Acts (p. 30). And he is not the only synoptist who brings material into line with his overall theology. "The parables in Matthew suit the gospel of Matthew, while those of Luke agree with Lucan themes", so that there is some difficulty in supposing that either go back directly to Jesus (p. 196).

It seems, then, that an evangelist was quite capable of adapting his material so as to make it provide for needs facing Christians of his own time. These included the need for effective criticism of rival religious bodies, whether within Christianity or outside it. Sanders and Davies think that, on this basis, Mark, in the pericope on plucking grain on the sabbath (2:23–28), attributed to Jesus sayings defending the church against Jewish criticism that it did not keep the sabbath laws; and that on the same basis Matthew was led to represent Jesus as vilifying orthodox Jews: "the scribes and Pharisees are fiercely attacked in Matthew 23, which doubtless reflects real conflict in the life of some branch of the church". On the other hand it will have been the need to combat the view of some group that was still within the church that occasioned the logion of Matthew 5:19, where Jesus is made to insist that all provisions of the Jewish law, down to the last iota, must be kept; i.e. this saying probably originated as a "rebuke" directed to a part of the church which did not teach full observance of it (p. 194).

Sanders and Davies thus allow, and even stress, that some "early Christians, besides altering and reapplying stories about and sayings of Jesus", also "simply made up material and attributed it to him" (p. 138). They say:

> The early Christians needed guidance on all sorts of issues. They could turn to Scripture or to their leaders, and they did so. Their queries resulted in letters, then in collections of them, and finally in pseudepigraphical letters—written by others in the apostles' names. This we know from the Pauline corpus. When the resolution of a hard problem was reached, it appears that nevertheless many wanted assurance that the Lord himself approved the solution.

For instance, in the case of the question whether Christians should be required to keep the Jewish food laws,

> The real decision-making was long, laborious and contentious. It was simpler to have Jesus himself declare "all foods clean", and Mark or a predecessor either created a saying which had this effect or gave an authentic saying a context in which this was its meaning.

This could be done in good faith, because

> People who "discovered" a new saying or a new meaning . . . believed . . . that the Spirit of God spoke through inspired humans or that the Lord spoke directly to them, and thus could honestly attribute to Jesus things which came to them from some other source than his pre-crucifixion teaching. (pp. 138–39)

Sanders and Davies do not dispute that the earliest Christian writers are remarkably silent about statements attributed to Jesus in the gospels when these statements would have served their purposes very well. They give examples.

i. "Paul argued with Peter and the other Jerusalem disciples about whether or not his converts (and other Gentile converts) had to observe the laws of circumcision, food and 'days'. This topic is the occasion of Galatians, where the case against these parts of the law is argued extensively, and it comes up again as a major part of Romans. Yet Paul on the issue of the law does not quote Jesus, much less tell stories in which Jesus defends his followers for not observing (for example) the sabbath" (p. 132). For instance, " 'the Son of man is Lord of the Sabbath' (Mark 2:28) could have stood Paul in good stead in debating whether or not keeping 'days' was required (Galatians 4:10; Romans 14:5–6)" (p. 323); but he does not quote it, neither does he refer to the statement that led Mark to say (7:19) that Jesus had declared all foods clean. (One might add that Jesus's table-fellowship with publicans and sinners would have been equally to the point, and that all that Paul can allege in order to establish the "freedom" of gentiles from the law is that Jesus's Crucifixion has put an end to it. As in the earliest documents generally, it is not to Jesus's manner of life, nor to his teaching, but only to his death—in circumstances unspecified—that appeal is made in support of an important doctrinal matter.)

ii.   In 1 Peter "there is a good deal of exhortation to bear up under suffering. Thus the author writes, 'Yet if you should suffer for your virtues, you may count yourselves happy' (3:14). How appropriate it would have been to have written: 'Jesus said, "Blessed are those who are persecuted for righteousness' sake, for theirs is the kingdom of heaven!"' " (p. 132)

They think that the author of 1 Peter may have had this beatitude in mind, even though he "does not take the opportunity of quoting it—much less a full text of beatitudes." They also think that Paul sometimes seems to echo one of the beatitudes, even though he does not refer to them. But surely it is more likely that, when he wrote, they had not yet been put into Jesus's mouth. Paul tells his Christian readers to "bless those that persecute you", bids them "judge not" and urges them to "pay taxes". In such instances he might reasonably be expected to have invoked the authority of Jesus, *had he known* that Jesus had taught the very same doctrines. It seems more likely that certain precepts concerning forgiveness and civil obedience were originally urged independently of Jesus, and only later attributed to him and thereby stamped with his supreme authority, than that he really gave such rulings and was not credited with having done so by Paul, nor indeed by other early Christian writers. This hypothesis is strengthened when we find that the evangelists who do so credit him do not agree as to what he said. "Lists of beatitudes", say Sanders and Davies, "are quoted only in Matthew and Luke", where "the lists are different". Furthermore, "prayer for persecutors is most likely to arise in a time of persecution", so that "conceivably these traditions arose during the period of the persecution of the early church" (p. 322), that is, later than Jesus's Galilean ministry. And so the logion "love your enemies and pray for them that persecute you" (Matthew 5:44) or "bless them that curse you" (Luke 6:28) may not have been spoken by him at all. Sanders and Davies drop a hint to this effect when they say that it represents a very high ethical standard, and that "once one grants moral and spiritual stature to others beside Jesus", interpretation of the evidence is not as simple as has often been supposed.

Sanders and Davies refer to a number of Pauline passages which show that Christian congregations of Paul's time included "prophets" who made pronouncements in the name of (the risen) Jesus. But they stress that Paul himself rarely resorted to such practice or made use of such pronouncements in his own apologetic. They try to turn to account his failure to produce words of Jesus to support his doctrines by arguing that this silence shows that he was not disposed to invent such sayings (p. 132), so that when he does cite a saying by the Lord, "he provides the greatest possible independent attestation of it" (p. 323).

There are in fact three occasions when Paul explicitly quotes "the Lord" and attributes to him something resembling what he is made to say in the gospels. He tells that the Lord has ruled severe restrictions on divorce (1 Corinthians 7:10 and 12); but Sanders and Davies admit that there are "very substantial disagreements" between him and the synoptics here, and also between the synoptics themselves (p. 131) so that, although "there can be no reasonable doubt that Jesus said something on divorce", we do not know exactly what, but merely that "he was against it". His "teaching was revised as it was applied to different situations" (pp. 327–28). Again, at 1 Thessalonians 4:15–17, Paul says "by the word of the Lord" that "we that are alive" at the second coming "shall in no wise precede them that are fallen asleep. For the Lord himself shall descend from heaven with a shout . . . and the dead in Christ shall rise first; then we that are alive, that are left, shall together with them be caught up in the clouds, to meet the Lord in the air". Jesus in fact gives no such detailed assurances in the gospels, and what he there says about his second coming bears only a general resemblance to this passage: for instance Matthew 16:27–28; "for the Son of man shall come in the glory of his Father. . . . Verily I say unto you, There be some of them that stand here, which shall in no wise taste of death till they see the Son of man coming in his kingdom". A third passage is 1 Corinthians 11:23–26, where Paul quotes words which he "received from the Lord"—words which represent Jesus as instituting a eucharistic practice, a cultic act which existed as a regular part of Christian worship in Paul's time. No such implications are found in Mark's version of these words, where they are merely spoken by Jesus in a particular situation the night before his death, and point out what he will do after death.

Now it is perfectly feasible that all three of these sayings in Paul originated as words spoken by the risen Jesus through the voices of Christian prophets. Sanders and Davies themselves note that "many scholars" regard the saying about the coming end in this way, and are "possibly correct" to do so (p. 330). The saying about divorce could have originated in like fashion, as the obvious way of supporting a ruling on a socially important subject which Christians of Paul's day were anxious to inculcate. As for the eucharistic words, once a eucharistic practice had been established, it would be natural to suppose that Jesus had ordained it.[33] By the time the gospels were written, Christians were much more concerned with the supposed details of his incarnate life than had earlier been the case; and so I find it natural enough that they should have come to suppose that the pronouncements of the risen one through the voices of Christian prophets had already been given by him during his incarnate life. This would account for any overlap between what Paul states as "words of the Lord" and doctrines the gospels represent as pre-Crucifixion teachings, and would mean that what Sanders and Davies call Paul's "independent attestation" of such teachings is not independent at all. They, however, remain confident that "when we read Paul we can distinguish quite well between sayings which go back to the historical Jesus and new sayings from the Lord" (p. 140).

In the course of their attempt to discern facts underlying stories of Jesus's ministry, Sanders and Davies note that the gospels, although biased in his favour, "give us a glimpse of views held by those who were biased against him". They think that we may have "considerable confidence" that what is common to both portraits is historically sound (p. 302). On this basis they conclude that his "ability to perform miracles"—or "what many saw as miracles"—"is *proved,* since not only his followers, but also his opponents, knew him as a miracle-worker" (p. 331). This is unsatisfactory for two reasons. First, belief in miracles was, in antiquity, part of the way in which reality was comprehended, so that allegations that someone worked them would be met by hostile commentators with a denigration of them as mere magic, not with a denial that he worked any. Thus it is not surprising that Jesus's opponents are made to say (e.g. at Mark 3:22) that he worked them through the aid of evil spirits. Second, in none of the epistles I have mentioned as independent of the gospels is there any suggestion that he worked miracles, even though in some of them miracles are regarded as of great importance for the spread of the Christian message. Even the earliest (the so-called "Apostolic") Fathers fail to mention any miracle of his. Paul comes close to denying that he worked any when he insists that he can preach only

"Christ crucified"—a Christ who submitted to a shameful death, not a Christ of signs and wonders (1 Corinthians 1:22–23). We saw how he implies that Jesus had lived so obscure a life that he passed unrecognized by evil spirits, and how incompatible this is with gospel stories where he is repeatedly recognized by evil spirits when he miraculously casts them out from persons in whose bodies they had lodged (above, p. 101). It is surprising that Sanders and Davies find the healing stories in the gospels "quite modest, when compared to other healing stories, and relatively free of magical details" (p. 196). They concede that the early church probably elaborated on this aspect of Jesus's life, but nevertheless "avoided excessive elaboration" (p. 173). There is, however, little left of the "ministry" in Mark if the miracles are deleted.

Another criterion that Sanders and Davies employ is that "a passage or theme is shown to be historically reliable if it is directly against what the evangelists wished to be so" (pp. 304–05). Religious conservatism often leads to the inclusion of such contradictory material, and in 1921 H.P. Smith gave, as Old Testament examples, the two creation stories in Genesis and the two accounts of Saul's coronation in Samuel. On the two latter, he commented:

> In one we read that a king was a gift of God's grace for the deliverance of the people (1 Samuel 9 and 10). But another writer judged that this could not be, since Saul turned out to be a failure. He therefore wrote another account and represented the demand for a king as evidence of the incurable waywardness of the people (1 Samuel 8 and 12) . . . A devout man who possessed both documents could not bring himself to let either one be lost and therefore combined them. Probably if he reflected on the discrepancies he was able to satisfy himself with harmonistic hypotheses such as commentators delight in to the present day.

As to the two creation stories, Smith says that it is quite probable that the author of the more sophisticated of them "would have been willing to see his account displace the other. But again, religious conservatism, for which we cannot be too grateful, refused to let either one perish, and combined them" (1921, pp. 11–12).

In such cases, the surviving material that "goes against the grain" of the views of the final compiler represents earlier tradition which may be no more reliable than later variants. Sanders and Davies, however, think that Jesus's saying at Mark 7:27 is authentic because it implies that salvation is reserved for Jews and so conflicts with Mark's acceptance of the gentile mission: it shows "beyond reasonable doubt" that "the historical Jesus . . . limited his own mission to the people of Israel" (p. 305). The situation at this point in Mark is that a pagan woman has asked him to cure her daughter, and he remonstrates, saying "it is not right to take the children's bread and throw it to the dogs". Mark, they justly say, is "not likely to have invented" this saying, which is "extremely derogatory towards Gentiles" (p. 306). But this does not make it authentic. Since Christianity emanated from Judaism, it is understandable that an early layer of Christian tradition believed that Jesus was concerned to save only Jews, and that sayings to this effect came to be attributed to him. Mark may have included this particular saying partly from the kind of religious conservatism to which H.P. Smith drew attention, but partly because the pagan woman shows exemplary faith by persisting in her request, so that it is finally granted. Haenchen has noted that Matthew developed this Marcan pericope so as to emphasize the strength of her faith even more, and that both evangelists intend, by this story, "to encourage the Christian reader not to lose faith when a prayer remains unanswered in the first instance" (1968, p. 275).

Sanders and Davies themselves declare that the evangelists' standards of accuracy were like those of rhetoricians, in that "the 'truth' of a given event or saying would be assessed according to the impact it made. If it testified to the value of faith, or inculcated high morals, or exemplified the Christian way of life, it would be used as true" (p. 38). This principle clearly annuls the evidential value of this Marcan episode. They add:

> And in a very real sense it may so be judged [as true] today.
> Numerous values are higher than empirical accuracy.

Not, I contend, apropos of statements which purport to be empirically accurate. We do not respect persons who invent or mis-state facts in order to inculcate their policies. Sanders and Davies insist that they are historians, not apologists, but I detect in the sentence I have just quoted the theological cloven hoof. They are confident that their study of the synoptics supports belief in a minimal Jesus. They think that Christianity would be destroyed if it were to be shown that Jesus never lived (pp. 302–03). But will their minimal Jesus suffice as a basis for it?

vii. THE EVIDENCE OF JOSEPHUS: CHARLESWORTH

Many commentators have supposed that at least the Crucifixion of Jesus under Pilate is adequately attested by a well-known passage in Josephus's *Antiquities of the Jews* (Book 18, Sections 63–64, or Chapter 3§3), which follows a reference to Pilate's maltreatment of the Jews, and reads, in the translation of the Loeb Classical Library:

> About this time there lived Jesus, a wise man, *if indeed one ought to call him a man.* For he was one who wrought surprising feats and was a teacher of such people as accept the truth gladly. He won over many Jews and many of the Greeks. *He was the Messiah.* When Pilate, upon hearing him accused by men of the highest standing amongst us, had condemned him to be crucified, those who had in the first place come to love him did not give up their affection for him. *On the third day he appeared to them restored to life, for the prophets of God had prophesied these and countless other marvellous things about him.* And the tribe of the Christians, so called after him, has still to this day not disappeared. (Italics mine.)

Only the most naive commentators can still argue that Josephus, an orthodox Jew who at the beginning of his autobiography classes himself with the Pharisees, could have written the obviously Christian words I have italicised.[34] The remaining question is whether the whole passage is Christian addition to his original, or whether he said something at this point about Christians, even about Jesus, which has been reworked by Christian hands. Josephus lived in Rome, where there were certainly Christians well before the date when he completed the *Antiquities* (AD 93),[35] so that there is no reason why he should not have heard of Christian views. Indeed, the Christian tradition that Jesus had suffered under Pilate was current by then, so that he could—as Tacitus did a generation later—have merely repeated what Christians were by then saying about the circumstances of Jesus's death.

However, there are reasons for regarding the passage as wholly interpolated. Only three manuscripts of it are extant, none earlier than the eleventh century, and all traceable to a single root (Bammel 1974B, p. 29), and Christian scribes will have had time enough to tamper with it. Also, "the passage is not mentioned by Christian writers before the fourth century, despite its obvious value to them"; and "it breaks the continuity of the narrative, which tells of a series of riots" (Feldman 1984, p. 690). Section 65 (immediately after the passage) seems to belong directly after 62 (immediately preceding it). Prior to the passage (which comprises 63 and 64) we have a description of two riots, and after it of two others, "all of them termed Θόρυβος, whereas in sections 63–64 the Christian movement is not called a Θόρυβος" (p. 696). Thus 65 begins with the words: "Some other dreadful event" (ἕτερόν τι δεινὸν), which presupposes some Θόρυβος immediately preceding.

J.H. Charlesworth, Professor of New Testament at Princeton Theological Seminary, has recently published a discussion of the passage in which he deletes from it those words that are obviously of Christian origin, but regards the remainder as basically authentic.[36] In order to link it with its context of "troubles" for the Jews, with which it would otherwise have no connection, he has to render the passage translated in the Loeb edition as "those who had in the first place come to love him did not give up their affection for him", as ". . . did not cease to cause trouble."[37]

Charlesworth thinks that his case is greatly strengthened by the recent discovery of a less obviously Christian version of this whole passage which is quoted from Josephus in Arabic translation—a translation probably itself made from the Syriac into which the original Greek had been rendered—by the tenth-century bishop Agapius in his Arabic *World History*. Charlesworth quotes the translation of it given by Professor Pines, of the Hebrew University (Jerusalem) who drew attention to it:

> Similarly Josephus (Yūsifūs), the Hebrew. For he says in treatises that he has written on the governance (?) of the Jews: "At this time there was a wise man who was called Jesus. His conduct was good and (he) was known to be virtuous. And many people from among the Jews and the other nations became his disciples. Pilate condemned him to be crucified and to die. But those who had become his disciples did not abandon his discipleship. They reported that he had appeared to them three days after his crucifixion, and that he was alive; accordingly he was perhaps the Messiah, concerning whom the prophets have recounted wonders."

The statement that "the disciples did not abandon his discipleship" seems to offer no opportunity of understanding any explicit reference to them as trouble-makers to the Jews such as Charlesworth was so anxious to find in the Greek. And the statement that Jesus "was perhaps the Messiah" is no more likely to have come from an orthodox Jew than the affirmation in the Greek that "he was the Messiah". Origen, who said that Josephus "did not believe in Jesus as Christ", could not, says Bammel (1974A, p. 147) have had access to a text which went as far.[38] Bammel thinks that Agapius's version of the passage may have originated in an Islamic environment, as it states that "Pilate condemned him to be crucified and to die" (the last three words are not in the Greek). As we saw (above, p. 107), the Koran denies that Jesus was put to death; hence the contrary assertion became of vital importance to Christians in Islamic times (p. 146).

Bammel has argued elsewhere that Josephus actually wrote something pejorative about Jesus at this point in his book, and something even more pejorative about his disciples, and that this represents "the oldest literary denunciation of Christians" (1974B, p. 20). To reach these conclusions, Bammel has both to amend the text and reinterpret it in a manner that is scarcely plausible.[39]

In view of all the uncertainties, we are not surprised to find Winter concluding that "we cannot reliably guess" what Josephus may have written here (p. 438). Winter did not live to comment on the discovery of Agapius's version, which Charlesworth hails as "an antidote for a poison affecting our Western culture"—the poison represented by the view that "Jesus's life was completely fabricated out of prophecies and myths". As an example, he mentions "an influential book by R. Augstein, the former editor of *Stern*" which, he says, claims that "Jesus is merely the projected dreams and dogmas of a superstitious people" (pp. 97–98).

Charlesworth really ought to read works which he finds disagreeable more carefully and comment on them more fairly. The dust jacket of Augstein's book describes him as the editor not of the *Stern,* but of the *Spiegel,* a much more serious journal; and the argument of that book is, not that Jesus never existed, but that "*that* Jesus which theologians offer us never lived".[40] What Augstein does say is that it would not be the sheer folly that it has so often been declared to be if one were to deny Jesus's historicity, as so little about him can be established (1972, p. 47); and that Schweitzer's pronouncement of 1913—that modern Christianity must reckon with the possibility of having to give up his historicity—still holds good (p. 49).

In the same context where he misrepresents Augstein, Charlesworth makes a dismissive mention of me as a contributor to the "poison", saying that I "issued a book that simply claims that Jesus never existed" (p. 98). Although on another page he says that "in scholarly works I expect both sides of an argument to be explored" (p. 52 n8), he does not even state, let alone "explore" the arguments underlying the view he designates as poison. This is the method favoured over many centuries by apologists confronting views incompatible with their own.[41]

Charlesworth believes that "the sheer existence of the Gospels . . . proves that, from the earliest decades of the movement associated with Jesus, there must have been *some* historical interest in Jesus of Nazareth" (p. 13). But these gospels cannot prove that such interest existed a generation or more before their time, in documents where Jesus is not even said to be 'of Nazareth' and which, while allowing him a vague undefined historicity, are concerned with his atoning death, his Resurrection, and his second coming. Charlesworth allows that "we have begun [sic] to see more clearly that the Gospels were written to serve the needs of communities decades removed from Jesus" (p. 10). This is in some ways convenient, as it enables us to deny that he vilified the Pharisees: "the harsh portraits" of them in the gospels "reflect not so much Jesus's time as the clashes between the Christians and the Pharisees after 70 CE" (p. 46). Again, there were admittedly "early Christian prophets who spoke in the name of the risen one", yet their "emotions and enthusiasms" did not go "unbridled. They were *at least somewhat* controlled by eyewitnesses who anchored enthusiasm in real history" (p. 11, author's italics).

It is easy to be contemptuous about other people's ideas. The history of scholarship should teach us all tolerance and humility. Theories are often regarded as reckless by those who underestimate the significance of the facts on which they are based. Charlesworth is among those who have done excellent work in disproving the traditional Christian view that Jesus was "the perfect person" who fell victim to Jewish malice—"strangled by a legalistic society, trapped in the Jews' sanhedrin, and murdered following diabolical outcries for his blood from the Jewish leaders and their followers" (p. 2). He quotes with disgust Jerome's definition of Jewish prayers as "the grunting of a pig and the crying of donkeys" (p. 47). Evidence against such a low view of Judaism has long been available, but, as Neill and Wright have noted, apropos of its long neglect: "facts, good historical arguments, clear organisation of ideas—all may count for little or nothing, unless there are people who want, perhaps for quite different reasons, to listen and take notice" (1988, p. 374).

I will not here repeat the full discussion of the non-Christian evidence concerning Jesus (including a second and shorter passage in Josephus) which I have given in my books on Jesus and on Christian origins. The sparseness of genuine early Jewish and pagan testimony about him is only what is to be expected if, as is surely the case, Christianity remained too small and obscure to attract much attention until the second century. The non-Christian material does not help us to decide whether Jesus did in fact live and die in Pilate's Palestine, and its importance has been exaggerated because the Christian notices are so obviously shot through with legend.

viii.   CONCLUSION

According to Locke's *The Reasonableness of Christianity as Delivered in the Scriptures* (1695), "an attentive and unbiassed search" of scripture shows that, through prophecy and miracle, God has disclosed truths which we cannot but accept.[42] That the Old Testament foretells anything concerning Jesus or Christianity is a standpoint no longer acceptable to very many Biblical scholars,[43] many of whom have also ceased to believe in the miracles recorded in either Testament. Yet Locke's standpoint persists among apologists. Maurice Wiles points in this connection to Swinburne's *Faith and Reason* (Oxford: Clarendon Press, 1981), where it is argued (pp. 177, 183, 193) that Christian doctrine needs, as a basis, "God's announcement to man of things beyond his power to discover for himself", which can be known to be "true without qualification" or are to be accepted "because of the prophet's authority", established by "some kind of miraculous signature symbolically affirming and forwarding his teaching and work". Wiles comments on this: "I do not see how any theologian who has given serious attention to the work done by biblical

scholars could begin to pursue the work of Christian
theology in the way that Swinburne proposes". And he
himself candidly admits to having "no clear-cut recipe to
offer of how we may give a reasonable account of faith in
God and of Christian belief" (1987, pp. 48, 51).

Wiles, a Canon of Christ Church Oxford, has elsewhere
bluntly declared that "the kind of information about Jesus
that theology has so often looked to New Testament
scholars to provide is not available", and that "there is an
oddity, which we must not allow our sophistication to
obscure from us, in affirming of a particular historical
person that he is the embodiment of the divine and at the
same time acknowledging that our knowledge about him in
himself is at every point tentative and uncertain". He
suggests that it might be better to turn from Jesus to what
he calls "the whole Christ event", understood as both his
life and its "impact on the world of the first century"—the
"transforming impact" of his death and resurrection being
particularly "enormous"—and to "the Church's experience and understanding of Christ down the ages" (1974,
pp. 48–52). He justly points out that, although he is
thereby proposing a "substantial degree of doctrinal
change", fundamental changes of doctrine have characterized Christianity's history:

> How does our faith compare with that of a Tertullian, for whom the
> basic character of Christian existence was to belong to a small
> group, living in the extreme end of time, in self-conscious separa-
> tion from a world about to perish? And what of Augustine, for
> whom the goal of the whole dramatic scheme of salvation was the
> preservation of a fixed number of the elect to make up the number
> of the fallen angels? And what of Gregory the Great, for whom God
> had communicated to men through the elaborate allegories of the
> scriptural record whose human authors were no more than a pen in
> the hand of their real divine author? (p. 106)

Wiles's proposals are, then, not to be rejected simply
because they are radical. But are they just? It is striking in
how many different contexts one meets the argument that,
while particulars may be dubitable, "the whole" in which
they are set, or can be set, somehow resolves the perplexi-

ties they occasion (cf. above, p. 131). Wiles suggests that the move from concern with Jesus alone to concern with "the whole Christ-event strengthens the case for giving some special evaluation to that series of events as a whole" (p. 54). But H.D. Lewis has objected that it is difficult to speak intelligibly about a 'Christ event' without a recognizable figure as the key to it; and that, as to Jesus's "transforming impact", there have been many transformations, some not so estimable as others, and that the whole weight of the truth about him cannot be made to rest on the quality of life of his followers (1981, pp. 47–50). Lewis is a strong advocate for what he calls "the traditional figure" of Jesus, yet even he cannot avoid embarrassment at some aspects of the records, as when he complains of "a too literal interpretation" of what he takes to be "certain metaphors about judgement and the fate of evil-doers" (p. 81). I have read Wiles with much sympathy and, I hope, profit; in particular his account in an earlier book (1967) of how Christian doctrine was formed is illuminating. But Lewis's criticism of him does seem just.

What Biblical scholarship has shown is that the New Testament includes a number of "Christologies", or ways of regarding Jesus, that are incompatible. They are very clearly outlined by Dennis Nineham, who says expressly that they simply cannot be "harmonised into a single coherent picture which could then be labelled 'the primitive Christian faith'" (1976, pp. 155, 163). He draws two conclusions. First, "Jesus . . . cannot have given any clear and precise account or interpretation of himself. In particular, he cannot have thought and taught about himself what later orthodoxy attributed to him. If he had, the wide variety of views about his origins, nature and work among his devoted early followers would be quite beyond explanation". And second: "No picture of the historical Jesus has yet emerged—or ever seems likely to—which comes anywhere near commanding universal, or even general agreement" (pp. 164, 165). These insights do not prevent Nineham from suggesting that "contemporary Christians have limitless truth to glean from the Gospels" (p. 168). I would argue that he makes insufficient allowance for the consequences of the fact (of which he is well aware) that the different christologies of early Christianity can be arranged in a chronological order which shows that those represented in the gospels are by no means the earliest. Although parables and exorcisms are absent from the fourth gospel, the other three, for all their differences, make Jesus a teacher in Palestine in the earlier part of the first century who spoke parables and performed what—in Nineham's words—"he and his contemporaries regarded as exorcisms and other miracles"; and all four maintain that he was condemned by Pilate to be crucified. Nineham concurs with the "general agreement" that these are historical facts (pp. 138, 166). But these are not the earliest relevant documents, and Nineham himself insists that "the reader of the Bible must remember that the meaning of words is always relative to the situation and experience of the person who wrote them and of his contemporaries" (p. 207). I therefore suggest that the words of the pre-AD 90 epistles, which repeatedly mention Jesus's Crucifixion as a historical fact without placing it in a first-century situation, and which certainly do not attribute parables or exorcisms to him, put a large query over the historicity of a Jesus who lived, acted, and died about AD 30. Although theologians will not go this far, quite a few of them will acknowledge the force of the remark made by H.J. Cadbury, in a book significantly entitled *The Peril of Modernizing Jesus* (1937, p. 40):

> I am not disposed to join those who deny entirely the historicity of Jesus, but one must be prepared to admit that the religion which became the Christianity of the Roman Empire may have had but slight relation to the historical actuality of its Founder.

5

THE NEW TESTAMENT ON HUMAN DESTINY AND HUMAN NATURE

i. BODILY RESURRECTION

In 1963 the London publisher Constable issued a volume entitled *Objections to Christian Belief* which was twice reprinted within its first month. All four contributors were Christian theologians, and although J.S. Bezzant (at the time a New Testament Lecturer and Dean of St. John's College, Cambridge) was the only one of them to give any candid account of real objections, his contribution made up for the others by its outspokenness. His description of the "scheme of salvation" according to "traditional Christianity" mentions the following doctrinal points (pp. 82–83):

1.   Scripture as a verbally inspired record of divine revelation.

2.   The fall of the angels.

3.   The creation of Adam and Eve by direct acts of God, their succumbing to temptation by Satan, whence the origin of original sin.

4.   God's response, namely to send his son as a sacrifice for sinful man.

5.   The rise of the Christian Church and its assurances to "those baptised in it who by grace persevered in the fulfillment of its commands" that they "would be secure in the life to come".

6.   Bodily resurrection of the dead in due course, and predestination of all to heaven or hell.

All this (and more in the following pages) is rejected by Bezzant as incredible (p. 84) and not to be re-instated because such beliefs may help some people to overcome their psychological upsets (p. 91). He notes the way in which some traditional beliefs—those, for instance, concerning "the other world"—have been quietly dropped by many preachers; and in this connection he admits that the known effects of physical accidents to the brain suggest that the dissolution of the body might end consciousness once and for all (p. 92). He is repelled by the theological doctrine, far from extinct, that the only ingrained bias in human nature is towards evil, and mentions "innumerable acts of devotion to duty by multitudes of men and women" which are not to be discounted by "theories based on short passages in the writings of an apostle" (pp. 97–98. We shall be studying some of those that he has in mind). What purports to be revelation is unacceptable if it "contradicts what we have reasonable grounds for regarding as knowledge or reasonably grounded belief" (p. 109). In particular, God cannot be regarded as revealing to man "notions destined to be found ethically and otherwise defective by man himself" (p. 100). Refuge from these and other difficulties is not to be sought in forms of words to which no intelligible meaning can be attached; what is "simply unintelligible" is not to be represented as "a profound mystery" (p. 94).

Bezzant candidly confesses that there are "at present no convincing answers" to these and other objections to the Christian revelation, and that an acceptable "natural theology" is also not available. But from a sense of loyalty he will not desert his master now that things are going so badly against him; and so he declares that "it is entirely reasonable for any man who studies the spirit and the facing of life as Christ faced it, and his recorded teaching, to decide that by him he will stand through life, death or eternity" (pp. 109–110). He here takes not only the "life" but also the "teaching" for granted, and perhaps supposes that his premiss that the ancient literature in which these are recorded is only "partly mythopoeic" (p. 107) entitles him to this much.

In this chapter, I wish to consider some of the doctrinal items listed above, beginning with the resurrection of the body. The so-called Apostles' Creed—its connection with apostles is legendary[1]—clearly affirms this doctrine, to the embarrassment of some commentators. Jessop shows unwarranted optimism when he says that, with the virgin birth, it constitutes the two items in that creed "which would alone be now regarded as controversial" (1960, p. 129).

Resurrection is often discussed in the context of an alleged contrast between Greek and Hebrew ways of thinking—a contrast widely accepted, so its critics say, because taught to students of theology at an early stage in their courses, before they have any real knowledge of either Greek or Hebrew literature. The "Greek mind" is held to be "abstract", whereas Hebrew thinking is "concrete"; and this, it is supposed, explains why Hebrews believed that body and soul form interdependent units, as against the "Greek" view that the soul is separable and capable of independent existence. (The soul was originally a hypothesis to account for certain observed phenomena—cf. above, p. 42—but came in time to be taken for an entity as indubitable as the heart or the liver.) From what is taken to be the Greek premiss, there could be a final judgment of bodiless souls, but from the Hebrew standpoint resurrection is necessary to eternal life, as a full personality requires some sort of body.

What is here called the Greek view is really that of Plato and his followers. It is not the view of Aristotle, who held that soul and body are correlative: "We must no more ask whether the soul and the body are one than ask whether the wax and the figure impressed on it are one" (*De Anima,*

Book 2, Chapter 1). As for the Hebrews, emphasis on any kind of post-mortem survival comes only in the latest parts of the Old Testament, notably in Daniel, where it takes the form of bodily resurrection of the dead and was occasioned primarily by the need to give assurances that martyrs for the faith (particularly those of the Maccabean rebellion) would be compensated for their sacrifice. Later Judaism, reflecting further on such martyrdoms, reached the conclusion that the soul can exist separately from the body. Such reflections, says Barr, went somewhat as follows: "The martyr is dead, and though he will live again by the resurrection, the resurrection has not yet come. But meanwhile he is with God. How is he with God when his body lies in the dust?" (1966, p. 52). It was an attempt to answer such questionings that inspired, for instance, Wisdom 2:21–3:9, where we learn that the righteous only seem to die, but in reality pass to the fulness of immortality: their souls are in God's hands and rest in his peace. Similar thinking underlies 4 Maccabees, a Jewish work, written probably about AD 40, where "future resurrection of the body (2 Maccabees 7) is replaced by immortality and an eternal life that begins at the moment of death" (Nickelsburg 1981, pp. 176, 226).[2]

Since the body, as it exists in life, obviously perishes, a body that is resurrected some time after death must be something imperishable substituted for it. Paul speaks in this connection of a "spiritual body" (1 Corinthians 15:44). "Flesh and blood", he says, "cannot inherit the kingdom of God" (Verse 50), and so the dead will be raised "in glory" (Verse 43). The meaning is that "Christ will change our lowly body to be like his glorious body" (Philippians 3:21, RSV). Those Christians still alive at his second coming—and Paul expects himself and many in his audience to be among these—will have their bodies changed from animal to spiritual ones. Hence "the dead shall be raised incorruptible, and we shall be changed" (1 Corinthians 15:52). In this way, although we may die, and "the earthly tent we live in" be destroyed, we shall not be left "naked" (2 Corinthians 5:1–3).

Bodily resurrection is still accepted by some of the more fundamentalist sects: the Seventh-Day Adventists, for instance, refer to the Pauline passages I have quoted and on this basis declare that "like Christ, the resurrected saints will have real bodies".[3] But the Platonic view of a disembodied soul is now more prevalent among those Christians who still believe in any kind of post-mortem survival at all. They are not particularly numerous. "The twentieth century", says Barr (1966, p. 54), "is one in which the question of individual destiny after death has become a matter of very little interest, while the idea that the separated soul after death is individually immortal has become an object less of vehement denial than of total indifference". This, according to Badham (1984, p. 66) is not surprising, for "since the demise of the mediaeval Christian world-view, no alternative overall picture of reality in which life after death could be supposed to fit has gained any wide general support."

A number of Christian doctrines have been defended by the argument that they are not accessible to reason and must be accepted by faith alone. There are two quite different grounds on which a doctrine may be so classed. It may be self-contradictory or unintelligible, like transubstantiation and the Trinity—an unintelligible fiction which keeps Christianity monotheistic—or it may be perfectly clear but in conflict with commonly accepted moral principles. It is in this latter sense that predestination, original sin, and hell are irrational, and it is these that will occupy us in the remainder of this chapter.

ii. PREDESTINATION

Predestination, or "election" as it is also called, is today an even less popular doctrine than immortality. Stendahl says that, in "established" churches and in countries where formal Christian faith is professed, belief in election "is sustained with the greatest difficulty" (1953, p. 64). The traditional Anglican view is given in the seventeenth of the Church's 39 Articles of Religion, to all of which candidates for ordination are still required to assent. The statement there is that "before the foundations of the world were laid", God decided "to deliver from curse and damnation those whom he hath chosen in Christ out of mankind." Part of the scriptural basis for this is Ephesians 1:4–5, where God is said to have chosen "us", that is, Christians, "before the foundation of the world", and to have "foreordained us" in this way "according to the good pleasure of his will". God's choice was what theologians call "gratuitous", in that it did not depend on the merit of those chosen. Thus it is affirmed at Romans 9:9–13 that, of the two sons of Isaac, God hated the elder and loved the younger and determined, "when they were not yet born" and "neither had done anything good or bad", that the elder should serve the younger. The sequel stresses that election depends neither on an individual's will, nor on his exertions, but on whether God has decided to be merciful to him or not.

In the previous chapter, Paul speaks of those who are

> called according to God's purpose. For whom he foreknew, he also foreordained to be conformed to the image of his Son. . . . And whom he foreordained, them he also called: and whom he called, them he also justified: and whom he justified, them he also glorified (8:28–30).

"Called", "justified", and "glorified" are Pauline technicalities: Paul never speaks of his "conversion" to Christianity, but of his being "called" to it; and naturally this event was foreordained: God "separated me even from my mother's womb", and then in due course "called me through his grace" to preach Jesus (Galatians 1:15–16). God "justifies" his elect by condescending to regard them as righteous, even though he knows that they are sinners; and he "glorifies" them by giving them his splendour. (The past tense is inappropriate here, as they do not already possess this splendour, but was presumably used to fit the tense of the other two verbs.)

Paul is concerned in this passage in Romans to give those to whom he is writing a sense of security, to assure them that their salvation is based on God's purpose and hence not in question: "If God is for us, who is against us? . . . who shall lay anything to the charge of God's elect?" (Verses 31, 33). The Anglican Article 17 generalizes these assurances, saying: "The godly consideration of Predestination and our Election in Christ is full of sweet, pleasant, and unspeakable comfort to godly persons". And Best observes, in his commentary on Romans: "Many great Christians have drawn strength from the belief that they fitted into God's plans" (1967, p. 135).

The election of some implies the rejection of others; and if the former was decided before the world was created, so was the latter. Those rejected include some Christians, persons who "gained admission" to the church, even though they "long ago were designated for . . . condemnation" (Jude 4, RSV). This makes God positively deceitful: by allowing persons to hear Christian preaching and in consequence join the Church, he is raising their hopes for a salvation from which he has already decided to exclude them.

Paul speaks of God enduring, for a long period of time, "vessels of wrath fitted unto destruction" (RSV "made for destruction") in order to show more clearly "the riches of his glory upon vessels of mercy, which he afore prepared unto glory" (Romans 9:22–23). Paul repeatedly contrasts "those that are perishing" with "us that are being saved" (1 Corinthians 1:18; 2 Corinthians 2:15). This "them" and "us" mentality does not, as Shaw observes (1983, pp. 38, 169), sound like loving one's enemies, and the complacency underlying it stems from Paul's conviction that he and those who hearken to him are in the clear: "we whom he has called" are vessels of mercy (Romans 9:24).

The contrast between the groups is already apparent in what is regarded as the oldest of Paul's epistles, and hence the oldest extant Christian document, namely 1 Thessalonians: "Jesus delivereth us from the wrath to come" (1:10); and whereas (since the day of the Lord will come like a thief in the night) calamity will suddenly come upon "them" while they are talking of peace and security, "you" are all sons of light (5:2–5). The same contrast informs 2

Thessalonians, ascribed to Paul, but probably the work of a later writer. The recipients are told to keep aloof from certain persons who "received not the love of the truth, that they might be saved", in other words, they did not accept the writer's preaching, "the tradition which they received of us". But then God, instead of trying to help them, put them under a delusion so that they "believe a lie" and so (in the wording of the NEB) "may all be brought to judgement, all who do not believe the truth but make sinfulness their deliberate choice" (2:10–12 and 3:6). Here, as in Paul's genuine writings, the idea that God blinded them is characteristically combined with the doctrine that their errors are all their own fault. "When Paul has in mind the assurance of salvation, God's action in giving it to men and God's grace in so doing, he can employ predestination terminology. When he has in mind the human need for decision for Christ's lordship, the terminology is that of 'faith'" (Sanders 1977, p. 447). Sanders also notes that Paul speaks of all being saved only when he is carried away by the force of his analogies. "As in Adam all die, so also in Christ shall all be made alive" (1 Corinthians 15:22). He really means no more than "all who are in Christ will be made alive", as other passages containing the same analogy show.[4]

This doctrine that God punished the human race with eternal death for Adam's sin, and relented with "the free gift" of "eternal life in Christ Jesus our Lord" (Romans 5:12 and 6:23; cf. Genesis 3:19), leaves one asking why the possibility of redemption was so long postponed. Modern sectarians have been scorned by mainstream theologians for believing that divine saving activity was resumed after long abeyance at or near the time when their particular sect was founded. Hutten notes in this connection that the decisive dates include: for the Swedenborgians, 1757; for the Mormons, 1829; for the Adventists, 1844; for Jehovah's Witnesses, 1874; and he asks whether the holy spirit was "having a breather" (eine Erholungspause) throughout the long centuries since the Resurrection, with the exalted

Jesus sitting idly at the Father's side (1957, p. 94). But the New Testament writers are in no better position than these sectarians, as the period between Adam and Christ's ministry is much longer than all that has elapsed since, given even the Biblical chronology.

Predestination is represented in the gospels as well as in the epistles. I have already commented on Mark 4:11–12 (above, p. 84). Apocalyptic passages in Mark and Matthew, referring to Jesus's return at the end of the world for the final judgment, specify that angels shall gather together "the elect whom he chose" (Mark 13: 20, 27 and the equivalent in Matthew). At Matthew 15:13 Jesus declares: "Every plant which my heavenly Father planted not shall be rooted up"—a logion given only in Matthew and which Beare regards as a "vagrant saying" which this evangelist, "after his fashion, has worked . . . into a context which he thought suitable" by making it a criticism of Pharisaism (1981, p. 339). One of Matthew's parables involves a man forced at nil notice to attend a wedding celebration, so that he naturally comes not wearing a wedding garment. On this ground he is condemned to be "cast out into the outer darkness; there shall be the weeping and gnashing of teeth. For many are called, but few chosen" (22:13–14). The reference can only be to salvation or membership of the Messiah's kingdom. That this is a privilege to be accorded to "few" is reiterated at Matthew 7:14: "for narrow is the gate and straightened the way that leadeth unto life, and few be they that find it". The whole idea of an elect in any case implies a minority. Matthew's Christ is, as Beare says, "on the whole a terrifying figure" (1981, p. viii).

Of course, the 27 books of the New Testament are not entirely consistent in their teaching on this whole question. Thus the author of the Pastoral epistles—they are ascribed to Paul in the canon but are actually the work of a second-century Christian—declares that God "willeth that all men should be saved" (1 Timothy 2:4). The penultimate sentence of the Anglican Church's Article 17 seems to have this passage in mind when, in spite of the predestinarian stance of an earlier sentence, it declares: "We must receive God's promises in such wise as they are generally [that is to say, universally, for all mankind] set forth to us in Holy Scripture". Commentators regard such double-think as a sign of superiority. "Our English articles", says Bicknell, "move on a higher level. If we compare them with other performances of the age, we must see in them an example of the special Providence that has watched over the Church of England" (1955, p. 17). However, the possibility of universal salvation has the— for Jerome, as for many others—unacceptable implication that eventually prostitutes might achieve equal status with the Virgin Mary.

Paul believed that, in addition to predestining men to salvation or damnation, God predestines some to sin, that is, to commit offences against him. The Old Testament represents him as proposing to harden Pharoah's heart so that he will refuse to let the Israelites leave Egypt, and to harden the hearts of the Egyptians generally, so that they will pursue them when they do leave (Exodus 4:21 and 14:17). God's purpose in so acting was, says Paul, to show his great power in liberating the Jews in spite of this opposition, and to cause his own name to be publicized throughout the whole world:

> For the scripture saith unto Pharaoh, For this very purpose did I raise thee up, that I might show in thee my power, and that my name might be published abroad in all the earth. So then he hath mercy on whom he will, and whom he will he hardeneth. (Romans 9:17–18)

Ziesler comments: "Paul appears to find no difficulty in having God exploit an evil for a good purpose" (1989, p. 243). But the significant point is surely that it is an evil of his own making that he exploits.

Paul makes this mention of Pharaoh in the course of his discussion of why the Jews have rejected Christianity. If Jesus was the Messiah whom Israel expected, why had God allowed his own people to miss the promised salvation? Paul's explanation is that God has deliberately hardened the hearts of most of them, as he did Pharoah's, made them blind to the truth (11:7). His purpose in so doing was to cause Christian missionaries to turn away from Jews and so save gentiles (11:11); and the result of this will be that the Jews will eventually see what they have been missing and so will finally come to accept Christianity and be saved (11:25–26). "Just why it is supposed that seeing Gentiles within the Christian community will prompt non-Christian Jews to join them is hardly clear" (Ziesler 1989, p. 273).

Paul is aware that, if God "hardeneth whom he will", he may be accused of injustice. How can those Jews who rejected Christianity be blamed for doing what God has carefully arranged that they shall do (9:19)? His answer is that it is impertinent to put such a question:

> O Man, who art thou that repliest against God? Shall the thing formed say to him that formed it, Why didst thou make me thus? Or hath not the potter a right over the clay, from the same lump to make one part a vessel unto honour, and another unto dishonour? (9:20–21).

Forster and Marston maintain that this is merely a reply to a bumptious questioner who "denies God's right to use some people, *who have themselves chosen* paths of rebellion or faith, as special demonstrations of the effects of such choices" (1989, pp. 19, 23n, italics added). But the context makes it clear that it is God who has done the choosing, and serious commentators admit that the figure of potter and clay "implies the omnipotence of God in regard to individual destiny to a degree not apparently reconcilable with the reality of man's free acceptance or refusal of the Gospel" (Robinson 1926, p. 133). God predestines some to sin, yet he is just; Israel rejected Christianity because God blinded the nation, yet it is to be blamed for rejecting the clear message (10:16–21).

Some scholars deal with such discrepancies by positing additions to Paul's text by other hands. John O'Neill, for instance, excises chapters 9–11 of Romans holding that predestinarian teaching is incompatible with Paul's known ideas (1975, pp. 13ff). But most believe that Paul simply put down ideas as they came to his mind without working them into consistency. Schopenhauer once said of Aristotle that "he thinks pen in hand" (Er denkt mit der Feder in der Hand).[5] Paul seems to have done something of the kind, and so found it possible "both to maintain human freedom and responsibility and to believe in divine providence, and leave it at that without trying to provide a theoretical reconciliation of the two" (Ziesler 1989, p. 28).

Best suggests that, although Paul makes men "appear in part as puppets to be used by God for his own purposes", this "difficulty" is perhaps partly met "when we allow that the purpose is for the good of the puppets". But the puppet does not in fact always benefit. Pharoah was not "hardened" for his own good, and those Jews who were blinded and so rejected Christianity till their dying day were surely not thereby benefited. Admittedly, Paul says nothing about the ultimate fate—damnation or salvation—of those whom, in the furtherance of his purposes, God causes to sin. Yet as he regards such sin as reprehensible, he can hardly have looked favourably on the prospects of its perpetrators. Some commentators deal with these objections by saying that he is here concerned primarily with peoples, not individuals. Yet individuals are affected. Best regards the whole matter as an "apparent paradox" to which "there is no easy solution"; that is why Paul "finishes by confessing (Romans 11:33–36) that God's ways are far beyond man's understanding" (1967, p. 136).

Because of its scriptural basis, the doctrine of election has figured prominently in Protestant theology. Calvin believed in double predestination: each person is either a member of the elect or a reprobate (one whom God has decided to damn). He nevertheless allowed divine providence some unclear but reassuring function. His successors were not always so careful, and some of them maintained explicitly that God had finally decided, even before the fall of Adam, who was to be saved and who condemned. This, says Rowell, "had the effect of abolishing any possible connection between moral choice and salvation", and so encouraged immorality (1974, p. 27).

Today, if the doctrine of election is defended, its relation to human responsibility is regarded as a mystery which embarrasses some commentators, while others would not willingly be deprived of it and greet anything which appears to baffle the reason as an ally:[6] inability to understand, so far from being regarded as a matter for concern, is welcomed as a licence to believe.

iii.   HELL

The blessed in heaven have been supposed to be worshipping God and enjoying a beatific vision of the divine reality; but this has sometimes been suspected as conducive to boredom if prolonged to eternity, and Hick allows that "deep conceptual difficulties emerge when we try to visualize a society of perfected individuals in a totally stress-free environment from which pain, sorrow and death have been banished" (1985, p. 203). It has been supposed by Tertullian about AD 200 and by some medieval Catholics—Badham (1984, p. 62) mentions Peter Lombard and Aquinas in this connection—that the saints in heaven would witness the sufferings of the damned and would enjoy the experience. Such a view derives from Revelation 14:9–10 ("If any man worshippeth the beast and his image . . . he shall be tormented with fire and brimstone in the presence of the holy angels and in the presence of the Lamb"). It is, of course, repudiated with horror by most modern aplogists. Badham calls it "the most dreadful aberration of the Christian conscience" (pp. 61–62).

Realistic and effective torment of the damned is easy to envisage and has certainly been described in considerable detail. Matthew, we saw (above, p. 83), consigns them (at 25:41) to "the eternal fire prepared for the devil and his angels". Attempts have been made to soften this by arguing that the Greek word for "eternal" here ($\alpha\iota\acute{\omega}\nu\iota\text{os}$) or its

Hebrew equivalent is often used in the Bible in contexts where it cannot mean infinite time. Jude, for instance, alluding to the destruction of Sodom, Gomorrah, and other cities, says (Verse 7) that they "suffered the punishment of eternal fire". But Matthew is drawing a parallel between "eternal punishment" for the damned and "eternal life" for the righteous (Verse 46); so if the punishment is not to be regarded as everlasting, neither is the after-life of the blessed, and it is very improbable that this is what he had in mind.[7]

Revelation 14:11 and 20:10 seems to remove any ambiguity by specifying torments lasting "for ever and ever". However, the Greek here has, literally, "for ages of ages", and Walker (1964, p. 143) has noted that some resourceful exegetes insist that "age" here means "the duration of the world", so that "ages of ages" means some multiple of this—a long but nevertheless finite time. The idea, he says, seems to be that "it is a 'barbarous and cruel' opinion to suppose that God torments the damned eternally in punishment for a short life of sin; but it is presumably in harmony with His 'astonishing Love towards Mankind' to have them burnt and eaten by worms for several ages" (p. 101).

Some English versions of the New Testament occasion confusion by translating both "Hades" ($\H\alpha\delta\eta s$) and Gehenna ($\gamma\acute{\epsilon}\epsilon\nu\nu\alpha$) as "hell". "Hades", the Greek equivalent of the Hebrew "Sheol" is merely the abode of departed spirits, and, in the New Testament, the resting place of the dead, pending the resurrection and last judgment. Thus at Revelation 20:13, the seer sees Hades giving up its dead so that they may be judged. It is Gehenna that is the place of eternal punishment. The relevant article in Grant and Rowley's *Dictionary of the Bible* informs us that Gehenna is the name of the valley to the south of Jerusalem where the kings Ahaz and Manasseh are said to have offered their sons to the god Moloch. It later became the site where the city's refuse was burned, so that both the sinister associations from its past and the smoke continually rising from it made it an appropriate symbol for woe and judgment. Once the Jews had come to believe—by the second century BC (cf. above, p. 156)—that their martyrs would be recompensed in an after life, a natural corollary was the belief that their persecutors would be punished after death; and so Gehenna was the name given in Jewish apocalyptic of the inter-testamental period to the supposed place of punishment in the hereafter. The New Testament is, however, not entirely consistent in distinguishing Hades from Gehenna, as, in the parable of Lazarus and Dives, the rich man is said to suffer torment in Hades (Luke 16:23).

Jesus's descent into hell was added to Christian creeds only in the fourth century (although the idea is represented in Christian tradition from the second). Pannenberg notes that in the baptismal creed of the church of Rome, which goes back to the second century, there was no mention of it (1972, p. 90). What is meant by "hell" in this context, and what Jesus is supposed to have accomplished there, is far from clear.[8]

The Catholic doctrine of Purgatory is often regarded as a mitigation of that of hell, but it is really a refinement of the doctrine of heaven. It concerns persons who were absolved from their sins before death, but died before they were able to do penance, and who atone for them by suffering pain in Purgatory. This does not really increase the number of the saved, for, since those affected died in a state of grace, they are not among the damned, even though, according to St. Thomas and other theologians, the smallest pain in Purgatory is greater than the greatest on earth. The doctrine is advantageous to priests, in that it increases the importance of the Last Sacrament which they administer, and encourages the practice of financing Masses as pleas for curtailment of time to be spent in Purgatory. Without it, prayers for the dead would make little sense.

The whole idea of hell as a place of torment, let alone of eternal torment, is now thoroughly unpopular. Küng stresses (1984, p. 165) the immense harm it has done over centuries, terrifying many and causing them to terrify many others. It has also meant that the faithful must at all costs be protected from any deviation from the true faith, and this justified the most ferocious persecution of the unorthodox. In the seventeenth century Bayle pointed out that, while natural reason or honour may often restrain an atheist from injuring his neighbour, "a man who is persuaded that by exterminating heresies he is advancing the kingdom of God, and that he will gain the highest degree of glory in paradise, after having been admired on earth and overwhelmed with praises and gifts, as the protector of truth—such a man, I say, will trample under foot all the rules of morality" (Quoted by Walker 1964, p. 184). If one has no religion, one at least cannot have such an obviously bad one.

However, Jessop rightly protests that we cannot remove hell from the Christian outlook "without being disloyal to a steady theme of Scripture" (1960, p. 111). But even he—although he will have none of "our modern euphemisms for sin and irresponsibility", and deplores any "pretty doctrine" on these matters—interprets hell as meaning no more than exclusion from God in the after-life. As he thinks that minor sinners may well not suffer there as much as major ones (pp. 107–09), partial "exclusion from God" must be a distinct possibility, although what it would entail is not clear. One may have the beatific vision, or one may be deprived of it, but what do half measures on the matter mean? The Catholic Limbo—the place to which infants who die without baptism are consigned for all eternity—is at least clear on this issue. They belong among the damned, because uncleansed from original sin, but they are not tormented, merely deprived of the vision of God.

Catholic theologians have had great difficulties over hell because of very explicit pronouncements of earlier centuries that have been accepted as infallible. The Council of Florence decreed in 1442 that "no-one outside the Catholic Church—neither heathen, nor Jew nor infidel, nor anyone in schism—will partake of eternal life: rather will he be consigned to the eternal fire prepared for the devil and his angels if he does not join the Church before his death". This is included among the Church's infallible pronouncements in the documentation assembled by Neuner and Roos (1958, pp. 222–23). Attempts to take the sting from it are typified by Karl Adam, who argued in his standard work on the "essence" of Catholicism that all who have received "grace" are within the Church, and grace is imparted to all who obey their conscience (1934, pp. 205ff). In other contexts he would of course not allow such latitude. Catholic parents are required to lead their children into the Church, and this is held to mean considerably more than teaching them conscientious behaviour. "Join the Church" means "obey your conscience" only when it is a question of escaping the implications of awkward texts.

We have heard a great deal in recent years about a crisis in values caused by decline of belief in God. T.S. Eliot would have us believe that "there is no such thing as just Morality. . . . For any man who thinks clearly, as his Faith is, so will his Morals be" (1951, p. 367); and that it is "our religion" that "imposes our ethics, our judgement and criticism of ourselves, and our behaviour toward our fellow men" (p. 393). But it is surely obvious that, whether theists or not, most persons can see that observance of public order and respect for legality serve the best interests of both the individual and the community; and that all societies must have ethical values, as society would be impossible without them. Furthermore, it is in the interest of each individual to stress social obligations in cases where he is not personally involved, so that even individual egoism to this extent helps to preserve public morality. If, however, it is maintained that, without theism, "anything goes", then it is reasonable to ask what there is about God that will stimulate moral action. Are we to hold that mere belief in him, without expectation that he will reward or punish our behaviour, is in itself conducive to virtue? Or does he impose rewards and penalties? It can hardly be argued that he causes the unjust to suffer and the just to prosper here and now. Are we then still to believe that there are rewards and punishments in a supposed hereafter? The New Testament views on these, far from being an asset to ethics, have been largely abandoned because the general ethical outlook now finds them unethical. "Today", says John Hick, "theological ideas are subject to an ethical and rational criticism" which forbids the "moral perversity" of doctrines formulated when "theology was exempt from moral criticism" and when, in consequence, God could be supposed to behave with "an unappeasable vindictiveness and insatiable cruelty which would be regarded as demonic if applied analogously to a human being" (1985, p. 200). Theology, then, has trailed behind ethics rather than leading it, on this and, as we shall see (below, p. 202), on other matters too.

Küng writes, apropos of what is to be understood by hell: "The old mythological ideas have been abandoned, but there is little evidence of new, clear answers" (p. 165). Punishment may have one or more of three intentions: curative (to reform him who is punished), deterrent (to keep him and/or others from inappropriate behaviour) or vindictive (to allocate what is considered just retribution for offences). This last alternative has an emotional origin, namely the satisfaction of vengeful anger, and there must —at any rate today—be some hesitation in predicating it of a deity held to be wholly good[9] (although the orthodox doctrine of Redemption presupposes the validity of vindictive justice: God demanded the vicarious punishment of his son to expiate man's sins). The curative alternative is applicable to a post-mortem situation only if the victims are not regarded as irrevocably damned, and now that older ideas of hell have been quietly dropped, this alternative has become a possibility. However, the principal argument that survives today seems to be: punishment of the dead as a deterrent to misbehaviour by the living. But what reasons are there for supposing that distant prospects of any kind have a strong influence on behaviour? And a punishment that is to consist merely in "exclusion from God" or deprivation of the beatific vision is a deterrent only for the tiny minority who are spiritually-minded.

iv. THE EFFICACY OF HUMAN INITIATIVE

According to the tenth Anglican Article, the condition of man after the fall of Adam is such that "he cannot turn and prepare himself, by his own natural strength and good works, to faith and calling upon God" without the prevenient (that is, antecedent) "grace of God by Christ". It has, of course, to be allowed that non-Christians may possibly behave properly; but it is denied that this will lead to their salvation: works that "spring not of faith in Jesus Christ" are "not pleasant to God" (Article 13). "Holy scripture doth set out unto us only the Name of Jesus Christ whereby men must be saved" (Article 18).

The "grace" necessary to remedy man's corrupt nature is clearly not given to all. 1 Peter 2:8 has it that "such as disbelieve . . . stumble at the word, being disobedient, whereunto also they were appointed". (The RSV has: "they were destined" to disobey the word.) We may recall in this connection Paul's doctrine that God has mercy on whomever he will and hardens the heart of whomever he will. One fact of experience underlying such a view is that, however good a preacher's sermon may be, his teaching will not convince his entire audience. This experience is probably reflected in the statement put into Jesus's mouth at John 6:44: "No man can come to me except the Father which sent me draw him". In this gospel, Jesus repeatedly refers to those "given" to him by the Father (17:6 and 9); and it is these who will be saved (6:44b).

Brandon suggests that a similar experience—the obduracy of many in rejecting the preacher's message—may well underlie the predestinarian views expressed in the Koran,[10] which also envisages even the foreordination of the precise length of each person's life.[11] Hence when, in

July 1990, pilgrims to Mecca died in a tunnel disaster there, King Fahd of Saudi Arabia declared:

> It was fate. Had they not died there, they would have died elsewhere and at the same predestined moment (Quoted in *The Observer,* London, 8.7.90, among "Sayings of the Week").

The so-called "Hadith", the "tradition" of Mohammed's teaching that had not been preserved in the Koran, implies that even every action of every person has been predetermined by God. If so, it would be futile to urge people to change their ways, although Mohammed and his followers have always done this.

It is not only religious thinkers who display this inconsistency. Marxists believe that men in a certain economic condition inevitably behave in a certain way, yet they abuse them for doing so. They combine what they call a "materialistic" interpretation of human behaviour with the commonplace moralising of the older historians. And although they claim to be coldly scientific in their treatment of social questions, they are in fact as much affected by primitive emotions as many of their opponents. They do not speak like fatalists but like agitators.

The impotence of human initiative divorced from God's assistance was established as Christian orthodoxy only after protracted controversy. About 400 AD the monk Pelagius urged mankind to fulfill all duties by moral effort, exercising their own free will. He held that Adam's sin had injured only himself, so that infants at birth were in the same condition as Adam before his fall. On this view, unbaptized persons will not be damned if they lead moral lives; universal or almost universal sinfulness is due only to the following of Adam's bad example, and is quite unnecessary, as our wills can resist sin.

If, then, the possibility is allowed that man can, by his own moral efforts, remain sinless, he has no need of the saving grace which Christ had supposedly purchased by his death on Calvary. God "sent his Son to be the propitiation for our sins"—so 1 John 4:10 and many similar passages. But if man can be sinless, the whole Christian scheme of redemption becomes superfluous. Hence Augustine opposed Pelagius and proclaimed the universal corruption of human nature as the result of Adam's Fall, and the individual's inability to help himself unless divine grace aided him. These ideas are represented in the ninth of the Anglican articles, which declares that "original sin standeth not in the following of Adam (as the Pelagians do vainly talk); but it is the fault and corruption of the nature of every man that naturally is engendered of the offspring of Adam; whereby man is very far gone from original righteousness, and is of his own nature inclined to evil". This salvages the scheme of redemption, but is hard to reconcile with human responsibility for evil-doing; so there were perhaps many who followed the seventeenth-century French Calvinist Pierre Jurieu in finding it wise "to dogmatise like St. Augustine and to preach like Pelagius".[12]

In this chapter I have been concerned to outline some of what were for centuries fundamental items of Christian doctrine, most of them based on the very earliest of the extant sacred literature. Bezzant rightly says that these doctrines have been "so shattered" that the bare recital of them has "the aspect of a malicious travesty" (1963, p. 84). That they are so unacceptable is the reason for the rise of the kind of vague alternatives to them considered in the next chapter. Yet they still have their defenders. Canon Knox says that criticism of the Thirty-Nine Articles is often "really a quarrel with Scripture" (1967, p. 64) and therefore inadmissible. And the old dogmas continue to be recited in the liturgies in which they are enshrined, perhaps because these latter are spoken on solemn and sometimes very emotional occasions which inhibit a critical attitude. Nevertheless, it must seem, as Rees has noted (1949, pp. 115–16), "puzzling to all but the most orthodox" to hear at an Anglican wedding that God joined "our first parents, Adam and Eve" together in marriage "in the time of man's innocency", and to hear God given "hearty thanks" at an Anglican burial for delivering the deceased "out of the miseries of this sinful world".

PART THREE

MAKE-BELIEVE

6

IDEAS AND PSEUDO-IDEAS

i. PROVIDENCE AND THE IDEA OF GOD

Jews and Christians have supposed that God, however strange his methods might appear, was in reality guiding the whole course of history for the ultimate advantage of, in the first case the Hebrew people, and in the second the members of the Christian Church.

There is great psychological force in the conviction that one is on the winning side, and that victory will come in the end. Even the most sober of historians have found it difficult to refrain from introducing a guiding providence into their interpretation of human affairs. Ranke, for instance, who declared his task to be ascertaining what actually happened, wrote:

> There are certain periods of history that tempt us to scrutinise anxiously, if we dare thus to express ourselves, the plans of God in his government of the world. . . . The development [described in Ranke's book] was indispensable to the complete naturalisation of Christianity in the West. (1896, p. 24)

If we are expected to take this seriously, then it must be observed: 1. that, unless we have inside information concerning the purposes of God, we cannot form any opinion concerning his educational methods; and 2. that we can judge whether a particular process is indispensable only when we have observed its application in a variety of different conditions. 'The naturalisation of Christianity in the West' is a unique effect in our experience, and we cannot therefore decide whether the process that led up to it was the only possible one. Ranke continues:

> The task of bending the refractory spirits of the northern tribes to
> the pure laws of Christian truth was no light one: wedded, as these
> nations were, to their long-cherished superstitions, the religious
> element required a long predominance before it could gain entire
> possession of the German character.

The assumption that the northern tribes were in fact finally
'bent to the pure laws of Christian truth' is a rash one; and
the term 'religious element' conveys no definite idea and
might quite easily be supposed to include the 'long-
cherished superstitions' with which it is contrasted.

The most interesting thing about this passage is its
evidence—unless it is a mere rhetorical flourish—that
Ranke still thought of history as the record of God's
dealings with mankind, as the education of the human
race, and of the task of the historian as the justification of
the ways of God to man. However, the apologists of
providence seem to ascribe to it nothing but gross miscal-
culations, as when Merivale declares:

> Providence was preparing mankind for the reception of one law and
> one religion; and for this consummation the nations were to be
> trained by the steady development of the Roman administration.
> (1853, p. 151)

Such attempts to explain the past by reference to an
anticipated future involve the assumption of a known
purpose in the mind of God. 'Purpose' sounds very intellectual, and those who think that to speak of the 'hand' or
the 'eye' of God is mere metaphor often have no compunction in understanding his 'will' or his 'mind' literally,
although some apologists in effect concede that will and
mind are really just as animal. Watt, for instance, first says:
"When God 'hears' prayers this does not mean that he has
an organ which picks up sound waves, but that somehow or
other [sic] he becomes aware of the desires of the human
suppliant." He then goes on to admit that even God's
'becoming aware' is as much "a secondary usage" as is his
'hearing.' "Such terms are not descriptive in the strict sense
but only evocative, that is, suggesting or hinting at some-

thing whose precise nature is beyond our comprehension." However, he tries to turn this admission to apologetic account, positing, as a "corollary," that, when words are used in this way, "what appears to be contradictory is not necessarily so; the application to God of the term 'transcendent' does not necessarily exclude the term 'immanent'; and, for Christians, the term 'father' does not necessarily exclude the term 'mother'" (1988, p. 81). This should satisfy everyone.

Bezzant is aware of the objection that "Christianity overpersonalises the Divine," and he notes that "no thoughtful person can ignore the fact that the universe, as modern astronomy reveals it, reveals no sign of *personal* activity." However, he believes that "personality is the highest category we know which the world-ground has produced", and so he decides to "ascribe personality to its originator", without "overpersonalising him" (1963, pp. 103–06). The difficulty for the theist is that an abstract God without human qualities is really of very little interest: prayers and sacrifices can be supposed effective only when dealing with a being having human emotions and human intelligence, even though it is his superhuman powers that make it worth while to cultivate him. God is still often conceived by superimposing the idea of authority or chieftainship on that of soul or spirit. In even modern religious poetry, the language used in addressing him is modelled on that in which the subject addresses a monarch seated on a throne, giving orders to attendants, punishing rebels, and rewarding his faithful followers. The supplant seeks protection in exchange for submission, execrating the deity's enemies and imploring his help against his own enemies. To abandon the idea of a God with personality would be, says Bezzant (p. 109), to hold that the cosmos "has no meaning or enduring value." One naturally asks to whom or what this value or meaning is to refer; but theologians are unwilling to admit that the cosmos is indifferent to human interests.

The animal nature of purposive behaviour is obscured by residual unwillingness to admit that animals other than man have minds, that they are capable of the kind of planned behaviour that Köhler and others have observed in them. Thus the late Bishop Stephen Neill says that the "traces of purpose" we see among them are "rudimentary" and "seem to depend more on instinctive response than on conscious planning." (1984, p. 21). This may be true of invertebrates, but with the higher mammals, as we saw, the role of instinct is very often to prompt the mind to reflection and thus guide the behavior only in a generalized way.

For Neill, purpose is one of the "categories within which Christians find themselves thinking all the time, and without the use of which they cannot think as Christians at all" (1984, p. 20). But purposes imply motives or desires: someone acts with a certain purpose because he feels some desire and believes that the action will lead to its fulfilment. We posit desires and beliefs of this kind in order to explain behaviour that converges upon a fairly constant terminal phase, although reaching it by many different routes. It is this variety of intermediate stages that compels us to rely on what we call the "aim" in order to characterise the actions. Neill tries to turn this variety to theological account. We cannot, he says, see from the initial stages of a man's behaviour what his purpose is: the heap of papers he puts on his desk does not betray that he intends to write a book; so likewise we cannot determine God's purpose in history when we know only a limited number of phases of history, and when he created human beings with free will which enables them to thwart his purpose (p. 21).

Today there is still a public prepared to accept Croce's view that the rise of Christianity was "the greatest revolution that the human race has ever accomplished", "something so great, so wide and so deep, so far-reaching in its effects, so unforeseen and so irresistible in its development" that it has been thought "a miracle, a revelation from on high, a direct intervention of God in human affairs" (1949, p. 37). As the author of some seventy books, Croce was an influential commentator; but nothing in his exposition suggests that he studied the rise of Buddhism, Mohammedanism, Brahmanism, or Confucianism, and so discovered that Christianity's rise was the greatest of all. And as he holds this rise to have been "unforeseen," it seems that he discounts the prophecies. He goes on explicitly to shed a few superfluous articles of faith—"myths" such as "the kingdom of heaven, the resurrection of the dead, baptismal regeneration, the expiation and redemption which atone the sins of those elected to the kingdom, predestination, grace and so on" (p. 39). Nevertheless, we are to believe that not even the invention of writing and mathematics "bear comparison" with that of Christianity; and the revolutions and discoveries "which have followed in modern times . . . can only be conceived as dependent on the Christian revolution and derivative from its original and lasting stimulus." On this level of irresponsible assertion there can obviously be no argument. This is the technique so well understood by the dictators whom Croce detested, not to be content with modest mis-statements, but to make them so comprehensive and extravagant that people are more ready to believe them true than to suppose that anyone could try to deceive them with such falsehoods.

The claims Croce makes for Christianity are perfectly clear. Pseudo-ideas would not be of any advantage to them. As, however, they are grotesquely excessive, pseudo-ideas are needed as support for them. And so we are told that Christianity caused "the conception of spirit" to prevail, "so that God himself was no longer conceived as an abstract identity with no distinguishable qualities and therefore impassive and inert, but was at once identity and difference, because living and the source of all life, one in three" (p. 39). It is not given to all of us to comprehend the distinction between an identity which is abstract and has no distinguishable qualities and one which is at the same time a difference. Identity means sameness, and two things are identical if they are the same. How, then, do we picture to ourselves an abstract sameness that is impassive and inert because it has no distinguishable qualities? And how do we conceive a sameness which is also a difference?

ii. RELIGION AS IMAGINATION: SANTAYANA

George Santayana (1863–1952) was an influential Spanish-American philosopher, author of 22 books and of numerous articles in periodicals. An early collection of his essays is entitled *Interpretations of Poetry and Religion* (1900), and all my quotations from him are taken from it.

An encyclopedia entry claims that "to the most abstruse subjects he never failed to bring an acid wit and a romantic beauty of style." His figurative style does not lend itself to the clarification of 'abstruse subjects'. For instance, having called religion "an imaginative echo of things natural and moral," he says: "If this echo is to be well attuned, our ear must first be attentive to the natural sounds of which, in religion, we are to develop the harmony" (p. 235). The processes of 'attuning an echo' and 'developing the harmony of natural sounds' are quite unclear; and how does one develop this harmony 'in religion'?

A great deal in Santayana's arguments turns on a supposed distinction between faculties of "understanding" and "imagination." "Ideas of the understanding," he says, are those which "prove serviceable in practice" and are "capable of verification in sense," whereas other ideas "remain ideas of the imagination." He finds that the more powerful minds are often "swayed by emotion" and desire to find a "noble" solution to all questions. Since the understanding cannot always supply the kind of solution required, these sublime spirits "pass beyond" it and "draw the wider views, the deeper harmonies" they crave from the imagination, for "there is no other faculty left to invoke" (pp. 5–6). Hence

> The imagination . . . must furnish to religion and to metaphysics those large ideas tinctured with passion, those supersensible forms

shrouded in awe, in which alone a mind of great sweep and vitality can find congenial objects. Thus . . . the intuitions which science could not use remain the inspiration of poetry and religion. (pp. 6–7)

He holds that prophecy and revelation are nothing but imagination; but this does not, it seems, invalidate them. They differ from science only in being unverifiable. The "intuitions" of the man of religion or the metaphysician may be just as true as the findings of the man of science, only they cannot be demonstrated; and by dwelling on such intuitions a man becomes "conscious of a certain moral transformation" which may be highly satisfying, for it gives him "a certain warmth and energy of life. This emotion . . . he calls faith or high philosophy, and under its dominion he is able to face his destiny with enthusiasm, or at least with composure." (p. 8).

In this context Santayana writes of "the higher reason" of the metaphysicians which, he says, is their name for the imagination, in particular for when it is "employed to anticipate or correct the conclusions of the understanding" (p. 7). But these conclusions are surely science, and are characterized by the fact that they can be verified. Does that which can be and is verified need to be 'corrected' by what cannot? If so, how are we to choose between the verified and the unverifiable? The only method hinted at in the passages from which I have quoted is to estimate the amount of moral uplift derived from the belief.

As we shall see, Santayana supposes that the 'truths' of imagination are true in a quite different sense from those of understanding, and may even conflict with them. But it is already clear that he is akin to those apologists who hold that *reason* is not everything, that *emotions* can teach one to comprehend truths which are outside the scope of reason and logic; and that with the *imagination* we can discern truths that to reason appear as falsehoods and illusions.[1] The terms in such arguments are familiar psychological ones, and psychology has one great advantage over other sciences, namely that many of its technical terms are taken from popular language where they are of very uncertain meaning, so that it is possible to scatter them through one's discourse without exposing oneself quite so palpably as if one tried the same method with the technical vocabulary of the chemists. The opposition between imagination and what Santayana regards as more rational processes is illusory. Verification of a proposition often depends upon imagination: it may involve putting together in imagination a set of conditions which will have to obtain if the proposition is true, and then seeing whether these conditions can in fact be observed or constructed (cf. above, p. 17). Even perception depends upon imagination. Our eyes and ears can give us only a momentary picture of our environment, as it is presented to us when we are in one particular position. Our memory and imagination allow us to build up a more adequate representation in space and time.

Santayana could not have been unaware that ordinary thinking involves the formation of images—or at any rate memories, if it is other than visual experiences that are being recalled—and is prompted by some interest. In a novel situation, fear may prompt us to withdraw, while curiosity leads us to explore further. Reason in such a case is merely the imagination, which draws on our memories to predict the consequences of either course of action. Reason, then, may justly be said to be "the same as imagination, except that we use the latter term where no strong aim or desire determines the sequence of images or memories. When we are under the influence of a desire or fear (not so strong as to turn our behavior into panic) there is a kind of selection of memories, and this is called reasoning"; whereas "when there is no such selective guidance of what we recall, we call the process imagination or daydreaming" (Englefield 1985, p. 57).

Contrary to what Santayana implies, the poet—if he is concerned to tell a coherent story—works in essentially the same way as the reasoner, in that the pictures or memories that pass through his mind are strictly controlled, all those deemed irrelevant to his purpose being set aside. How did the teapot on the kitchen floor get broken? A number of theories occur to me, all of them tentative reconstructions of the past. If my main concern is to prevent the recurrence of such accidents, I shall look for the true account. But if I want to write a story for a magazine, then I shall try to think of something unexpected, diverting, or uncanny. As Medawar implies, the only difference is that in the one case I quickly dismiss all theories obviously incompatible with the known facts, and in the other I dismiss only those that are commonplace or uninteresting.[2]

People who cannot think in an orderly way are apt to suppose themselves more imaginative than others. But the difference is really no more than that between the imagination unchecked, and the imagination checked and controlled by experience and memory. It is this difference that Santayana himself has vaguely in mind, saying for instance, that imagination "may loosen our hold on fact and confuse our intelligence" (p. 225). But on the whole he prefers what he calls imagination, as the vehicle of poetry and religion, to reason, although some of his grounds for praising it now seem distinctly dubious. Thus he says:

> Without poetry and religion the history of mankind would have been darker than it is. . . . By what a complex and uninspired argumentation would the pure moralists have to insist upon those duties which the imagination enforces so powerfully in oaths sworn before the gods . . . ; what intricate, what unavailing appeals to positive interests would have to be made before those quick reactions could be secured in large bodies of people which can be produced by the sight of a flag or the sound of a name. (pp. 8–9)

In the year 1900, these effects of flag and name on "large bodies of people" may have seemed desirable, but more recent experience has made us less inclined to overvalue them. And attention to the historical record might have made even Santayana less complacent about the beneficent influence of religious beliefs.

Santayana believes that, although it may not be possible to harmonize the two, we need neither question the findings of science nor give up our religious beliefs:

> That counter-Copernican revolution accomplished by Christian-
> ity . . . which put man in the centre of the universe and made the
> stars circle about him, must have some kind of justification. And
> indeed its justification . . . is that what is false in the science of facts
> may be true in the science of values. While the existence of things
> must be understood by referring them to their causes which are
> mechanical, their functions can only be explained . . . by their
> relation to human nature and to human happiness. (pp. 91–92)

This "science of values" which may contradict "the science
of facts" is meant to include moral values: there are moral
truths as well as factual ones. But surely a moral truth must
be some kind of maxim, some guide to behaviour, some
generalization about right and wrong. And maxims will be
of little use if they conflict with factual truths. A maxim is a
statement of what we should do, our aims and desires
(moral or other) being assumed; and it will be valid only if
it is related to a natural law, to a statement in general terms
from which we may infer what will happen in certain
definable circumstances. Thus it is a natural law that water
expands when it freezes, and it is a maxim not to allow
one's pipes to freeze when filled with water. It is a natural
law that ether takes fire if brought within a certain distance
of a naked flame, and it is a maxim to keep ether in glass
stoppered bottles away from open fires. There is no natural
law that one must not handle ether near a flame, and if
one's intention were to cause an explosion the maxim
would be reversed; but the law remains in either case the
same. Maxims, then, are based on laws and take the form
'do this, if you desire that.' The corresponding law would
be: 'if this is done, that will follow.' The two statements are
equivalent from the practical point of view, and it is often a
matter of indifference which way we state the correlation.
There can be no question of the maxim affirming what the
law denies.

Santayana next introduces the Christian doctrines of
heaven and hell, saying that "the idea of torments and
vengeance is happily becoming alien to our society and is
therefore not a natural vehicle for our religion" (p. 94). But
he is not willing to admit that these doctrines were so much

mischievous superstition. He thinks they are based upon the fact, ascertained by "intuition," that there is another life far more important than this one—a life "reached by the intuition of ideals, not by the multiplication of phenomena" (p. 96). How anything can be reached by either of these means remains unclear. The other life "is an eternal state, not an indefinite succession of changes." Life as we know it involves change, but

> Transitory life ends for the Christian when the balance-sheet of his individual merits and demerits is made up, and the eternity that ensues is the eternal reality of those values. (p. 96)

Christianity supposes—in this, far superior to "the Oriental mind"—that the values exist independently of any mind as "eternal essences, forms suspended above the flux of natural things." Yet Santayana cannot quite bring himself to represent this as the Christian position. He says that, for Christianity, "each life has the potentiality of an eternal meaning" which is actualized if it is "expressed in the phenomena of this [present] life," and that if this happens, "the soul is eternally saved," otherwise it is lost. What this salvation or perdition involves in hard cash we are not told.

All this has some relevance to Santayana's view of moral values. He believes that "moral distinctions are absolute" (p. 98), and that "the complexities of life" obscure this "truth," for they sometimes make the attainment of one good incompatible with the attainment of another, and even link it with the perpetration of an evil, as when to do a great right we have to do a little wrong. But the Christian "clear vision of Heaven and Hell" does away with "the confused vistas of the empirical world," where good and evil seem inextricably entwined, and makes the determination of our destiny "depend upon obedience to recognised duties" (pp. 100–02). He omits to say that the principal duty thus enjoined was belief in the dogmas of Christianity, although he does concede, speaking in quite general terms, that "these duties may often have been far from corresponding to those which reason would impose"

(p. 102). The Christian crusaders and the warriors of Mohammed were both offered the same eternal rewards, each for slaughtering the others.

Let us revert to the question: what is a moral truth? I have said it must be some maxim which guides behavior. It is not a moral truth to say that the immoral will be punished and the others rewarded, although it may be true. But Santayana implies that it is in fact a fiction: heaven and hell are to be included among what he calls "Christian fictions . . . which made man understand, as never before or since . . . the necessity of discipline" which, in his opinion, the "barbarous religions" of the East were unable to do (p. 98). So the Christian dogmas are justified because they induce people to behave properly. But what constitutes proper behaviour? What are the maxims on which it is based? Santayana is quite evasive here, and says that "it is . . . a moral truth . . . that some things are really better than others" (p. 100). As, for him, moral distinctions are absolute, he must mean better absolutely, not better for certain persons or under certain circumstances. He seems to wish to say that every action which is not indifferent is quite definitely either right or wrong and that there can be no doubt about it in any case. "The odious circumstances which make the attainment of many goods conditional on the perpetration of some evil . . . cannot rob any good of its natural sweetness, nor all goods together of their conceptual harmony" (p. 101). And the purpose of all this is to justify the Christian doctrine of hell! He has no sympathy with "the good souls that wish to fancy that everybody will be ultimately saved" (p. 103) and implies that it upsets our sense of justice to think that the wicked as well as the virtuous will be rewarded.

The aim of Santayana is fairly obvious. The beliefs of Christians have come into conflict with the discoveries of science. The crisis which started at the time of the Renaissance reached a climax in the nineteenth century, when many attempts were made to find some way of accepting the discoveries of science without giving up the beliefs of religion. Santayana's is merely a particularly feeble attempt of this kind. He denies that the Christian religion can be affected by scientific discoveries, for there is scientific truth and truth of the imagination, and they are independent. The dogmas of religion are not scientifically but morally true, that is they are fables inculcating moral principles, and are morally true in so far as they do in fact do this. Few Christians would derive much comfort from believing that the gospel story was a mere invention, designed to discourage immorality, so Santayana is careful to avoid saying this in plain language. On the other hand he is equally careful not to commit himself to literal acceptance of this story, so he says: "Christian fictions . . . were mistaken for accounts of external fact," and "the supernatural was an allegory of the natural" (p. 98). He even says that the great mistake of the Christians has been failure to appreciate that their dogmas are fictions; for he writes of "the fallacy, . . . the natural but hopeless misunderstanding of imagining that poetry, in order to be religion, . . . must first deny that it is poetry" (p. 115). This kind of writing naturally appalled religious folk, and Santayana has recorded that William James called the volume in which this doctrine is stated "a perfection of rottenness" (Arnett 1968, p. 104).

At times, what Santayana writes puts one in mind of J.A.T. Robinson's subsequent talk about 'the ground of our being', which will occupy us in a later section of this chapter. These phrases, or variations on them, get passed on from one generation to the next. He says (and we recall that, for him, poetry and religion are allied):

> The great function of poetry, which we have not yet directly mentioned, is precisely this: to repair to the material of experience, seizing hold of the reality of sensation and fancy beneath the surface of conventional ideas, and then out of that living but indefinite material to build new structures, richer, finer, fitter to the *primary tendencies of our nature,* truer to the *ultimate possibilities of the soul.* Our descent into the *elements of our being* is then justified by our subsequent freer ascent toward its goal; we revert to sense only to find food for reason; we destroy conventions only to construct ideals. (p. 270)

The three phrases I have italicized are not explained by
Santayana and are in themselves quite meaningless. And
what is the "goal" of our being? Why are the elements of
our being below and its goal above normal elevation? In
what manner do we, by reverting to sense, find food for
reason? Santayana clearly supposes himself to be thinking,
but in reality he is only making up sentences. But they are
sentences which suggest sublime conceptions of the human
soul and its superiority to mere nature, and of its supernatural powers when inspired by poets and philosophers. Such
writing may have a strong emotional appeal, and like all
that is meaningless, it has the great advantage that it
cannot be refuted.

iii.   RICHARDSON AND
'EXISTENTIAL KNOWLEDGE'

The late Dean of York Alan Richardson realized that, if
theology is to be taken seriously, it must "justify itself at
the bar of rational scientific enquiry" (1947, p. 7). By
'theology' he means "the study of Christian existence in
history and today" (p. 50), and he calls it "an empirical
science" (p. 16). All scientists, he says, approach their data
with ideas of their own, with unproven hypotheses "probably arrived at . . . by flashes of insight or 'intuitions'" (p.
46). Biologists and psychologists, for instance, operate with
"categories"—he later calls them "categories of interpretation" (p. 230)—such as progress, purpose, natural selection and the unconscious. The historian, as scientist, must
likewise "bring to the facts that he handles a perspective, a
point of view, a scale of values" (p. 94), otherwise he would
not be able to select what he regards as significant from his
material. And the theologian is in large part historian,
since the Christian faith "is bound up with certain happenings in the past," and if these "could be shown never to
have occurred, or to have been quite different from the
biblical-Christian account of them, then the whole edifice
of Christian faith, life and worship would be found to have

been built on sand" (p. 91). Because, then, all scientists bring interpretive hypotheses to their data, science, including history "is based on an act of faith . . . not formally different in quality from the faith about which the religious man speaks" (pp. 43, 47–48, 99).

The scientist could reply that the difference is that all his hypotheses are provisional, that he is prepared, even anxious to modify them if he can find evidence falsifying them. There is no way of testing a theory save by provisionally assuming its truth, inferring the consequences, and comparing these with the facts. Richardson is in fact quite aware that the historian must learn to "criticise the assumptions of his own thinking and the scale of values and principle of selection which he has adopted" (p. 104). History is written "on the assumption that one interpretation of the evidence can be shown to be more credible than another" (1966, p. 76); and "that perspective from which we see most clearly all the facts, without having to explain any of them away, will be a relatively true perspective" (1947, p. 105). He is aware too that, in science generally, "progress . . . is made by the constant criticism and modification of hypotheses" (p. 43). He is glad to note this as the basis of his claim that the Christian apologist has no need to bring "Christian truth" into line with the latest scientific ideas, as "scientific theories and conclusions have no permanence" (p. 16). But if theology is an empirical science, are not its theories and conclusions equally ephemeral?

Richardson contrives to avoid this inference by insisting that criticism of a scientific hypothesis "must come from within and not from without the particular scientific discipline itself, since those who venture to criticise from outside . . . have not the technical competence" (p. 43). Hence theological hypotheses may be criticised only by theologians: their technical competence needs to be so vast that it would be impertinent for outsiders to venture opinions.[3]

In this connection Richardson introduces his concep-

tion of "existential knowledge". This does not contradict
scientific knowledge, but is of a more personal kind—the
knowledge, for instance, of a game which the players rather
than the observers have. He quotes with approval an
authority who holds a proposition or truth to be existential
when "I cannot apprehend it or assent to it from the
standpoint of a mere spectator, but only on the ground of
my total existence" (p. 52n). This vague idea becomes even
vaguer in Richardson's later publications, as we shall see.
But he believes that "only those who possess what we have
called existential knowledge of the Church's faith and life
are in a position to articulate its true meaning" (p. 62). If
the theologian is to come to his work, like any other
scientist, "with a high regard for its dignity and value," it
follows "in practice—if not absolutely in theory—that he
will be a convinced member of the believing and witnessing Christian community" (p. 61).

The principal hypothesis which the theologian brings to
his data is the category of revelation, without which
"theology as a science stands or falls." "If there is no
distinctively Christian revelation in history, the special
categories of theology will not be needed" (p. 57). Revelation provides the "prior enlightening of the eyes of the
mind" which enables the relevant facts and their meaning
to be seen "in their true perspective" (p. 107). It is,
however, for Richardson, not an arbitrary category, but is
shown to be a true one by the material to which it is
applied; for the theologian as historian is confronted with a
Jesus whose Crucifixion under Pontius Pilate plunged his
disciples into a despair documented at Luke 24:20–21; and
yet the Church rapidly established itself. "The only credible explanation," he says, is that their despair was changed
to triumph by Jesus's Resurrection. Faith in him did not
create belief in this event, but the event created faith in him
"and therefore also the Church which arose to bear witness
to his resurrection" (1966, pp. 76–77).[4]

Richardson is able to make 'revelation' the most plausible hypothesis here and elsewhere only by speaking of "*the* apostolic interpretation of the events to which the apostolic testimony bore witness," and of "*the* biblical-Christian account" of certain past happenings (1947, pp. 91, 107, Italics mine), when in reality conflicting accounts are given of them. The Nativity and Resurrection narratives are among the striking examples, and their divergencies are best understood by supposing that each of the narrators believed that Jesus was virgin-born and resurrected, but had no reliable information on the subject. Similarly, all four gospel passion narratives appeal to prophecies, but the actual ones quoted differ, showing that, although the authors believed that the events fulfilled prophecy, each one of them could do no more than hunt out what could be represented as plausible passages. They also depict Jesus's death as accompanied by supernatural signs, but no one sign is recorded in all four gospels.

Just as the Bible speaks with a divided voice, so do also its interpreters. Theologians do not say the same things about Jesus's birth, his Resurrection, and his overall significance, even if they belong to one and the same (for instance the Anglican) religious community. And so the outsider who wants to form an opinion on such matters has no option—impertinent though this be from Richardson's standpoint—but to form his own, even if he restricts the rational part of this process to deciding which of the conflicting authorities to follow. If discordant voices create mental confusion in a listener, there is irresolution, escape from which is possible by reliance on an external will. Religion requires of us a choice in matters that are not trivial. If the intellect gives an ambiguous answer, one is tempted to resign one's will and resort to authority. And one is told that it is a virtue thus to 'humble' oneself.

In the first chapter of this book, I tried to show that abstract ideas are relatively remote from their sources in experience and may not correspond to reality; and that this allows pleasing theories to be built on unrealities.

Richardson's view that there is "existential knowledge" which differs in quality from scientific knowledge is one such theory. Although he calls theology an empirical science, he at the same time insists that religious truth "is not primarily a matter of verifiable propositions about God and human destiny, but is rather an existential awareness of man's situation as over against God and the world, which can be expressed and communicated only under the forms of imagination and symbol" (1963, p. 308). Elsewhere he says: "Existential knowledge . . . arises from an 'I—Thou' encounter, and is based on the utter individuality of every single separate person" (1957, p. 15). We have earlier seen how this idea of individuality has been made the basis of attempts to protect historical phenomena from scientific scrutiny. When he says that 'existential' knowledge of a game is the knowledge the players, rather than the observers, have of it, he is supposing greater interest and emotional involvement on the part of the players. This may well not be the case, judging from the behaviour of, for instance, present-day football crowds. The real difference is one of what in Chapter 1 I have called *aspect* (above, p. 3). The conditions in which two persons can view or experience the same event on equal terms are, either that the experience should involve only sound, smell, or temperature, or that, if the event is visible, it shall be far enough away to reduce the difference of aspect to zero. Even then, the experience which *any* two people have of an event may be materially different; for the perception of an event involves more than the mere reception of sensory stimuli. The previous experience of the person and his mental habits, not to mention inherited peculiarities of sense-organ and brain, affect his new experience, which is to some extent moulded and accommodated to harmonize with them. Perhaps therefore we may say that no two persons can ever have quite the same experience. To base anything on a distinction between experiences that are common to players and those that are common to observers—when each member of each of these two groups perceives different aspects of the game and may well come to it with different expectations—is rash.

iv. *HONEST TO GOD* IN RETROSPECT

A. GOD

J.A.T. Robinson caused something of a furore when, as Bishop of Woolwich, he published his *Honest to God* in 1963 and introduced it with an article, entitled 'Our Image of God Must Go', given pride of place in the Sunday Newspaper *The Observer* on 17th March of that year. This title was apparently the editor's choice, not Robinson's, whose article does not commit him to the position that traditional Christian views of God are completely unacceptable. He was, however, aware that a number of awkward questions were being asked and that it was no longer possible to ignore them; so in the article he declared himself ready to discard "the whole supernaturalist scheme", and said that the word 'God' has become "impregnated with a way of thinking we may have to discard if the Gospel is to signify anything." It is important for him that the gospel should signify something; we must find some new way of thinking which will permit it to make sense. *What* it signifies seems to be of secondary importance; for in the 'Observer' of a fortnight later he gave an assurance that he did not wish to disturb people who are satisfied with the old way of thinking: "I do not want to sweep away any picture of God which makes him real." If any traditional idea about him effects this, then "well and good. I am concerned for those for whom it makes him unreal or false." So his purpose was not so much to question traditional ideas as to suggest alternatives for those who found them unsatisfactory.

He says in the first of these two articles that "God is ultimate reality" and that "mathematics is God." This might be regarded as cold comfort by some even of the more sophisticated believers, but it seems to reconcile religion with science. He believes that "reality . . . can finally be reduced to mathematical formulae". One wonders what 'finally' here means, as nobody has yet shown how even an amoeba or a mushroom spore can be 'reduced to mathematical formulae.' He also says that "depth is what the word 'God' means," and that "to speak of God in terms of 'depth' instead of 'height' may have a profounder appeal to modern man brought up on 'depth psychology' ". Such upbringing normally means no more than learning to talk of Freud and Jung; and Robinson's argument, here as so often, is based merely on the associations of a word with other words: 'depth' suggests concern and involvement, while 'height' suggests remoteness and indifference (cf. pp. 45–6). Verbal associations can be very strong and may prevail over the associations between ideas; and these in any case are often but remotely related to anything in nature.

It is remarkable with what confidence he and the theologians he quotes determine the meaning of a word. A word can mean just what the user at any time wishes it to mean. Robinson may, if he chooses, use the word 'God' to signify any idea he has, but by so doing he does not abolish all the ideas which have been expressed by the word before. So long as he is able to make us understand the idea he has in his mind, we may readily agree, for the purposes of his argument, to use the same word as he does. But if we cannot understand his idea, we shall only cause confusion by using his word. In fact neither 'ultimate reality' nor 'depth' denote such clear ideas that they can be regarded as contributing very much to our understanding of the word 'God'.

The book which these articles introduce was rapidly translated into many languages. John Bowden mentions, in this connection, German, French, Swedish, Dutch, Danish, Italian, and Japanese, and says that "yet more languages followed later" (1977, p. 15). In the book, as in the articles, Robinson insists that he has no intention to disturb the orthodox or raise doubts in the minds of believing Christians, but that his concern is rather with persons who "imagine they have rejected the gospel" because of its apparently "incredible" statements (p. 8). The God "those who call themselves atheists" feel they cannot believe in is, he says, so often one particular "image of God instead of God" (p. 126). He wants to convince such persons that an inability to believe what is stated in the Bible or the Prayer-book does not disqualify them from calling themselves Christians and presenting themselves at church. This situation is hardly new, and he himself recalls (somewhat obliquely, p. 9 and note) the efforts of Bishop Colenso in a similar direction a century earlier.

Robinson speaks of traditional Christian beliefs as a "language" (p. 24), and seems to think that Christianity must be conveyed to different people in different languages. By employing, as he does, the language of Bonhoeffer, Tillich, or Bultmann, an atheist may find himself able to call himself a Christian. As atheists are becoming more numerous, it is perhaps wise to make provision for them. But the old familiar language of the Bible remains more intelligible to most of God's children, particularly to his "older children" (p. 43); so we must not give it up, although he allows that those whom it satisfies will become progressively fewer, and that, without "the kind of revolution" he is advocating, "Christian faith and practice . . . will come to be abandoned" (p. 123).

Let us look more closely at what he says about God. He tells us that people used to believe that the earth was flat and the sky a kind of canopy hung with lanterns, behind which there was a place called heaven in which God dwelt. But when this view of the universe was revised it became necessary to be less explicit about God's localization. Instead of being supposed to be 'up there' he was removed to 'out there'. The locality of heaven was less clearly specified but was still supposed to be somewhere beyond the stars. Now that the astronomers have explored a little further and still found no suitable site for heaven it becomes necessary to look in another direction. But these changes of view about the whereabouts of heaven do not, according to Robinson, constitute any radical change in belief about God. They were and are only metaphors. A change of metaphor is a matter of convenience and each age must choose its metaphors to suit its own way of thought. The earlier change in spatial metaphor from 'up there' to 'out there' was, however "undoubtedly important in liberating Christianity from a flat-earth cosmology" (p. 17). Christianity was thus 'liberated' from an erroneous belief. Later it was liberated from the belief in God 'out there' beyond the stars, and then it was liberated by Bishop Colenso from various beliefs concerning creation, Adam and Eve, and other Old Testament legends. The older method of dealing with such liberating efforts was to demolish the liberator. That is no longer possible, and so the modern apologist undertakes to dispose of the inconvenient dogmas himself—a dangerous process which, once started, may well be carried very far. Hence Robinson's anxiety to show that the "recasting" he proposes "will . . . leave the fundamental truth of the Gospel unaffected" (p. 124).

It is clear from the above that in some passages Robinson suggests that the Biblical writers never intended their accounts to be taken literally in the first place. The "more sophisticated" of them, he says, "would have been the first, if pressed," to regard their picture of a three-decker universe (heaven above, earth beneath, and waters under the earth) as "symbolic language to represent and convey spiritual realities" (p. 11). "For St. Paul, no doubt, to be 'caught up to the third heaven' was as much a metaphor as it is to us," and "everybody accepted what it meant to speak of a God up there, even though the groundlings might understand it more grossly than the gnostics" (p. 12). But can we really believe that these writers were consciously speaking in metaphors when the whole Christian Church for centuries afterwards understood them to have been speaking literally? Were these writers so enlightened that they did not share the common ideas of their age? Robinson admits that the "three-decker" arrangement was at one time "taken literally" (p.

11)—perhaps by the less sophisticated sacred writers themselves. But such beliefs became in time "embarrassing" and had to be regarded as metaphors. This must mean that the form of words in which they were expressed continued to be used, but with a different meaning. This secondary use of the formula becomes in turn "embarrassing" and yet another meaning has to be given to the words (p. 16). It seems that the embarrassment arises when there is some danger of having to give up using the formula. Hence as long as a new meaning can be found for the old words, there need be no embarrassment. A given meaning is apparently much less important than the words!

We have seen from the *Observer* articles what meanings Robinson gives to the word 'God', and he reiterates those views here, saying that "by definition"—presumably Robinson's definition—"God is ultimate reality." The argument is that there must be some reality that is ultimate, so that we cannot question whether it exists, only what it is like (p. 29). And the answer is supplied by the word 'depth': "the word 'God' denotes the ultimate depth of all our being" (p. 47). It follows that one can be an atheist only if one denies that our being has any depth (p. 22). It also follows that God is not "a supreme and separate Being" (p. 17). Robinson writes a good deal about "transcendence" and says that Tillich's great contribution to theology is "the reinterpretation of transcendence in a way which preserves its reality while detaching it from the projection of supranaturalism" (p. 56). The word, then, is a valuable one, and even when it is not allowed to imply anything supernatural, it must be supposed to stand for some reality. God, says Robinson, "is not outside us, yet he [the masculine pronoun seems unavoidable] is profoundly transcendent" (p. 60).

In this connection, Robinson appeals to what he calls "depths of revelation, intimations of eternity, judgements of the holy and the sacred, awarenesses of the unconditional, the numinous and the ecstatic." These, he says, "cannot be explained in purely naturalistic categories without being reduced to something else" (p. 55). Any explanation of anything must of course be in terms of something else. A hunk of cheese is not explained by saying that it consists of numerous fragments of cheese. What Robinson has in mind is presumably the doctrine that explanations should be given in terms somehow comparable to what it is that has to be explained; that a mechanical explanation may serve to account for a material motion, and a material structure may be held to be put together out of material components, but molecular motions cannot account for ideas or feelings.[5] And he is arguing that it is not permissible to explain the phenomena in question by noting, for instance, that mystical revelations are commonly preceded by a protracted state of anxiety which is then relieved by harmonizing conflicting notions; they are to be explained only by being referred to some non-animal essence in man which is not created by a god external to us, but is in itself God. This is as much explanation by appeal to 'something else' as any relevant naturalistic theory. But it presumably has the advantage that no 'reduction' to something else is involved.

He goes on to extend the meaning of the word 'God' to relationships between persons. Statements about God, he says, are "acknowledgements of the transcendental, unconditional element" in such relationships (p. 52). So he reaches the conclusion that the love and trust of others inherent in human relationships form the essence of man, identical with God (pp. 49–50). If, then, the doubters can recognize that a relationship of goodwill with one's neighbour is something of great value, then they may call themselves believers. In some passages he even implies that belief in God means no more than right behaviour; for "prayer and ethics are simply the inside and the outside of the same thing" (p. 105), and prayer is "openness to the ground of our being" (p. 102), alias God, alias love. "To pray for another is to expose both oneself and him to the common ground of our being" (p. 99). It is far from easy to envisage this 'thing' of which prayer and ethics are said to be the inside and the outside.

B. JESUS AND NEW TESTAMENT 'MYTHS'

Robinson faces what he calls "the problem of Christology," namely to show "how Jesus can be fully God and fully man, and yet genuinely one person" (pp. 64–65). I have noted elsewhere (Wells 1988, p. 89) that the simple answer is that the whole thing is an absurdity, that no one in his senses should try to solve such a pseudo-problem, and that the real problem is how such a contradictory conception got into the minds of rational beings—a problem for the psychologist and the historian. The latter will perhaps note that the idea of Jesus as both man and God may have become problematic from considerations such as the following: According to Jesus, Moses wrote the Pentateuch (Luke 20:37, and other passages with similar implications), and either this guarantees the Mosaic authorship, or else Jesus was mistaken. But if he was truly God, would he have made such a mistake? If, however, in taking our human nature fully, he possessed no more information about the Pentateuch than any other person of his day and age, and should not be expected to speak with divine knowledge on this or any other matter, then all his pronouncements are deprived of authority. Charles Gore, later Bishop of Birmingham, gave great offence in his Bampton lectures of 1891 when he argued, taking Philippians 2:7 as his text, that Christ, at his incarnation, became subject to all human limitations.

Robinson's solution to the 'problem' is that Jesus is God and man not in the sense that a supramundane personage came to earth in human form (although this is clearly enough the doctrine which Paul states in his epistles and which is even put into Jesus's mouth in the fourth gospel), but because so much of his behaviour proceeded from what Robinson has specified as the essence of the human personality, indeed of all reality, namely love. (I shall be asking (below, p. 206) why love is the essence, rather than greed, pride, love, gormlessness, etc. collectively.) Hence Jesus is "the disclosure of the final truth, not merely about human nature, . . . but about all nature and all reality" (p. 128). He is the man who lived for others, "the one in whom Love has completely taken over, the one who is utterly open to, and united with, the Ground of his being. And this 'life for others, through participation in the Being of God,' *is* transcendence" (p. 76).

One can understand what might be meant by "life for others" but not by the phrase "through participation in the Being of God." And Jesus as the man of love is a view of him based on a very one-sided selection of the utterances ascribed to him in the gospels (cf. above, p. 83). Robinson does not go into this question, but he is aware that many of Jesus's maxims conflict with what he calls "the new morality," which is chiefly distinguished by the disappearance of various restraints and prohibitions of things which former generations of Christians regarded as sinful. It used to be thought that, by eschewing all forms of pleasure, one became more fit to enter the kingdom of heaven; and those who could abstain from sexual activity were specially respected. Such an attitude persisted well into the present century, as is shown by the contributions of Robinson's Church at successive Lambeth Conferences to the question of contraception. It was condemned as inimical to "self-denial" at the Conferences of 1908 and 1920; a sub-committee of the 1930 Conference went so far as to allow that "each couple must decide for themselves"; but not until 1958 was what Alan Wilkinson calls "the bold step" taken of "proclaiming that what most people had been doing for more than a generation was right after all," so that in the end, on this as on other ethical matters, Church and society reached similar conclusions, "but the Church usually took longer (despite its claims to be guided by the Spirit)" (1988, pp. 128–130). Its tardiness resulted of course in erosion of its authority. It was seen to be merely reluctantly accepting a situation to which opposition had become hopeless.

Robinson, anxious not to be in the rear of the permissive climate of the 1960s, is at pains to show that older ethical attitudes were not an essential part of Christianity —he calls them "the equivalent in the ethical field of the supranaturalist way of thinking" (p. 106)—and for this purpose he argues that it is a mistake to take Jesus too literally; that Mark 10:11 is not the total veto of divorce and remarriage that it appears to be; that "here as elsewhere" he is not really laying down any inflexible rule, and his sayings "make no attempt to adjudicate on conflicting claims" (pp. 111–12). In other words, no universal maxims are possible, and what is right depends on the circumstances. Yet Robinson recoils from this conclusion, for it leads to "every kind of ethical relativism" and to "a morass of . . . subjectivism" (p. 113).

What the New Testament teaches on matters of social importance is likely to depend on which of its books one consults. Matthew, adapting the Marcan passage to which I have just referred, allows the wife's "fornication" as a ground for divorce. Either Jesus made this qualification—in which case he was very inadequately reported on this socially important matter by Mark—or else it represents the view of an early Christian community which did not regard marriage as indissoluble and was prepared to authenticate its standpoint by ascribing it to Jesus.

The New Testament speaks of Jesus's sacrifice on the cross as delivering believers—only believers (John 3:36)—from God's wrath (Romans 5:8–9; 1 Thessalonians 1:10). 1 John 4:10–11 states that, because God loved us sufficiently to send his son as the remedy for the defilement of our sins, it follows that we in turn are bound to love one another. The modern reader is likely to find this reasoning bewildering, however admirable the sentiment, and to think that, although it is desirable that we should love, or at least be just, friendly and helpful to each other, God's sacrifice of his only son hardly contributes to this end; and that millions who have never heard of this extraordinary action have believed in loving one another and have done their best to live up to this belief.

With such musings Robinson would sympathize, for he declares that "the whole schema of a supernatural Being coming down from heaven to 'save' mankind from sin, in

the way that a man might put his finger into a glass of water
to rescue a struggling insect, is frankly incredible to man
'come of age.'" He nevertheless believes that there are
"genuine and deep-seated realities in the existential situation" which are "expressed" or "projected" by such a
schema (p. 78). His view that God is the ground of our
being, that this is love, and that Jesus, as the man of love, is
utterly united with it (p. 80), enables him to say that Jesus
reconciles God and man, but not as "two parties . . . who
have to be brought together" through "an objective trans-
action supposed to have been accomplished outside us in
time and space" (p. 78).

Robinson calls this latter idea a "myth" and allows that
the New Testament contains a good deal of such myth
which he nevertheless regards as "an important form of
religious truth" (pp. 32–33). He refers (p. 24) with approval to Bultmann's view that the gospel myths are a kind of
"language" in which the evangelists tried to express "the
real depth, dimension, and significance of the historical
event of Jesus Christ" (p. 34). But this theory leaves us
asking: what *was* the historical event, and who were the
men who were thus able to judge of its depth, dimension
and significance? We know nothing about the gospels'
authors and so cannot possibly know whether they were
able to estimate correctly the depth etc. of the supposedly
historical event, and if they were so capable, how they
would set about 'expressing' it in the 'language' of myth.
Those who interpret this mythological language can give
completely free rein to their imagination, as when Robinson repeatedly introduces his formula 'the ground of all
our being' for the purpose of saying, for instance, that
heaven means "the union-in-love" with this ground, "such
as we see in Jesus Christ," while hell means attempts to
escape from it—futile attempts as it is in fact inescapable
(p. 80). He regrets that there has been a tendency to drop
hell altogether from Christian teaching, instead of thus
finding an "effective translation" for "the Devil and his
angels, the pit and the lake of fire" (p. 16).

Another example of ingenious re-interpretation is what he makes of the story of Jesus's virgin birth. This "symbol", he says, "can only legitimately mean . . . that the whole of his life is a life 'born not of the will of the flesh, nor of the will of man, but of God'" (p. 77). He concedes that this quotation from John 1:13 refers to "Christians", and that it is they who are there said to have been "born not of the will of the flesh", and so forth. To see any suggestion of virgin birth here (in a gospel which in any case makes no mention of Jesus's virgin birth) would mean ascribing such a birth to all believers. The people for whom the gospel stories were written, indeed all the church congregations throughout the Christian era, never understood the virgin birth story as meaning that they were born of God and not of the flesh; so, if that was the meaning which the story was designed to convey, then the writer failed completely and calamitously.

C. VERBIAGE

In mathematical textbooks I find chapters of which I can understand almost nothing. I do not suppose them to be meaningless, for I know that books of a more elementary kind were just as unintelligible to me when I first tackled them, although I now find them clear. On the other hand there are books whose obscurity is of another kind, books which appear more obviously meaningless the better I become acquainted with them and with the subjects with which they deal. No one would deny that these two kinds of obscurity are to be found—the one due to the ignorance of the student and the other intrinsic. Apologists exploit the fact that, without complete and exhaustive analysis, the two kinds are often not easily distinguished.

Honest to God is essentially a restatement of views that can be found in Tillich, Bonhoeffer, and Bultmann, and the kind of revelation which needs their interpretation will be revelation only to those who have sufficient faith in them as interpreters. Furthermore, Robinson admitted that their views were not altogether clear, even to him: "I am struggling to think other people's thoughts after them. I cannot claim to have understood all that I am trying to transmit" (p. 21). There can therefore be little chance of his key abstractions being valuable ideas, and his phrase "the ground of all our being" is a signal example of a misapplication and distortion of a real idea which we adopt in our practical reasonings. When we have ascertained the properties of an object, we expect them to remain constant at least for a time, for otherwise no experience or experiment would teach us anything. Since many things do in fact change very rapidly, we cannot take this principle too far. But in order to preserve it, in order to be able to rely on our general laws, we try to analyze the less constant things into more durable constituents, and in this way we come to speak of what a thing is, of its being. Such a distinction between more and less durable elements is a matter of our convenience, and there is nothing absolute about it. In the case of man, it is arbitrary to suppose that he has a basic nature of love and kindness, and that his less pleasing tendencies are ephemeral or in some other sense less fundamental. But this is what Robinson implies when he writes of "our relationship to the ground of our being". Such a view seems to have arisen as a convenient fiction invoked for those of our actions of which we are ashamed. If I do you a kindness, I will claim that this represents my true self. But if I lose my temper and assault you, I readily suppose that my baser instincts manipulated this true self. Nineham makes this point in his criticism of Robinson. He queries the plausibility of "talking of reality—the only reality we experience—as being at its deepest level personal, concerned and gracious", and asks: "what is the relation between reality 'at its deepest level' and reality at the more superficial levels, where it often seems anything but caring and gracious?" (1988, p. 155).

Robinson even writes of "the structure of our relationship to the ground of our being", saying that "built into" this structure is "an indestructible element of personal freedom" which "gives us (within the relationship of dependence) the independence . . . to be ourselves" (pp.

130–31). When the term "structure" is used meaningfully, it implies a recognizable set of elements or units, and some principle according to which they are grouped or combined. Thus one may explain the different properties of diamond and graphite structurally, saying that both consist of the same units (carbon atoms), but grouped in entirely different ways. "Structure" cannot mean any sort of relationship between parts, otherwise one might speak of structure in the burblings of lunatics or in the contents of a dustbin. It is therefore important to specify both the units and their relationship, or else the mere statement that something has a structure conveys no information except a belief that there must be something for which this word stands, if only we knew what it is. The scientist is always being pulled up by the necessity of making his theories accord with brute facts. But the person who theorizes as Robinson does has no such obvious check, and can get away with what is meaningless, provided it sounds impressive.

A telling feature of Robinson's style is the way he will use three common prepositions instead of one to express a relationship: something is encountered "in, with and under" something else (pp. 53, 60, 114). In intelligible contexts the meaning of such prepositions is suggested by the words they serve to link; but if these latter are words like "the transcendent", "the unconditional", and hence themselves not sufficiently clear, then the prepositions can convey nothing. J.S. Mill (1872, p. 454) had occasion to note that "a large portion of all that perplexes and confuses metaphysical thought comes from a vague use of those small words". We meet the same three prepositions again when Robinson says that the Holy Communion should be "the place at which the common and the communal point through to the beyond in their midst, to the transcendent in, with and under them" (p. 86). In this type of writing, one thing is said to "point to" another when an author wishes to posit some connection between them but has no intelligible relationship in mind. And phrases like "the beyond in their midst" no doubt suggested to Robinson what he called a "dialectical relationship" (p. 85n) rather than mere playing with words. This kind of thinking involves few restraints on inference, analogy, generalization or any of the logical processes which are so difficult to perform reliably with true abstractions, and so facilitates the attainment of any desired conclusions.

One cannot understand Robinson's ideas without allowing for the strong emotional drive which informed his thinking. He repeatedly relies on association between words of strong emotional colouring, putting side by side words which normally do not at all suggest the same things, in such a way as to imply that they do. He writes of something's "depth and ultimate significance" (p. 60), of its "ultimate depth and ground and meaning" (p. 114), even of its "creative ground and meaning" (p. 47). All these adjectives and nouns sound important, and the suggestion is that the manifold associations of each one of them somehow belong together and contribute to an overall sense. Similarly, he calls experience of God an awareness of "the transcendent, the numinous, the unconditional" (p. 52), again juxtaposing important-sounding terms for the same purpose. One notices too his fondness for such words as 'finally', 'ultimately', 'deep down', 'in the last analysis'. Analysis involves breaking up a complex whole into simpler parts or aspects in order to find familiar elements in what is at first unfamiliar—not just splitting it up into fragments (one cannot analyze a clock or piano with a sledge-hammer), but looking in it for those elements one has met elsewhere. Were one to say that the human body is, in the last analysis, made up of carbon, oxygen, nitrogen, and so forth, one would mean that these are what is left if we carry the analysis far enough. But there is no intelligible analysis in such statements as: "to be convinced of the personality of . . . God" means "in the last analysis knowing that 'home' is Christ" (p. 130) or (here I paraphrase Robinson) "reality in the last analysis is personal" (pp. 29, 38). My readers may think that such short extracts do not do him justice, and that the context of such passages provides an essential clue to their meaning. But in nearly every case where I have quoted, an extension of the passage only introduces new obscurities.

D. THE SEQUEL

Robinson's style of argument was not new. I have mentioned predecessors to whom he was avowedly beholden; and a generation earlier Collingwood (1924, pp. 146–47) had argued that Jesus's birth, miracles and Resurrection are merely "imaginative symbols", and that "no more pitiable manifestation of thought exists" than atheism or rationalism, which takes them literally. Atheists and rationalists are thus a set of duffers chronically engaged in the flogging of dead horses. Today Bishop Jenkins of Durham and Don Cupitt of Cambridge continue the tradition of reinterpreting gospel stories into what are called profound truths. Bishop Jenkins's views are set out with commendable brevity in his article "Re-Searching the Question of God" (pp. 82–95 of *In Search of Christianity,* edited by Tony Moss and printed for London Weekend Television by Firethorn Press, 1986). He there declares that the Bible contains "symbols and stories" not to be taken in "some unchanged and always received sense", but to be used in "an ever-expanding exploration in response to and in search of the dynamic mystery of God". He calls God 1. "the ultimate reality", 2. "the creative possibilities within all present realities", i.e. possibilities of improving present situations, and 3. "the promise of a final reconciliation between facts (what is) and value (what is worthwhile)", in other words, the assurance that such improvements can be achieved. It is hard to see how inferences can be drawn from the premisses that God is a reality, a possibility and an assurance—"a presence who is also an absence and a promise". Nevertheless Jenkins continues: "Ultimate reality, therefore, is to be thought of and worshipped as love, glory, holiness, justice, and truth". Jenkins's religious ideas are an amalgam of such abstractions with Biblical "slogans" ('Jesus is Lord' is one of his examples) and concern for social justice, evidenced in what he calls Jesus's "passion for people" which he says he himself shares. He regrets that we cannot yet reconcile science and religion ("our problem . . . is that the reality of the worshipful God . . . and the realities of the autonomous processes of matter and energy do not come together"), nor the "reality" of God with the reality of undeserved suffering. Yet Jesus "somehow (sic) puts us on to the knowledge and experience that God is precisely involved in overcoming the contradictions and obstacles and in bringing the realities together".

The editor of the volume in which this paper appears records that many people have written to Jenkins "to thank him for trying to grapple with beliefs which they found hard to accept today". It seems, then, that there are many who will accept pretentiously worded sentences as replacements of plain statements they find unbelievable. But as those now profundities are far from clear, one result of this kind of argumentation is complete confusion in the minds of its many followers who, holding on to a belief that there is a force in the universe that is on the side of the virtuous and will somehow in the end justify and reward them for their trust, find this framework much too vague to preserve them from muddle when they state their position more specifically. As Andrew Brown has observed (in *The Independent,* 27 December 1988), "what appears to have happened is that religious language has lost all agreed meaning, so that people are able to assent to all sorts of contradictory propositions without noticing anything odd".

Even if a particular individual is not thus muddled, uniformity of belief between different individuals has declined. One of the 17 contributors to the volume (edited by Eric James in 1988) celebrating the publication jubilee of *Honest to God* notes that "many a vicar might be surprised to know how many of his congregation are agnostic about some of the doctrines he expounds, and quietly do their own personal 'demythologising' as they go along" (Baker 1988, p. 4). Another apologist, the present Bishop of Salisbury, has put this point with bluntness unexpected from such a quarter:

> If the majority of clergy knew what their people actually believed, they could never preach as they do . . . The average English church-goer believes just as much as he or she can swallow as not improbable, namely that there is Someone or Something behind it all, that Jesus was a good man, and that the betting on survival after death is evens. These are not the vestiges of Christianity lingering in the dwellers on the housing estate, who have never been near a church since they were sent once or twice to Sunday School. This is, at bottom, what a large proportion of regular worshippers would sincerely uphold if pressed. (Baker 1970, p. 335).

Christians, then, have become aware that what Dennis Nineham calls "knock-down answers" are no longer available to a whole range of religious matters; and, as he says, from their own personal views on them, "unanimity is not to be expected". They will conform only in so far as they find it convenient and are not thereby expected to modify their way of life. Nineham notes in this connection that "the refusal of large numbers of Roman Catholics in the West to accept the papal line where sexual mores are concerned and to feel no guilt for their refusal surely foreshadows the shape of things to come" (1988, pp. 159–160, 225n).

Since the year of publication of *Honest to God,* apologists have repeatedly consoled themselves with the thought that the situation of the modern Christian, of not quite knowing what he may rightly believe, is nothing new. For hundreds of years during the rise of the Church, says Bezzant, "the decisions of bishops in council and other-wise were bewildering in their contradictions and there was an insufferable strife of tongues which must have made it impossible for the ordinary man to know whether or not he was an 'orthodox' Christian" (1963, p. 110). Such Church councils have been called about as reliable as annual general meetings of amateur dramatic societies.[6] Neverthe-less, Bezzant added, "Christianity survived; and it will survive present difficulties, objections and uncertainties".

It will indeed, so long as it is backed by powerfully entrenched organizations supplied with ample financial means.

Apologists who are not open to re-interpretive tendencies have responded to modern scepticism about the older doctrines by emphatically reaffirming them and strengthening their consciousness of themselves as a people apart. E.L. Mascall, for instance, while acknowledging the warmheartedness of Robinson's desire to claim all good men as his brothers, protested that "it is quite illegitimate to redefine Christianity in order to include within it all men of good will". He also protested that Robinson's "translations" of older doctrines—we met above what he called an "effective translation for the Devil and his angels"—are no translations but substitutions which enable him "to run with the theistic hare and hunt with the atheist hounds" (1965, pp. 110, 180). One contributor to the jubilee volume says that radical revision of traditional Christian doctrines was briefly popular in the 1960s because it was then seen as a means of halting decline in Church membership; but that, now that this decline has continued, such radicalism has come to be regarded as one of its main causes (p. 135).

What was new in Robinson's book was its success in communicating the kind of discourse it contained to an exceptionally large audience. In the decade following its publication, more than a million copies were sold in 17 different languages (Beeson 1973, p. 168). As a result it created what Bowden calls "a mood of expectancy", the feeling that "at last something was going to happen, there was going to be a breakthrough, the old moulds were cracking, a new age would shortly be dawning . . . Here was no abstract, academic debate, but something which amounted to an intellectual crusade". But in the upshot "nothing tangible emerged" and the churches soon seemed to be reverting to "a new conservatism as though nothing had happened" (1977, pp. 11, 17).

Robinson himself was, in other contexts, much less

radical than one would have expected from *Honest to God.*
David Edwards, who was editor of SCM Press when it was
published, says that "in the final analysis" (sic), Robinson
"believed in God the Father and Creator", not in God as
"a nice word to describe what is best in us"; and that he
regarded Jesus as "God's initiative in our salvation", not as
"only 'the Man for Others'" (1988, p. 94). While such
fluctuation is consistent with Robinson's avowal that *Honest to God* offers but one 'image' of God, not the only
possible one, his position remains unsatisfactory in that he
does there stress that traditional Christian beliefs are
outdated, even unintelligent—a "way of thinking" which
"can be the greatest obstacle to an intelligent faith" (1963,
p. 43). Lay radicals who met him were disappointed, John
Bowden tells us, to find that "in temperament he really was
an Anglican bishop and was in no way prepared to abandon his biblical theology" (1988, p. 45). Even in the
Observer article introducing *Honest to God,* he proposed to
retain what he called his "faith" and his "commitment",
and these, for a bishop, are surely comprehensive.

The emotional drive behind his thinking is perhaps
easier to detect in his writings on historical questions than
apropos of the more abstract matters which form the topic
of *Honest to God.* In historical investigations, facts have to
be established by inferences from records, reports and
traditions, and if, as so often, the inferences lack full
certainty, we are left free to lean to that version which
pleases us best. David Edwards notes in this connection
that Robinson "loved the New Testament so much that he
wanted to argue that it was all written before AD 70 and
that the Gospels (including the fourth) were much more
trustworthy historically than most of his fellow-scholars
were (or are) prepared to grant. He loved Jesus so much
that he took seriously the claim that the Lord's shroud, left
behind in the empty tomb, is preserved in Turin" (1988, p.
94).

A striking feature of this jubilee volume from which I
have been quoting is that so few of its articles say anything

at all about the central theses of the book whose publication it is celebrating—perhaps because, as Bowden says, in
his contribution to it (1988, p. 46), the Church has
"completely forgotten" two of the three theologians
(Bultmann and Tillich) to whom Robinson was so much
beholden, and now regards the third (Bonhoeffer) as "primarily a devotional writer". The way other concerns have
come to the fore is almost comically illustrated when two
other contributors observe that Robinson's book is no
feminist document. "There is but one woman mentioned
in it" (p. 70), and its cover illustration is a seated *youth,* a
"symbol" that would hardly be used now "if one were
seriously thinking about honesty and the divine" (p. 133).

Nineham's paper is an exception to the general silence
about Robinson's arguments (cf. above, p. 206). The other
exception is the article by Alistair Kee. He thinks that, if
one believes that there is "more to life than colour-
supplement consumerism or tabloid voyeurism", then one
accepts that there is a "mystery which lies at the heart of
reality" and which requires to be solved not in terms of
biblical mythology (God as a supernatural being dwelling
in a realm above the earth) nor in those of obsolete
metaphysics (God as a "timeless and immutable" entity),
but in a manner acceptable to "the thought forms of our
time". Theologians, he says, have been unable to provide
any such solution because they have failed to break away
from the old mythological and metaphysical models (pp.
109–111), and so have not followed up the lead Robinson
gave them. I find myself better able to understand their
predicament and so even to sympathize with them than is
apparently possible for Kee. On the one hand there is
considerable malaise with the traditional doctrines which
have been taught for hundreds of years and for disbelief in
which many persons have been killed; but on the other
hand Christianity is based on a Bible in which these
doctrines are explicitly endorsed. To escape from this
impasse while retaining "Christianity" is apt to lead to
mere playing with words. Gordon Kaufman, a Professor of

Divinity at Harvard, illustrates what I have in mind when
he says:

> God . . . should not be understood any longer as one individual
> over and against all others but rather as the unifying symbol of
> those powers and dimensions of the ecological and historical
> feedback network which create and sustain and work to further
> enhance all life. Within this picture of human life and the world the
> meaning of the symbol "Christ" will have to be conceived rather
> differently than in traditional christologies.[7]

It will indeed.

In sum, what has to be set aside as myth really cannot
be brought back as some kind of profundity in disguise. All
the disagreeable teachings cannot be regarded as spoken in
some kind of irony. And what can no longer be accepted if
it means what it says cannot plausibly be regarded as
symbolizing something else.

v.   CONCLUSION

> I believe: help thou mine unbelief (Mark 9:24).

> Certum est quia impossibile est (It is certain because it is
> impossible) (Tertullian, c. AD 200, *De Carne Christi*).

> *Alice:* "One can't believe impossible things".
> *Queen:* "I daresay you haven't had much practice . . . When I was
> your age I always did it for half an hour a day" (Lewis Carroll,
> *Through the Looking-Glass,* Chapter 5).

A distinction needs to be made between belief and profes-
sion of belief. There is no great difficulty in professing
belief in incompatibles or in what is meaningless. In
George Orwell's nightmare world of *Nineteen Eighty-Four,*
twice two ordinarily equals four, but it can equal five if the
dogma of the Party demands this. Similarly, the Athanasian Creed insists (cf. above, p. x), on pain of hell-fire, on
belief, in a certain instance, in the identity of the numbers
one and three. Faced with dire threats they regard as
real—excommunication, torture, or worse—most sensible
people will give their assent to any sort of nonsense,
without changing their actual beliefs. But if their mental

processes are sufficiently confused, they may take verbal formulas for ideas, and then they can sincerely profess belief in what is meaningless, such as the proposition "God is ultimate reality". If this elicits the retort, "No, he isn't", its emptiness is revealed; for the idea of debating whether God is, or is not, ultimate reality, is manifestly ludicrous. But people today are so accustomed to pretentious nonsense that they see nothing amiss in reading without understanding, and many of them at length discover that they can without difficulty write in like manner themselves and win applause for it. And so it perpetuates itself.

PART FOUR

RELIGION AND POETRY

7

THE ORIGIN AND DEVELOPMENT OF POETRY AND DANCE

i. POETRY

Santayana was continuing a well-established tradition in arguing that there is an affinity between poetry and religion. Many have proposed what I call metaphysical theories of poetry, which contrast poetic with scientific truth and imply the belief that through poetry man has in some way access to a reality which is beyond the reach of any kind of purely intellectual inquiry. There are, however, also psychological theories of poetry, constructed on the assumption that poetical activity is a form of human behaviour which, if it is to be understood at all, must be explained in terms of the normal capacities with which psychology in general is concerned. Finally, there are pseudo-psychological theories, which purport to do the same, but employ for the purpose psychological conceptions of a vague and fanciful nature. The advantage of this latter method is that the psychological principles can be constructed to fit the theory, instead of *vice versa,* and the theory can be made to accord with what is felt to be the proper dignity of the poet and of his interpreter, the critic. Thus we find that theories of poetry which are propounded by poets or literary experts are usually either metaphysical or pseudo-psychological. The more sober psychological theories are put forward by anthropologists who are more interested in the origins of human culture than in the prestige of the poet.

I can illustrate this distinction from what the poet Wordsworth and the anthropologist Wundt have to say on the subject. Wundt will occupy us later. Wordsworth is generally sober and moderate and so one might expect him to be coherent. He argues for a strong affinity between poetry and religion:

> The concerns of religion refer to indefinite objects, and are too weighty for the mind to support them without relieving itself by resting a great part of the burden upon words and symbols. The commerce between Man and his Maker cannot be carried on but by a process where much is represented in little, and the Infinite Being accommodates himself to a finite capacity. In all this may be perceived the affinity between Religion and Poetry.[1]

Because, then, poetry and religion are concerned with things beyond the normal capacity of men to understand, both make use of "words and symbols". How these can help unless we understand what they mean he does not explain. He then compares religion and poetry and alleges the following characters:

RELIGION

1. makes up the deficiencies of reason by faith.
2. Its element is infinitude.
3. Its ultimate trust is the supreme of things.
4. It submits itself to circumscription.
5. It is reconciled to substitutions.

POETRY

1. is passionate for the instruction of reason (Presumably this means that poetry desires to do the instructing, not to be instructed by reason).
2. is ethereal and transcendent, but
3. is incapable of sustaining its existence without sensuous incarnation.

The first item under Religion is perhaps parallel to the first under Poetry: as religion supplies reason's deficiencies, so poetry supplies it with instruction. Religion tells us the things that reason fails to reveal, and poetry teaches reason to do better. The next features are infinitude on the one side and transcendence on the other; and last, both have to submit to some kind of limitations in order to be understood by finite men.

Now let us assume that all this is intelligible, and that we understand how something whose element is infinitude can be reconciled to substitutions, and how that which is ethereal may be incapable of sustaining its existence without sensuous incarnation, it still remains a problem why the possession of such propensities should involve incitements to kindred error: for this is what Wordsworth's next sentence maintains:

> In this community of nature may be perceived also the lurking incitements of kindred error—so that we shall find that no poetry has been more subject to distortion than that species, the argument and scope of which is religious, and no lovers of the art have gone farther astray than the pious and the devout.

Poetry and religion, then, are subject to the same errors, and—according to the final three clauses of the above quotation—where poetry and religion are combined the error is likely to be doubled. The argument seems to rest on some such reasoning process as the following: if two substances have similar properties, then a mixture of them will have the properties in a higher degree. Hence if both substances have the same defects or weaknesses, we may expect their combination to be inferior to either. If two men have the same characters and the same weaknesses, if they act in concert their actions will be worse than if either of them acted alone.

If it should be said that the combination of poetry and religion is not the same as a mixture of substances or the joint action of two persons, then we must ask for some more information concerning the effects of combining poetry and religion, and must not be supposed to know without further instruction. It is by such unmeaning analogies that this kind of reasoning is conducted. The analogy here is not frankly stated, as it would obviously be invalid. But if the analogy I have suggested is not implied, then the argument remains unintelligible. The writer's purpose is, however, clear. He does not think much of a good deal of religious poetry, but he cannot blame religion for this, and he does not wish to say that poetry is not adapted for religious expression. On the contrary, since he is a religious man and a poet, he wishes to believe in some essential affinity between the two, and yet also to account for the prevalence of poor poetry on religious topics or when inspired by religion.

Wordsworth, Coleridge, and Shelley agree that poetry is a very fine thing and that the poet is perhaps the most important member of society. But their ideas on the subject are nebulous and disguised for the unwary reader in picturesque language, as when Wordsworth says: "Poetry is the breath and finer spirit of all knowledge".[2] The explanations offered by these writers are made to rest on principles which are considerably less intelligible than that which has to be explained. It is easy to understand why they should wish to be regarded as something more than entertainers, who are not looked on as meriting particular respect. The poet was once revered as a seer, but when this claim, baldly stated, became absurd, his greatness remained, though undefined, and there was a fair-sized public to acclaim him and so keep the illusion alive. The superiority felt by both poet and audience over commonplace, uncultured persons counted for much, and still does. Bowra says:

> The Latin *vates* was both a prophet and a poet, the Romantic poets were equally prophets. To this conception of poetry Mallarmé implicitly gave his support. (1943, p. 28)

I have shown elsewhere that the poet Paul Valéry, who died in 1945, was anxious to follow in this same tradition, and that his present-day commentators treat his claims with respect (Wells 1985).

Poetry is but one of the arts, and philosophers have frequently discussed them all together. Kant called aesthetic pleasure "pleasure without interest".[3] If I look at a mountain or a painting of it and think it a good place in which to put up a funicular railway, I am thinking of some interest which the landscape can be made to serve. If, however, I have no practical aim, but appreciate the scene in and for itself, this is pleasure without interest. In general, nature has given animals desire for and pleasure in those acts or experiences which it is good for them or their race to indulge in, and fear of and distaste for acts and experiences which are harmful or dangerous. If there exists a form of pleasure which has nothing to do with biological advantage, where does it come from? It is futile to reply by inventing principles without regard to ordinary human experience, and to speak in the manner of Santayana of "the ultimate possibilities of the soul" (cf. above, p. 189). If we turn from the psychological processes of the audience to those of the artist, it is hard to believe that he never aimed at anything more than supplying his audience with disinterested pleasure. Something as prominent and as ubiquitous in human civilization as art must at some time have been more purposeful than that, however much purposelessness may be predicated of art as we know it today. Furthermore, although there is some ground for distinguishing utilitarian activities from those practised for fun, the distinction is not limited to certain forms of activity. Nearly all activities which are within the range of an animal's capabilities may be performed for their own sake, as play.

It has been plausibly argued that architecture, painting and poetry (lyric, epic, and dramatic) all originated in forms of activity having a definite practical purpose. Indeed, in the case of architecture this is obvious: buildings provide shelter from cold or from hostile beasts. Thomas Reid maintained, in the eighteenth century, that much of what we now call art is a specialized adaptation of what originated as a means of communication. Before either writing or even much in the way of vocal sounds were available for that purpose, pantomime, drawing, modelling would have to be used to convey ideas from one person to another, and when, later, vocal sounds replaced them, they became free to develop independently of communication and of each other. Models and drawings are then made for their own sake; miming dances and dramatic performances become a form of recreation or entertainment. I have gone into this fully elsewhere and have there noted that Reid is positing a process which Englefield has called cultural differentiation: the primitive ancestor is communication; acting, painting, and so forth are among its specialized descendants.[4]

In seeking the origin of poetry we must expect to find that the sophisticated product of modern literary activity has no single simple source. The various elements which enter into it are likely to have distinct historical and psychological beginnings. Furthermore, there is no constant character by which we can, at all times and in all countries, identify poetry and distinguish it from other forms of composition. We can, however, say that it has traditionally included the following features:

1.   A special *form* which depends on the distribution of sounds, quantities, stresses: metre, rhyme, assonance, alliteration and verse structure.

2.   A special *language* distinguishable, though not wholly different, from the language of common affairs.

3.   A special *subject matter,* or at least a restricted range of subjects regarded as appropriate for poetical treatment.

4.   An appropriate *manner of recitation,* differing in various ways from the normal inflections of common linguistic intercourse.

These may be called the objective characters of poetry, but what is usually regarded as its essential character is its emotional effect. This can hardly be distinct in kind from the emotions evoked by the common accidents of life, as there is only a limited number of fundamental emotions

available, and any particular state cannot be due to anything more complicated than a certain combination of
these.

Many have attributed poetry to some kind of artistic
instinct in man. Gummere and others have claimed that
poetry is rhythmical because rhythmical behaviour is instinctive.[5] But really it is only certain rhythmical actions,
such as breathing, which may be so termed. There are
many forms of activity which do not adjust themselves to a
regular rhythm, such as putting one's clothes on or cooking
the dinner. And many rhythmical actions are only secon-
darily so: rhythm has been imposed upon them as a result
of practice. If an operation (such as chopping or sawing)
requires the repetition many scores of times of one small
movement, it is easy to see that there must be some ideal
speed for each individual which combines the maximum
achievement with minimum fatigue, and that after much
practice the skilful workman will discover this. There are,
of course, other kinds of work which cannot be carried out
in this way, where every stroke of the tool must be directed
somewhat differently, or where many different movements
must alternate in an irregular manner. The more delicate
the operation is, the more likely is this to be the case. But
we cannot speak of instinct in any of these operations with
tools. All must have been acquired as habits. They certainly cannot be compared with the scratch reflex of the dog or
the swallowing reflex. If we are to explain artistic activity
in a biologically acceptable way, we must not invent
instincts to account for what is mysterious.

The features I have specified as the *form* of poetry are
most easily accounted for by supposing that they were
adopted for mnemonic reasons. So long as oral language
was not written, any longer compositions, if they were to be
preserved at all, must be committed to memory. It cannot
be supposed that rhyme, metre, and alliteration were
deliberately invented as an aid to memory. Like other
useful inventions, they must have arisen at first by acci-
dent, and not by design. Phrases and longer word se-

quences which happened to possess a rhythm or were linked with some kind of sound harmony would stay in the memory more readily. Other passages would be more liable to alteration in being repeated, and to avoid this might also be given a rhythmical character. Those who deliberately undertook to commit long speeches to memory might discover the value of such characters and gradually modify the traditional matter accordingly. Finally, as these forms had come to be associated with certain types of composition, they survived when the invention of phonetic writing had made it possible to preserve any speech forms.

To the literary theorist it is naturally disagreeable to suppose that elements of the poetic art which to him appear mysterious beyond all possibility of rational explanation are but a relic of an old device for memorizing verbal formulas. Nevertheless, it is certainly the case that the extant poetry of different peoples achieves, by quite different and independent means—it may be metre, assonance, alliteration, rhyme, or parallel clauses as in Hebrew poetry—the same end, namely the dividing of discourse into clear units that can easily be remembered.[6]

It is in connection with religious compositions that a *special language* would be developed. The language of poetry is generally archaic, and this is a natural result of the long preservation of sacred liturgies during many generations while the common language continued to change. Maintenance of the metrical form would have made it almost impossible to replace these archaisms with modern words, and where the text was sacred, only minor alterations could be permitted.

This archaism in language is but a particular case of the working of the principle of the special sanctity of the archaic. Whenever some magical performance, some spell, or religious rite is believed to be efficacious, it tends to be preserved very faithfully in every detail; for as the reason for its supposed efficacy cannot possibly be known, it is impossible to be sure that the omission of the smallest feature will not be destructive of the whole effect.[7] This applies particularly to communal practices. These must be administered according to immemorial custom, for who knows why the details were laid down and what would result if they were neglected? When belief in the efficacy of any practice depends on tradition alone and not on any genuine experimentation it is obviously only reasonable to keep to the letter of the rubric, to follow the recorded instructions as closely as possible. In everyday domestic affairs, one individual may experiment and innovate; no harm comes of it, and others follow his example. But in communal affairs experiments are not permitted, for all would suffer together if anything went wrong. Thus the precise form is carefully preserved, generation after generation, until the language is no longer current. Finally, because the sacred formulas are expressed in archaic language, it comes to be felt that this language is especially appropriate for them, so that new compositions may be deliberately archaic. The long association of archaisms with solemn matters had made them seem in themselves impressive.

Only a certain degree of archaism can be tolerated. Spenser used many old-fashioned words, but did not write in the language of Chaucer. In time the conventional language of the poet becomes artificial, hence unsuited for the expression of either ideas or emotions, and has to be to some extent modernized. Some poets then go to extremes and make as much use as possible of low and cant terms.

The language of poetry is often characterized also by unusual word order. The poet naturally contrived to make the metrical stresses fall on words or syllables which are naturally stressed. To achieve this, he would often find it necessary to introduce an unnatural word order: and in time this peculiarity came to be associated with poetry, and was then deliberately done where it was unnecessary because it was felt to be part of the poetic style.

Another feature of poetic language is its extended use of metaphor and simile. Such figurative language is merely description by reference to familiar things. It does not help the memory, but it can be understood as deriving from a feature of relatively primitive language. There must have been an early stage when the stock of words, particularly of words with a precise meaning, was limited, so that description would depend on comparison; for to describe a new thing or new idea in words, one could only compare it to something for which a word was already available. Of course, common needs in the face of a shared situation will have led to the invention of relevant vocabulary at a very early stage. But the poet is (and was) generally concerned to express things not commonly said: his audiences do not possess the thing and wish only to know its name. They do not know his meaning and there is no word available, and so he has to resort to suggestive analogies to things they do know. Comparison was, then, in the first place resorted to simply for the purpose of making oneself understood. But as the number of words increased, and also the number of ideas in the minds of most people, it became possible to communicate without it. As, however, the poetry of later times was modelled on early poems which necessarily embodied primitive features of language, the use of similes and metaphors was continued, because it was felt to be part of the poetic effect. Objects of comparison were then chosen not because they helped to make anything clearer, but because they were supposed to be picturesque or otherwise interesting.

As to the *subject matter* of poetry, what was memorized so as to be passed on to the next generation was matters of importance—magical formulas, or oracular utterances, religious liturgies, royal proclamations, tribal customs, and important occurrences of interest to the tribe. Religion is particularly important here, and in early times it was not something removed from communal life as it has often become. It was associated with special ceremonial occasions, when the community was gathered together for some common concern—harvest, initiation, marriage, funeral —and certain emotions were shared by all and intensified by the sharing. But all the common concerns of the community were embraced by it and periodically became the subject of special rites, with dancing, pantomime, recitations or song. The subjects of such representations were gods and heroes, memorable deeds, or awe-inspiring experiences. Thus poetry dealt with the important, the memorable, and excluded the trivial.

The ideas of the philosophers, of Xenophanes, Parmenides, and Empedocles did not derive from religious functions. It was not unnatural, however, that they should try to give authority to their ideas by expressing them in the poetical manner. The idea of special inspiration had probably always been associated with verse, the language of the oracles. Since recitation was the only way in which any composition could be widely circulated there were additional advantages in composing in verse. The philosopher is surely the descendant of the prophet, and he certainly gives himself the same airs. The man of science who calmly seeks after truth is perhaps in turn derived from the philosopher, but could develop only in company, as a member of a body of persons who, by their mutual criticism, could expose make-believe and exclude any kind of appeal to inspiration. But the philosopher or prophet who spoke with authority, not condescending to explain the reasons for his pronouncements, needed the assistance of elevated language.

That such features as metre, rhyme, and alliteration originated as aids to memory has repeatedly been asserted: in the eighteenth century by Condillac, Voltaire, and Herder, among others; by R. de la Grasserie in 1892; and by Schumann and Müller in 1894, on the basis of experimental evidence that these features do in fact aid memory.[8] Norden took the same view of their origin in 1898.[9] Recently, Vansina mentions what he calls "formal factors" affecting oral transmission which make what is transmitted resemble poetry.[10]

It has been queried whether extensive compositions could have been preserved verbatim without writing, but a number of recent scholars have replied affirmatively. Ruth

Finnegan mentions forms of sung poetry in South Pacific and other cultures where inspired composition is transmitted through exact memorization, and says that such accurate transmission "is perhaps particularly important in texts that have a definite religious value or function".[11] The Vedic literature of India is a signal example, transmitted in oral form for well over two thousand years. Staal specifies complicated mnemonic devices in it which prevented the loss of a single word (1986, pp. 265–66). Kiparsky notes, apropos of the Rigveda, that "it is not the *technique* (writing versus speech) that determines the fixity of a text, but rather the *function* which that text has in the society" (1976, p. 101). And Foote has shown that a legal function can be just as efficacious as a religious one in ensuring the exact preservation of wording. In an article on early Scandinavian law he notes:

> Scholars have concluded that the briefer, the more vivid and pregnant kind of legal statement, as in the Swedish laws, developed inevitably and inexorably because the laws were made, rehearsed, practised and transmitted in communities where writing was unknown or virtually so. As a recent generalization puts it: "They cite cases and provide decisions as these had been promulgated, memorized and proclaimed generation after generation, in a memorable, chiseled form that often has the lilt of poetry, . . . Some of the qualities of style appear to be directly connected with mnemonic effort. (1977, pp. 49–50)

The "qualities of style" he has in mind include "alliteration, assonance, rhythmic construction with syntactic parallelism" and "concrete and palpable images". He refers to Stähle's view that "forceful alliteration and syntactic effects could obviously make for easy memorization, and presumably came into being because of that".

The author of the article "Narrative Poetry" (in Premiger 1965) has objected that alliteration, assonance, and other qualities which have been regarded as originally mnemonic "are essential to the effectiveness of incantations", and so belong in verse that "had a magical purpose and was in some way connected with ritual". But connection with ritual does not exclude mnemonic origin, since the words recited at the ritual need to be memorized, and exactly memorized if they were magical formulas. He also objects that "the oral transmission of the tale indicates that prose can be handed on with as great ease as poetry". He overlooks the fact that tales—stories such as the *Babes in the Wood,* for instance—can be preserved without keeping the wording in which they are told. The preservative effect of metre and rhyme works on the language and was especially employed where retention of the exact verbal form was regarded as necessary. A tradition may be preserved quite independently of any particular verbal expression, and so may a story. A child can repeat nursery tales after having heard them often, but not necessarily in exactly the same words, since the ideas and events involved are simple enough to be expressed in his own language. But if he had to repeat the substance of one of the Psalms, there is no simple story that can be expressed independently of its words, and he would have to commit them all to memory. The poems of Homer do include such stories, the incidents of which can be rehearsed in prose. But these poems were surely composed deliberately at a time when the convention of metrical form had been established, not for the sake of facilitating memorizing, but because the form was admired and gave pleasure.[12]

Early this century Gummere protested that "the splendours of rhythm", its emotional effects, cannot be accounted for by "mnemonic convenience" (1901, p. 77). But rhythm is not always linked with emotion. Our breathing, walking, and running are rhythmical, yet not associated with any special emotion; and so if rhythmical *speech* excites emotion today, simply because it is rhythmical, we cannot hold that this is a necessary effect of rhythm.

Gummere believes that the rhythmical character of poetry derives partly from the "rhythm of work or play or dance in the life of primitive man" (p. 66). Dancing, for instance, if carried out by a number of people together, tends to become rhythmical, for only so can the movements of one individual be made to harmonize with those of his companions. And the rhythm can best be sustained if the whole company utter cries or sing in time with the rhythm of this dance (cf. below, p. 235). The sounds uttered will at first have been arbitrary, but as oral language began to prevail the meaningless vocal noises were gradually replaced by words which had some significance. Gummere's account (pp. 93–99) shows that in some cases mere strings of words would be used, words which by their meaning had some connection with the occasion, such as the names of animals hunted, or of crops harvested, or places, or activities. At a later stage the words could become connected to form some kind of story, and finally the story remained for its own sake without the dance.

All this means—and here Gummere is quite right—that rhythm in poetry cannot be solely mnemonic in origin. But his appeal to the dance points to the importance of the arousal of emotion by *association*. Dancing is not in itself a useful activity, and we explain its origin in relation to play or emotional discharge. If a certain kind of oral utterance has become associated with the emotional experience of dancing, then it is understandable that it should acquire the emotional colouring of the dance with which it is associated. If the dancing came to have religious associations (whatever may have been its first beginnings), then the religious solemnity could be transferred to any of the features of the accompanying songs, not only to their rhythm.

Association is equally important for explaining the emotional effects of the originally mnemonic features of poetry. Long association of such features with verbal sequences which were uttered only in strongly emotional circumstances ensured that the emotion should, in the end, come to be linked to those features themselves. Once they have become *associated* with the expression of emotion, they acquire the power to *awaken* that emotion, in whatever verbal sequences they occur.

We cannot, then, say that rhyme, alliteration, and so forth have always been linked with some form of emotional release. But if we can explain how they came into relation with emotional language, then we can account for their present effects. The general principle involved here is that, where any form of activity which is not apparently related directly to any fundamental need or instinct has become linked to strong emotions, then we must look in the past for circumstances in which it might have come to be associated with emotional experiences, that is to say, with experiences which *were* linked to a fundamental need or instinct.

There are three obvious factors in poetry which give pleasure: rhythm, imagery, and word-colour. The choice of words serves not only for the creation of rhythm, for with every word there goes a train of associated ideas with attendant emotions. Were the strict connotation of the word alone important, it would make no difference whether we called a man a Roman Catholic or a papist, a German land-owner or a Junker. And words can derive their emotional colouring only from our experience of their use. Some have become so sanctified by their environment that they are entirely withdrawn from vulgar currency, while others are so contaminated by low company that they may not appear in polite circles. The existence of different grades of speech, words with different associations although nearly the same meaning, is a natural consequence of the social use of language. It can hardly be doubted that the use of a conventional poetic language can produce effects. Aristotle was surely not deluded in supposing that these depended in part on the use of a special kind of vocabulary. From all this we can see the force of association.

ii. SONG AND DANCE

Poetry is traditionally classified in western literature into three chief categories: lyric, epic, and dramatic—or song, narrative, and play. It is obvious that these have influenced one another, and what they now have in common may be due to this mutual influence rather than to a common origin. Lyric poetry may be said to have its origin in the song which accompanied the dance; epic or narrative poetry to have come from stories of hunting, fighting, or other important enterprises related to the community, although narrative also arose from religious songs.

The commonest form of religious poetry—the hymn of praise—takes the form of enumerating the god's titles, stating his powers and achievements, giving thanks for favours received and requesting further favours. Examples can be found in the *Book of the Dead,* the Vedic hymns, and the Hebrew psalms. The form comes to be stereotyped because these hymns are repeated on special occasions, and may also have been supposed sometimes to have a magical efficacy in ensuring the granting of the favours requested. In any case, when addressing a potentate, one must avoid any form of words, any use of a wrong title, which could possibly give offence, and therefore it is never safe to improvize. The statement of the god's powers and achievements may develop into biography. His origin and adventures are recited, and the address becomes a narrative. Peabody notes in this connection that although the Vedas are "predominantly religious and consist in large part of hymns, magic formulas, prayers, curses, incantations, and the like", nevertheless, "within the span of recorded tradition, one can see narrative entering Indian hymns as a gloss, developing into episodic passages, and gradually increasing in relative importance" (1975, p. 31).

Wundt's discussion of these matters is still very helpful. He says that the song is distinguished from other forms of poetry by predominance of emotion, whereas in the other forms some kind of action or objective sequence of events is important. He regards it as the simplest form of rhythmical poetry, the only form universal among all peoples at all times, differing from music, which also expresses emotion, merely in its speech content, which at first may be very scanty and is sometimes restricted to interjections, mere vocal music. Bowra (1962, pp. 57–60,

270ff) agrees that emotion is the source of song, and that meaningless sounds characterize it in its earliest stage. It is still common to find meaningless songs accompanying dance movements. Rhythmic noise is much more easily produced than rhythmic speech.

The rhythmic element in the song, the repetition at short and regular intervals of the same sound or stress, may be due either to what Bowra calls "rhythmical action" (p. 29), that is to dance or marching accompaniment, the rhythm of which is imposed on the sounds; or to choral singing. If at a rowdy meeting, for instance, all were to chant the words of some slogan independently, nothing would be intelligible and there will merely be a great noise. But if all are to chant together, a regular rhythm must be established between successive words. This, of course, is not a natural expression of the emotion. A lone individual, calling out the same words in a state of great excitement, would not naturally adopt such a rhythm, but would follow the natural speech pattern, giving stress to some words and not to others. The rhythm, far from being an emotional expression, is a restraint accepted for the sake of intelligibility.

Nevertheless, choral singing is often an outlet for emotion. At ordinary times, when we speak solo, we have to keep our voice at moderate strength, but when we sing in chorus we can let ourselves go. The actual words may be of minor importance, and we may simply go on repeating the same phrase. But if we like to imagine that there is something more in our singing than the mere letting off steam by loud utterance, then we must vary the words and let them have some meaning. Before writing was available, this would have involved the considerable effort of learning a good deal by heart. But a compromise is reached when one or two individuals supply the variations and the rest merely sing a refrain. The refrain not only lets the audience join in, but also keeps their attention on the solo.

This primitive pleasure in mere vocal utterance is exploited in later religious rituals to engage the interest of the congregation: the throng responds with a refrain to the recitative of the priest.

The refrain is a special instance of repetition, and repetitions are not always related to joy in singing. If there was a magical efficacy in the words, the force of the magic could be enhanced by the repetition of particular spells. Hence "the vain repetitions of the heathen" (as the Geneva Bible renders Matthew 6:7), the Buddhist prayer-wheel and the Catholic recital of *Hail Marys* and *Pater nosters*. It is not possible to derive either of these factors from the other. There was on the one hand the sheer pleasure of utterance, and on the other the magical element in the words. Wundt, when he discusses the "cultic song", mentions the mnemonic utility of repetition, saying that the repetition was first intended to strengthen the effect, but became in time a merely formal feature, which nevertheless helped the memory (1923, p. 387).

Another source of rhythm in song is work. Many business activities, such as grinding, spinning, weaving, rowing, or threshing, involve repetition of identical movements, and these naturally become rhythmical: for the interval between two such movements tends to a certain minimum below which exertion is disproportionate to effect and above which there is a loss of efficiency. Wundt notes (p. 391) that an individual workman may accompany his rhythmical movements with a song that is adapted to their rhythm, and that communal work, which is often necessarily rhythmical, positively requires audible accompaniment. Men hauling the same rope must pull together. Each participant in a communal activity could conceivably correct his own movements by watching those of his immediate partners, but it is not possible to watch a great many at the same time, and if each merely watches his neighbour, this will not suffice to keep the whole company together. If, however, everybody accompanies his own movements with some audible sound—stamping, clapping the hands, slapping the body, shouting or singing—then the common rhythm is manifest and the individual can adjust his own movements to make them coincide. The best method is a system of sounds or cries which may be heard without any special effort of attention which would distract the worker from his own movements. A work song originating in this way is, says Wundt, an effective means for the creation and consolidation of communal poetry (p. 392). If each individual improvizes his own song, nothing will remain and no tradition will be established, but when many have to sing together, they must all learn the same words, and there will be a natural tendency for the younger generation to learn from the older.

There is another significant factor about such work songs. Preuss, whom Wundt quotes (p. 394n), spoke of their words as a description of the operation the song accompanied: Successive lines can refer to successive acts. If we are learning an operation which consists in a sequence of different acts which have to be performed in a particular order, it is helpful to learn a verbal sequence which corresponds. Here again, we need not suppose that this, any more than repetition, was invented as mnemonic device from purely theoretical considerations. But experience would show its utility, and the accidental discovery could then be exploited. As we saw (above, p. 48), Wundt is well aware that this is how inventions are characteristically made.

It is not essential that work or other songs should consist of intelligible words, but some songs, says Wundt, are deliberately unintelligible—those for instance, which are supposed to have secret magical effects (p. 385). Even if they were originally perfectly comprehensible, they were believed to be effective only when recited without tampering with the wording. They are then passed on from generation to generation and from tribe to tribe, and become unintelligible because the language of everyday usage changes rapidly among uncivilized peoples, where it is not protected by being fixed in writing (p. 386). Wundt adds that, once people have become used to using unintelligible formulas for magical or religious purposes, and have experienced the emotional effects which such mysterious utterances have, they come to think that religious formulas should be incomprehensible. He points in this connection to the preferred use in Christian Europe of liturgies couched in "a dead language, no longer understood by the faithful". Presumably he has in mind not only the use of Latin in the West, but also the Old Slavonic liturgies of the Eastern Church.

Song and dance go together, with rhythm as the connecting feature. Both may be a sheer expression of emotion, a mere joyful exercise, for instance, or alternatively be believed to have a special magical efficacy. Dancing in its modern form is usually play. It has often been a form of expression, a letting off of steam occurring when there is a store of energy to be released, perhaps from a superabundance of vitality in young people or in consequence of an excess of emotional excitement, either joyful or painful. When David danced before the Lord with all his might, it was presumably an expression of thanksgiving. The psychologist William Sargant has noted, apropos of such 'abreaction' by vigorous dancing, that "it was with wild hysterical dances that Britain greeted the Armistice in 1918", and that "Negro jazz came as a godsend to the war-neurotics of the period"—the waltz and the two-step being quite unsuitable for the release of strong emotion (1957, p. 52).

Forms of activity which do not alter the external situation in any way, but serve for the direct release of emotional tension, are what Wundt calls "movements of expression" (Ausdrucksbewegungen). Mere activity of whatever nature can reduce the nervous excitement by canalizing it into muscular action, and he includes dancing in such movements of expression. But he speaks (pp. 478 ff) not only of emotion finding release in dancing, but also of emotion being increased by it. Both processes undeniably occur. As Peter Brinson has said, "every dancer . . . has experienced . . . catharsis, the release of tension, in personal performance", just as "the experience of dance as stimulator . . . is part of life in any dance company as it is in many kinds of social dance, notably the emulation of disco" (1985, p. 207). Contagion is important here. When any situation arises which excites the emotions of a whole group rather than merely a few individuals, then the united expressions of emotion tend to increase the intensity of emotion in each individual. This is the psychological fact that underlies panic where fear is the emotion. It underlies the orgy where the sexual emotions are involved, and it underlies the choral dance where, for instance, rejoicing or mourning is the emotion.

Contagion is, however, not the only relevant factor, and heightening of tension can occur even in solo dancing. Disturbing emotions, such as fear or sexual desire, can be resolved only if action leads to some situation which removes their cause. But they can be diminished by violent activity such as dancing which swamps the original state of tension by another which is produced by the activity: sexual urges, for instance, can in this way be replaced or swamped by emotions more closely related to the dancing. The latter may be gradually increased, but at the expense of the former. When the dancing comes to an end through fatigue, the emotion which accompanies it quickly subsides.[13]

The apparent contradiction—expression releasing yet increasing the tension—is resolved if we recognize that all forms of pleasure involve a release of tension, and that to obtain the pleasure one must first produce the tension. At first the activity is indulged in for the release it brings, but as this is agreeable in the memory, the exciting conditions which make it necessary are sought, and measures are adopted to increase the tension for the joy of resolving it. Wundt writes of "sweating houses" built in the proximity of dancing places for the express purpose of intensifying ecstasy, and of the use of tea, tobacco, and special drugs. He also realizes that with war dances excitement is increased by "the noise of shields and weapons clashed together", accompanied by loud songs (pp. 478–79). He

summarizes the process of development clearly, saying that
first the mental disturbance, religious or other, gives rise to
the excited movements, which being repeated become
rhythmical; the pleasure of release becomes a secondary
motive, and artificial methods of excitation are resorted to
in order to generate the condition in which this pleasure is
possible (p. 483).

The dance may come to represent something definite. It
may become pantomimic or dramatic, miming important
events. These may actually have happened or they may be
expected to happen. Such anticipatory miming is often
magical in intention. In Wundt's view, the 'mimetic' dance
is normally choral, occasioned by common experiences (p.
487). The private joys and woes of an individual may find
expression in gambolling or breastbeating, but it is only
when many come together that the formalities of the
communal dance can come into existence. The great
occasions for such dances are, he says, seed time, harvest,
hunting, war and the initiation of the young men. How are
the supposed magical effects, such as ensuring good crops,
of such dances to be explained?

Englefield has argued that all magical rites were derived
from practices of a more effective kind (at least in early
times, before magicians had become professionals and had
introduced new methods and doctrines) and that mimetic
dances can be traced to primitive, pre-oral forms of
communication which were only later adapted for magical
purposes.[14] Following a number of eighteenth-century writers (I have mentioned Reid in this connection, above, p.
223f), he believes that man's first efforts at communication
must have involved only the use of signs that are self-
explanatory, not signs (like the words of language as we
know it today) whose meaning depends on convention; for
conventions could have been agreed only on an existing
basis of communication, which must, therefore, have been
possible without them. The obvious signs that are intelligible prior to all convention are gestures, which can be
deliberately employed to mimic actions and can be ex-

panded into more or less elaborate pantomime. If I want a man to jump high or to fetch water, I can convey my wishes by performing the gesture myself. Such gestural and pantomimic communication was, of course, effective only between human beings. The magical extension of it lies in supposing that a gesture that can influence the behaviour of a fellow man may be equally effective on other creatures and even on natural phenomena;[15] and so the savage jumps high in his ritual dances to encourage his crops to grow; he sprinkles water to attract rain, roars to encourage thunder, and whistles for the wind. All such ritual was an attempt to influence the crops and weather—either directly or by appeal to the powers behind the scenes supposedly controlling them—by the same means as were employed to influence fellow human beings. To convey the ideas of 'life' or 'alive' before oral language was available, resort would have to be made to such pantomime as: pretending to drop dead, and then springing up again. Thus gestures which originally served to convey to another person ideas such as 'restoration of fertility' or 'reproduction' developed into elaborate representations of death and resurrection as a means of controlling nature, of ensuring its burgeoning in the spring. When gesture language had been replaced by oral language for everyday communication, gesture survived in communicating with spirits, because the tradition of so communicating with them was by then well established. When also urban life had removed populations from obvious and immediate dependence on the annual growth of crops, the meaning of the old methods was obscured, and myths purporting to explain the dramatic rituals arose: the actors portraying death and resurrection were understood to be commemorating incidents in the lives of gods or heroes.

If it is in fact the case that communication depended initially on gesture and pantomime, then in those early days dramatic representation could have served such purposes as: to announce to the community that a hunting or warlike expedition is to be undertaken; to relate to the old men and the women the circumstances of a hunt or a battle afterwards; to commemorate an important event of any kind. The drama would take the form of a mimic representation of the conditions or events desired or reported. Such performances would become magical only if they were supposed to communicate some message to the unseen powers or to have some virtue in themselves to ensure the conditions desired. Before that, they may well have been employed as a means of informing one another, of confirming the common resolve, or enlivening the individual imagination prior to the carrying out of a joint enterprise. How else, without oral language, could people concert plans and resolve on a common course of action?

In all such cases, emotional expression would naturally combine with the motive of communication. As when a man relates in words the triumph of his party he becomes elated, so we may suppose that, before such oral description was possible, there would be mimic representation with like effect. Such excitement might serve a useful purpose. The war dance would not only constitute the public announcement of what was to happen, but would also enhance the courage and ferocity of the warriors. We find a certain amount of wild antics, resulting from emotional overflow and not brought fully under the control of the regular ritual, in war dances, funeral rituals and festivals of rejoicing.

In all such ritual, customs become established, and then the performance is undertaken—even after the invention of oral language will have made its original purpose unnecessary—because it is the custom and because of the pleasure associated with it. Here, then, we can see the importance of what Wundt called substitution of motives (p. 478): the occasion can develop from a serious operation with an important purpose into a festival, perhaps then emphasizing features which have little connection with the primitive sources of the performance. If the mimetic dance was at first a magical process based on the primitive form of communication, its activities were not always easily to be distinguished from the gambols and frolics of excited young people. On the one hand we have at first a communicative and then magical design which in time becomes obscure, if not entirely forgotten. On the other there is an emotional release combined with an enhancement of the emotional state to begin with. And so it is not difficult to understand how the serious pantomime could degenerate into an entertainment. In some cases—for instance of dramatic representations of death and resurrection—an opposite development could equally well occur. From being regarded as commemorative of incidents in the lives of the gods, they could come to be seen as a means of assuring participants and spectators of their own immortality. In this way we can understand the development of the mystery religions of antiquity. Thus, out of primitive ritual to ensure the fertility of the land by magical means, there could grow on the one hand forms of entertainment and, on the other, forms of religion.

iii. DEVELOPMENTS IN LITERATURE AND IN LITERARY CRITICISM

The arguments I have given concerning the origin and development of certain forms of what is now known as art point to the principle that any form of behaviour which does not serve a useful purpose presumably derives from one that did, or was at least believed to do so. To explain any new form of behaviour, we try to show that it could result from the modification of another form which we know existed. If a form is manifestly adaptive, then we suppose that we understand how it came into existence. Or it is non-adaptive, and then we ask how it may have resulted from a form which used to be adaptive, but, for one reason or another, ceased to be of great importance and so was subjected to modification.

If most of the activities known as art had, like those known as sport, at one time a business function, it is clear that their development took place under the influence of the play tendency, the essence of which is the indulgence in all kinds of activities for their own sake.[16] The activities are established first in relation to some business need, but are repeated when the need is not there. Every kind of performance, especially those which are complex and the result of a good deal of learning and experiment, are willingly indulged in for their own sake when they have been well learned and are no longer difficult. To run or swim as fast as possible, to jump, fight, or climb are activities which yield satisfaction in proportion to the skill and prowess of the performer. In society there is an additional factor as soon as a performer becomes aware of the respect or admiration which he may earn by exhibiting his powers. But apart from this, he finds pleasure in the mere exertion of them, and the more pleasure the more he is aware of his capacity.

It is the same with less vigorous forms of activity wherever some kind of skill is involved. The putting together of words for the expression of ideas, the fabricating of implements, tools, utensils, all such activities afford satisfaction to the artist as he becomes aware of the skill which he is exhibiting. He may not receive any applause, though if he does this will be an extra incentive.

This play tendency, which induces a man to go on with what he can do best even when there is no external call for it, leads to a differentiation. The business activity is restrained and guided at every moment by the need which initiated it and by the external situation. During play these restraints are removed, and the activity tends to assume the form which gives the greatest satisfaction. This may be defined as being that form of activity which involves the greatest exercise of power or skill.

In this way, games are invented and more and more specialized for the purpose of giving scope for the exercise of bodily or mental powers. Since the exercise of superior skill is a source of amusement to onlookers, the game then comes to be modified in accordance with a new requirement.

So also with the arts. The activities which earlier are

performed for their own sake are found to give satisfaction to others who cannot indulge in them very successfully themselves, and this leads to a modification of the activities, as in the case of games.

The psychological foundations of literary and artistic composition and appreciation are today largely ignored. If commentators introduce psychology at all, it is usually with reference to Freud or Jung. They commonly seek words and phrases which do not commit them to any clear position in regard to the aims of literature. They may not say that literature serves some moral, political or social end, for although novels and poems have been written for such purposes, these works have not as a rule been the most successful, and other kinds of book do the work much better. They may not say that literature is written merely to entertain an idle public, for this would make the position of the writer a very subordinate and undignified one. Nor may they say that the real merits of a literary work lie in the language, the style, the technical excellence; for this puts the writer on a level with the craftsman. Very often commentators simply take certain arbitrary formulas as to what is good or great and what is inferior and refer to them by means of a more or less elaborate jargon. These tendencies are well exemplified in Wimsatt and Brooks 1957, both in the critics whose views they quote and in their own opinions. They say, in the latter regard:

> The kind of literary theory which seems to us to emerge the most plausibly from the long history of the debates is far more difficult to orient within any of the Platonic or Gnostic world views, or within the Manichaean full dualism and strife of principles, than precisely within the vision of suffering, the optimism, the mystery which are embraced in the religious doctrine of the Incarnation.

They do not tell us exactly what this doctrine is, nor how a plausible literary theory "emerges" from history "within" it, but go on to say that what is required of "verbal art", if it is to be successful, "is not simply a complicated correspondence, a method of alternation, now sad, now happy . . . , but the oblique glance, the vertical unification of the metaphoric smile. To pursue the ironic and tensional theories in the way most likely to avoid the Manichaean heresy will require a certain caution in the use of the solemn and tragic emphasis" (p. 746).

As Douglas Hewitt has noted, in an article on present-day literary criticism, the professional lives of critics are often so arranged that they never have to deal with normal persons, but only with fellow practitioners or trainees (students). They live in what he calls "a large self-contained empire which does not need to export its wares to common readers" (1969, pp. 331–32). Their performance is partly due to the fact that they feel they need to do more than repeat the sounder observations of predecessors; and sensible originality about established classics becomes progressively more difficult. As University teachers, which they commonly are, they feel they must show that their "discipline" requires as much abstract knowledge as that put across by their colleagues in well-developed sciences. In consequence they pretend that any work which they discuss "is radically different in kind from what readers have always thought it to be", and "achieves its proper dignity" only as a result of their "critical meditation", which operates with considerable "stylistic complexity", in terms of "myths, archetypes, semantics, structuralism", and so forth. Hewitt gives examples and notes, apropos of the 'myths', that they are mostly "loosely Jungian" constructions,

> probably because the psychology of Jung (like all systems which claim to be all-embracing) provides a method which can be used to interpret into its own terms any phenomena whatever, and because neo-Jungian use of myth, religion and ritual is sufficiently loose and ambiguous to allow plenty of elbow room. . . . Moreover, Jungian interpretations can offer more easily than any others what is often sought—a sense of unction, of vast significances, of the substitute theology of a secular age, of—in short—religion on the cheap.

A further reason why the reader acquiesces in such performances is the enormous effort he has to make to understand them: "it is hard, after such a rough journey, to believe that he has not travelled a long way".

There is a parallel development—towards meaningless

originality—among the artists themselves. Although originality has often been admired in the arts, maximum effectiveness is achieved when it is tempered by a certain conformity to traditional rules; for although an artist who slavishly follows tradition will bore us, one who breaks with it completely will bewilder us. Artists and critics alike have repeatedly recognized that the best results come from giving an established tradition a new twist, so that the old form can be recognized in the new product, which is nevertheless refreshingly new. The German dramatist Friedrich Hebbel, for instance, stated that the public expects the poet to keep to some extent within the bounds of established conventions, while the poet may assume that these are in themselves no longer fully adequate to meet its expectations.[17] And Ernst Mach, speaking of a symphony by Schumann or a poem by Heine, said that a good deal of their charm comes from their "surprising variation of older turns and figures, which cheat our expectations in a pleasant manner. Without what is older and more trivial in them they could neither have arisen nor be understood" (1926, p. 161). But this combination of originality and convention becomes, over the centuries, more and more difficult. As the conventions are relaxed and modified again and again, the stage must eventually be reached when they are all annihilated and originality attained by means of every kind of freakish novelty. Over a century ago, the Austrian dramatist Franz Grillparzer pointed to the plight of modern writers when he said that to be novel without being artificial ("gekünstelt") was becoming increasingly difficult. He knew too that there is such a thing as original nonsense, and that originality is all too easy if no relation to reality is required.[18] Early in the present century, the poet Rilke advised a young poet not to write love poems, to "avoid those forms which have become current and habitual"; for "they are the most difficult: great and mature capacity is required to give of one's own where good, and to some extent, brilliant traditions are available in plenty". In other words, it is hard to be effective in a field where so many have already worked so well, whereas if what one writes is novel, it cannot be compared and contrasted with any standard model. Hence Rilke's advice is that the young man should depict his own "sadnesses and wishes", his "passing thoughts and belief in something or other of beauty".[19] One suspects that what this amounts to is: follow my example and write about nobody quite knows what; that's the way to get on.

The way the situation today has come to be the dissolution of all conventions can be seen from the so-called 'new novel', as expounded by Robbe-Grillet and others in France. It must not, he tells us (1961) "foster any resemblance" to the novel of yesterday. "We must move on"—in the sense, no doubt, of the policeman's injunction, since the direction of movement seems a matter of indifference to him. According to his account, the new novelist has nothing to say, but merely searches for a way of saying something—a way, he strongly suggests, that involves no plot, no attempt at characterization or analysis of feelings or study of milieu, in fact nothing at all that has ever been regarded as a merit in the novels of the past. He says expressly that, in the new novel, the events are not narrated by the author, but by one of the characters, preferably when in a state close to delirium. Presumably this has, for the author, the advantage that he can still work even when he is drunk. If this is to continue, it must mean the end of all art.

CONCLUSION

Vague statements about a close relationship between poetry and religion are by no means extinct. Richardson, for instance, says: "The language of religion is the language not of scientific prose but of poetry" (1957, p. 24). Such statements are made by people who think that, because both poetry and religion can have powerful emotional effects, something supernatural must be common to them. Religious prepossessions are also often obtruded, probably for the same reason, in discussions about art in general, as when John Bowden, having said that "there are other aspects of reality than the world as seen by science", goes on to quote the composer Michael Tippett as saying that "beauty is an absolute" (1970, pp. 16, 52).

The emotional basis of both religious and aesthetic experiences, it is held, makes them too personal, too subjective for scientific study. According to Dingle, science is concerned with experiences of which we can agree on a definition in terms of external existences, whereas experiences of God and of beauty are those with respect to which we can reach no such agreement (1931, p. 95). He thinks that it is without meaning to ask whether something is beautiful or even "funny", because the question implies a common standard of 'funniness' which does not exist (pp. 96–97). In fact, the conditions which elicit mirth do not differ entirely for each individual; if they did, professional humorists would have an impossible task. Likewise, people of the same race do not differ much in their ideas of human beauty; and as to music, poetry, drama, and other arts, it is not impossible to determine factors in any one of these capable of evoking a certain emotional response—not universally, but in some community or definable group of people.

Religious beliefs, like all others, may depend in part on loyalty to one's early teachers, respect for authority, desire to 'belong'—on factors which may be summed up as habit and uncritical following of tradition. This factor has often (and not only with uncivilized peoples) been prominent because persons who perform elaborate ceremonies to appease the gods cannot possibly know which elements in such a ceremony are efficacious, as in fact none at all are; and so they follow the traditional practice meticulously (cf. above, p. 226f).

In so far as reasoning is involved, religious beliefs are formed by the same processes as scientific ones. Both are based on evidence and include generalizations abstracted from the evidence. The difference is that the one looks only for confirmatory evidence favourable to certain preconceived theories, and the other constantly revises its theories by seeking out all available evidence. When, for instance, Christian convictions are supported by appeal to evidence which subsequently turns out to be not to the point, this evidence is then simply replaced by other of its kind, until that too has to be quietly dropped. Examples from the present century include the following: Serious philologists regarded the Greek dialect of the New Testament as the language of the Holy Ghost, as no ordinary writings in the same idiom were known—until papyrus discoveries showed this idiom to approximate to the non-literary Greek of the age. Jesus's parabolic teaching was held to be unique, and hence superhuman, until such a teaching method was shown to be that of rabbis who were contemporary with the gospels. And the Holy Shroud of Turin was adduced as evidence of his Resurrection, until carbon dating showed it to be a mediaeval forgery.

A common technique, amply illustrated in this book, is to avoid relinquishing what is regarded as valuable material by re-interpreting its significance. Another possibility is to claim (as do Sanders and Davies) that what is true need not necessarily be what the empirical evidence shows to be the case. Santayana made what he called truths of imagination independent of scientific truth; Collingwood declared the 'historical spirit' the sole judge of what purports to be historical truth, and insisted that there can be no science of history, nor of human nature. We are familiar nowadays with the notion that there are many kinds of reality, of which scientific or commonplace reality is the least respectable and the one that we are most entitled to ignore when it suits us. The motives behind this kind of reasoning include not only the support of religious beliefs of one kind or another, including philosophical beliefs which take the place of the traditional creeds, but also (as we saw in Chapter 7) vindication of the prestige of the man of letters as opposed to the man of science.

Science can be very troublesome. It tells us how, if we want B (e.g. drugs effective against disease but without harmful effects) we must also have A (exhaustive testing of them on animals or humans before they are marketed). But often we don't want A at all, and would prefer B just by itself. This kind of thing makes science unpopular, for what many people want almost more than anything else is their illusions; and when these are patriotic or religious, they will often accept physical deprivation without complaint, but turn in anger on anybody who touches their cherished beliefs. Lecky, in the course of pointing out how, in Greece and Rome, patriotism was the prevailing influence, notes:

> If we take a broad view of the course of history, and examine the relations of great bodies of men, we find that religion and patriotism are the chief moral influences to which they have been subject, and that the separate modifications and mutual interaction of these two agents may almost be said to constitute the moral history of mankind. (1897, ii, 100)

There is much in this as a view of paganism and Christianity. Patriotism in Greece stood for strife, bloodshed, and

intolerance, as in later Europe did religion, and as patriotism has also done there until quite recently. Both had their
martyrs and poets, both have been elevated to the rank of
ideals. They are not the sole sources of discord, but they
have hitherto been the chief, and are most deplorable when
their forces combine, as in Islam today. (The Islamic
Republic of Iran issued a postage stamp glorifying the man
who assassinated President Sadat of Egypt.[1])

We hear much today about 'worship of money', and the
complaint is not new (cf. 1 Timothy 6:10). Lecky spoke, on
the final page of his *History of the Rise and Influence of the
Spirit of Rationalism in Europe* (1865), of an undefined
"materialism" as a cloud hanging over rationalism, and on
this basis he panegyrized the times when men could be
found to sacrifice "with cheerful alacrity . . . all their material and intellectual interests to what they believed to be
right". But the obsession of illusory ideals, to which all was
sacrificed 'with cheerful alacrity', has brought suffering and
death to millions. It was just such an obsession which, in
1914, induced many to sacrifice themselves, and the rest
joined the tendency for fear of contempt and abuse.

Perhaps there is no evil which does not produce some
compensating good. The needs and interests of mankind
are so complex that an unmitigated evil is possibly an
unrealizable abstraction. But what Treitschke called "the
noble pursuit of arms" is fallen nowadays into discredit, as
is also his characterization (in the same context) of war as a
"rejuvenating spring for the moral forces of nations",[2]
however fine these things may have appeared to an enthusiastic and inexperienced Prussian patriot writing at a time
when a victorious and not too costly war, such as that
which his country had recently waged against Austria,
flattered the vanity of a state emerging into power.[3]

No such discredit has today fallen upon religious belief.
No one has described more vividly than Lecky the immense sufferings inflicted on humanity by the Christian
religion, or the primitive stupidity of some of its main
dogmas. Yet even he, as a Parliamentary candidate, de-

clared himself a Christian, and persisted in assuming that Christianity somehow constitutes an ideal moral scheme. The following passage typifies the ambiguity of his position, and represents a standpoint still strongly maintained:

> The Christian religion . . . has probably done more to quicken the affections of mankind, to promote pity, to create a pure and merciful ideal, than any other influence that has ever acted on the world. But . . . it is a no less incontestable truth that for many centuries the Christian priesthood pursued a policy, at least towards those who differed from their opinions, implying a callousness and absence of the emotional part of humanity which has seldom been paralleled and perhaps never surpassed. (1897, i, 326)

The rise to power of the so-called "third world" has made it more than ever apparent that Christianity is not the only world religion, and that "moral feelings based upon religion are of all things the most difficult to change when confronted by different feelings based upon a different faith. The tendency of a human being in this situation is to rally to his own group and suspect all others" (White 1948, p. 8). I will not deny that religious rapture may sometimes be an altruistic emotion in which—so William James in a famous book—"the sand and grit of the selfhood incline to disappear and tenderness to rule". He adds: "Like love or fear, the faith-state is a natural psychic complex, and carries charity with it by organic consequence".[4] But history tells of another faith-state which carries with it—whether or not 'by organic consequence' I cannot say—a mania for persecution and a powerful hatred for large numbers of one's fellows. Even as late as the second half of the nineteenth century, the Papacy called liberty of conscience and the right to practise one's own religion "deliramentum" (Bury 1930, p. 5). The spirit of kindness and goodwill is associated perhaps chiefly with the state of happiness and contentment, and the same symptoms are seen whatever the source of the happiness. Intoxication at a certain early stage seems to produce an expansiveness and a feeling of good fellowship less marked in the same individual when sober.

Many apologists who were not in a position to persecute tried at least to humble non-Christians. Milner, for instance, in his very popular *History of the Church of Christ* (published 1794–1809), is spiteful to all forms of ancient thought. One might have supposed that the Christian spirit would have welcomed all forms of kindliness and common virtue, all sincere attempts to understand the relation between man and God, and while regretting that philosophers like Epictetus, Plotinus, and Marcus Aurelius should have failed to understand the Christian message, would have been glad to find so much good in humanity even under unfavourable conditions. Some Christians did hold that all who have sought the truth sincerely have had their share of inspiration from God, that human reason, as God's gift, is not despicable, and so on. And today many more than of yore hold, with the late Bishop Stephen Neill, that the Christian "must rejoice in everything" that other faiths "possess of beauty and high aspiration" (1984, pp. 32–33). Tom Driver, at the end of a recent symposium on Christianity's relation to other faiths, distinguishes the following three stages in Christian thinking on the matter:

1. The "time-honoured Christian exclusiveness that held, and in many quarters still holds, that persons (some conservative voices say nations) that do not confess Christ are for that reason condemned and lost to all eternity".

2. "The so-called inclusivist position, according to which, although salvation can indeed be found outside the Christian fold, this is so by virtue of the fact that non-Christians are somehow included in the saving grace that comes from God through Christ".

3. The view that this second position "still represents an unwarranted attachment to a traditional kind of christology that is no longer in the best interests of the world or the church" (Driver 1988, pp. 203–04).

The symposium to which these concluding remarks are attached explores the possibilities of a recognition of the independent validity of non-Christian religions, and does so very tentatively, recognizing that many Christians regard such a venture as highly questionable—not surprisingly, as the New Testament says, of Jesus: "In none other is there salvation, . . . neither is there any other name under heaven, that is given among men, wherein we must be saved" (Acts 4:12. Locke's attempt to come to terms with this passage typifies the embarrassment it has occasioned among liberal Christians).[5] It is still widely believed that Christian influence is responsible for much, if not all that is good in non-Christian outlooks that have arisen in Christian environments. Canon Richardson attained the height of pompous condescension on this matter in 1947;[6] and later Bishop Robinson declared (with characteristic 'dialectic') that "we Christians find our identity by losing it in identification. . . . We are distinctive precisely as we are not distinct"; and suggested that one reason for this is that "modern humanists have largely taken humanist values from Christianity" (1972, pp. 17–19). That this is the reverse of the truth is in effect conceded by Gilkey, who points out that, until about a century and a half ago, Christianity's prime concern was to defend the faith, and that it is "largely with the help of the Enlightenment" that someone who killed in order to keep the faith pure came to be regarded as a misguided fanatic (1988, p. 38). Christianity has repeatedly flouted acceptable values as long as it could afford to resist them.

Christianity today, then, includes spokesmen who, in the words of Edwin Robertson, a Baptist minister and religious writer, modestly claim no more than that "the Christian . . . seeks with the seeker" (1989, p. 186). The Anglican minister and author John Bowden, although he does not wish "Christian belief" to be "put in the dock and questioned about its statements by others", would be glad to see "genuine conversation" between the parties (1970, p. 114). This is indeed devoutly to be wished, but conversation in the sense he is advocating is extraordinarily difficult. It can lead to fruitful results only when the participants are trying to solve the same problem without rivalry, without thought of personal prestige; and this commonly occurs only under the stress of dire need, when the solution of the problem is more important to the parties than the satisfaction any of them gets from proving his point or making his solution prevail. Otherwise the element of antagonism results in a change of motive: curiosity gives place to rivalry, and the desire to solve the problem is replaced by the desire to be its solver. In the presence of a rival, and in the consciousness of his opposition, there is apt to be a surplus of emotion which cannot be canalized into pure investigatory activity. Instead there is straying from the point into side-issues or irrelevancies, and arguments about what has been said by way of proving folly or inconsistency. This sort of thing does not happen only when the disputants are face to face, as I know very well from comments on my own work, some of which I have referred to above. There is a paradox here. One cannot do one's best in a vacuum, with no comment from outside: the mind works better under the stimulus of criticism and exchange of views; but comment is rarely such as to advance the subject. Liberal theologians are reasonable up to a point, but if their residual beliefs are impugned, they are capable of gobbling like turkeys, in the tradition of the kind uncle and the rest of the sorcerer's avatars, as portrayed in Stevenson's fable.

The Cardinal Archbishop of Turin has said that, in spite of the results of recent carbon dating tests, the Church reiterates her respect and her veneration for the holy shroud. If a mediaeval artifact can be thus treated, how much the more will first-century myths embodied in the New Testament retain their potency, and how much the less will the arguments of informed critics prevail against them! I have mentioned to clergymen serious objections to the reliability of the New Testament (objections that have in fact been made since the eighteenth century by reputable Christian scholars), only to find that they dismissed these objections as 'absolute nonsense' and obviously thought (as I did not name any critical scholars) that I had made them up myself through careless reading of the documents. There are thousands of such clergy, whose function is to maintain the traditionally accepted doctrines, and who address themselves to thousands of laity who have no idea how to form an independent opinion on these matters, even supposing that they had the leisure, the capacity and the inclination to do so. So long as beliefs are backed by a powerful organization of this kind, they can survive any amount of criticism.

NOTES

1.   Hume 1738, Part 1, Section 7 ('Of abstract ideas').

2.   Berkeley 1710, Introduction, § 10.

3.   This point has been argued in detail by Englefield 1985, Chapter 5, pp. 41ff, who also shows that there is no fundamental difference between the particular idea and the general, and that the former grades into the latter.

4.   Schopenhauer, *Über die vierfache Wurzel,* § 49, as cited in the bibliography: p. 154 of the German, and p. 226 of the English translation.

5.   Burke 1757: Cassel Edition, p. 184.

6.   Campbell 1814, Book 2, Chapter 7, Section 2 (Volume 2, pp. 125, 134); Englefield (1990, p. 80) quotes the following passage from Hume's *Treatise* (loc. cit. in Note 1 above) to the same effect: "I believe every one who examines the situation of his mind in reasoning will agree with me that we do not annex distinct and complete ideas to every term we make use of, and that in talking of *government, church, negotiation, conquest,* we seldom spread out in our minds all the simple ideas of which these complex ones are composed. It is however observable that notwithstanding this imperfection we may avoid talking nonsense on these subjects, and may perceive any repugnance among the ideas as well as if we had a full comprehension of them. Thus, if instead of saying *that in war the weaker have always recourse to negotiations,* we should say *that they have always recourse to conquest,* the custom which we have acquired of attributing certain relations to ideas still follows the words, and makes us immediately perceive the absurdity of that proposition".

7.   Although the Catholic doctrine of transubstantiation (the change of substance of the bread and wine at the eucharist) is said (in the twenty-eighth of the Anglican Thirty-Nine Articles) to be "repugnant to the plain words of Scripture" and to have "given occasion to many superstitions", Anglicans and Catholics have recently agreed on the following eucharistic formula: "The sacramental body and blood of the Saviour . . . are present as an offering", and "when this offering is met by faith, a life-giving encounter results". Bowden asks, appositely: "But what does this mean?" (1977, pp. 36–37, 68). As for baptism, Eric James addressed an ecumenical conference where it had been stated that "there is one Spirit and one indwelling of the Spirit which is given at Baptism". He commented: "I know this is biblical language, and I know that it is the biblical language which has been used in the Church for centuries. But as 'a child of our time', I do not really understand it; and, to be honest, if it means what it seems to mean (namely that there are "two sorts of humanity—those indwelt by the Spirit after baptism, and those who are not"), I simply do not believe it" (1965, pp. 129–130).

8.   Thus Locke says that "brutes . . . have not the faculty of abstracting or making general ideas, since they have no use of words or any other general signs" (1690, Book 2, Chapter 11, Section 10).

9.   Cf. Davey 1981, p. 302: "It should be quite obvious from everyday observation of animals that their behaviour is often determined not by specific features of environmental stimuli but by more general characteristics. For example, many wild animals, especially birds, will flee at the sight of a human being regardless of the size, shape or colour of the person, while they will happily remain in the presence of other animals". Hinde (1966, p. 414) mentions some interesting experiments by Herrnstein and Loveland, who, he says, reported in a paper of 1964 that they had "trained pigeons to respond to the presence or absence of human beings in photographs. The people might be anywhere on the photograph, were clothed or nude, adults or children, in varied postures, black, white or yellow, in fact so diverse that simple stimulus characterization seems ruled out. These experiments thus suggest very considerable powers of conceptualization in pigeons".

10.   This distinction between experiments on the ground and experiments in the mind had been very clearly stated by

Ernst Mach who, in a chapter of his book *Erkenntnis und Irrtum,*
explains how the scientific investigator carries out imaginary
experiments ("Gedankenexperimente") in his head; and in 1920
Eugenio Rignano developed Mach's view in his *Psychologie du
Raisonnement.* Englefield drew on both these writers, whose
elucidation of the thinking process has remained otherwise
unacknowledged (Popper developed his views independently.) I
know of no book on Rignano, and as for Mach, Blackmore
(1972, p. 179) regards his ideas concerning "thought experiments" as an unimportant methodological principle. Englefield
coined the term "internal peirasis" (the Greek word means 'trial'
and is more convenient than the phrase 'trial and error') for this
process of experimentation in the imagination, as against what
he called "external peirasis", which consists in actually performing the trials instead of merely imagining their performance
(1985, pp. 16ff).

11. William James says, misleadingly, that the most intelligent person is he "whose determinations are swayed by reference
to the most distant ends" (1901, p. 23). Eternal salvation is a
distant end, but the behaviour of many relatively unintelligent
people has been much determined by reference to it. What
matters for the measurement of intelligence is what might be
called the larger situation (of which what is at one moment
perceived is merely a morsel), not the more distant prospect. A
lively imagination can bring a distant prospect nearer, but a
small mind cannot embrace a large idea.

12. Strahler also notes perceptively that creationists direct
their polemic towards schools rather than universities, as school
teachers of biology are in a weaker position; they "work in
relative isolation from colleagues but in direct contact with
parents of the students in their classes, only the local community
being involved" (1987, p. 67).

13. The impossibility of making large-scale historical predictions has been argued in sufficient detail in Popper 1957.

14. I discuss these matters more fully in Wells 1959, pp.
276ff.

15. F. Engels, *Anti-Dühring,* second edition, Part 1, Chapter
13. I give a detailed criticism of Engels's arguments here in Wells
1959, pp. 209ff.

16. Pavlov 1927. 'Generalisation' is discussed on pp. 113, 186, and 'concentration' on p. 157. A very readable account of Pavlov's work is Jeffrey A. Gray's *Pavlov,* Brighton; Harvester Press, 1979. He notes (pp. 50–51) that Pavlov "showed that a dog could perceive the difference between a circle and an ellipse even when the axes of the latter were in the ratio of 9:8". The importance of Pavlov's distinction between the phases of generalization and concentration is stressed by Englefield (1985, p. 34).

CHAPTER 2: REASON AND INSTINCT

1. This distinction between the savage and the scientist is insisted on by Wundt, 1910, pp. 37, 62.

2. Tylor gives an excellent account of the development of ideas about the soul in the final chapter (entitled 'Animism') of Volume 1 of his *Primitive Culture* (cf. the bibliography under Tylor 1891). The difficulty in tracing this development lies partly in the continual alternation of the idea of the soul as a hypothesis (to explain observed phenomena) with the idea that the soul is an actual existing entity, well enough understood to serve in itself as an explanation of other things.

3. Tylor concludes his Chapter 10 by allowing that the evidence makes it "possible to treat myth as an organic product of mankind at large, in which individual, national, and even racial distinctions stand subordinate to universal qualities of the human mind."

4. "Man is man because he has no instincts, because everything he is and has become he has learned, acquired from his culture, from the man-made part of his environment, from other human beings" (Montagu 1968, p. 9). Montagu is concerned to refute the view that man is so innately aggressive that war is inevitable. He holds that "if one is born innately aggressive, then one cannot be blamed for being so" (p. xiii)—as if instinctive tendencies (such as sexual or acquisitive drives) were completely uncontrollable. He refers (p. ix) to Bernard 1924, who says (p. 515): "The most cursory analysis of the origin of the action patterns involved in such so-called instincts as the parental instinct, reproductive instinct, fighting instinct, instinct of self-preservation, the gregarious instinct, and the like, will show that by far the greater part of the action content is acquired", that is, "acquired habit". "By far the greater part" is an important

qualification, and Bernard expressly allows (p. 516) that "all acquired action-patterns must grow up as the differential phase or superstructure of inherited capacities and activity bases". What he is justly concerned to oppose is multiplying instincts in the manner of McDougall. There is no point in assuming, for instance, an instinct of expression, another of destruction, another of conservation, another of change, and so on, to explain the many and various peculiarities of human conduct.

5.   Locke 1690, Book 2, Chapter 7, Sections 2–3.

6.   Hume 1751, Section 9, end of Appendix 1.

7.   There is now a considerable (if largely unilluminating) body of literature on the subject of leadership: see the summaries by Stogdill (1977) and Bass (1981). Gibb (1969) gives a selection of relevant material, and Bell (1950) a summary of views of the leader from Aristotle onwards.

8.   G. Freytag, *Bilder aus der deutschen Vergangenheit* (first published 1859–1867), Volume 2 (i), ad. init.

9.   Apologists have repeatedly represented Pascal as a scientist who—in the words of Malcolm Muggeridge—had "seen through and scornfully rejected the pretensions of science" in religious matters (1975, pp. 19–20). Pascal's science was in fact limited to mathematics and physics and did not extend to historical criticism. Coleman's recent study has documented his "cavalier attitude towards biblical scholarship" and his "dramatic ignorance of church history" (1986, pp. 67, 169). Pascal's thesis—that if the unbeliever is wrong he risks future torment, whereas if the believer is wrong he will be no worse off after death for having believed—is available to the Moslem no less than to the Christian.

10.   Isaac Newton, *Observations on the Prophecies of Daniel*, London, 1733, p. 25 (Chapter 3). P. Borthwick, editor of the 1831 edition of this work (published by Nisbet in London) adds here the stern note: "It would have been well for the sceptical theologians of the German school, and for their less learned followers amongst ourselves, had they attended to this warning of Sir Isaac" (p. 25).

11.   William James, *Varieties of Religious Experience,* chapter on 'Saintliness' (Doubleday edition, as listed in my bibliography, p. 252).

12. *Ibid.,* chapter on 'Mysticism' (Doubleday edition, p. 350).

13. Judith O'Neill (1975, p. 9) thinks the thunderstorm story, which Luther told only 35 years after the event, may be apocryphal, as in later life he often forgot how things had really happened. But she does not dispute that he "became a friar not freely, but walled around with the terror and agony of sudden death".

14. Maspero (1916, p. 113) quotes a passage where a mournful and inert soul is represented as lamenting that "since I came into this funeral valley, I know not where or what I am. Give me to drink of running water. Let me be placed by the edge of the water with my face to the North, that the breeze may caress me and my heart be refreshed from its sorrow".

15. John Bunyan, *Grace Abounding to the Chief of Sinners,* ad. init.

16. E.T. Cook, *The Life of John Ruskin,* New York: Macmillan, and London: G. Allen, 1911, i, 271.

17. Cf. Bury's *A History of Greece,* Chapter 8, ad init. (p. 322 of the edition cited in the bibliography).

18. I discuss this more fully in Wells 1988, pp. 193ff.

19. On Bonhoeffer, see Wells 1988, Chapter 6.

CHAPTER 3:   THE BIBLE—WITH OR WITHOUT ILLUSIONS?

1. On the development of allegorical interpretation of both Old and New Testaments, see Lofmark 1977.

2. Richardson, for instance, says: the "passionate atheist . . . may cause some of Christ's little ones to stumble, but if he is judged by the intention and not by the result, no millstone shall be hung about his neck" (1966, p. 63). This amounts to correcting Jesus from the commentator's own moral consciousness, teaching him, not learning from him.

3. Bicknell and Carpenter, for instance, say that "Jesus displayed an unfailing love to all men" (1955, p. 175). More

recently a scholar has stated that "the New Testament must still be taken as an absolute standard if the conduct required of Christians today is still to be Christian conduct, grounded in the name of Jesus Christ" (Schrage 1988, p. 2).

4. Cf. Downing 1968, p. 35: "In every account of major events, where Acts and the Pauline epistles overlap they are . . . in conflict." He gives detailed evidence for this, and adds: "Once it has been decided that Paul, writing to contemporaries who could and even would be very likely to check his assertions, is to be preferred, great suspicion is thrown on Acts as a whole. If a witness is proved untrustworthy at every point where his evidence can be checked, it is surely illogical to go on accepting his unsupported evidence at other points". The opposite view—that Acts is completely reliable—is argued by Sherwin-White 1963, p. 189, whose critics (including Downing himself, p. 91) have protested that he succeeds only in showing that Acts gives an account of conditions, prevailing and recent, in the Roman Empire that might have been expected of any well-informed person at the time of writing. See, for instance, Finley 1968, p. 195: "Mr. Sherwin-White has been able to demonstrate that the New Testament is very accurate in its details about life at the time, whether about geography and travel or the rules of citizenship and court procedures. Why should it not be? It is made up of contemporary documents, regardless of the accuracy of the narrative, and so reflects society as it was. That still does not tell us anything about the narrative details, and they are what matter".

5. Bishop Michael Marshall (1988, p. 5) has said that "today, in some areas of Anglicanism the scriptures are not merely critically studied but virtually written off as culturally conditioned and as almost totally irrelevant to any discussions on matters so widely ranging and diverse as homosexual lifestyle, women bishops and inclusive God language".

6. Whittaker (1990, pp. 36–37) holds that the credibility of religious views "depends, at least in part, on their power to inspire affirmative sentiments about life and to promote the prospects of a meaningful existence . . . What else could, or should, the credibility of a life view depend on if not its capacity to deepen one's sentiments, to elevate one's passions, and to shed meaning into a troubled existence?" This criterion would make the convictions of enthusiastic communists or fascists credible.

7. Stark and Glock 1970, pp. 141–42, 161–62. They note that it is only in "the most conservative" (Fundamentalist) Christian bodies that knowledge of the Scriptures is very high (p. 154).

1. Neill and Wright, in their very informative survey of New Testament criticism from the late nineteenth century until their own time of writing, have noted that "it is still universally agreed that our picture of the earliest Church must begin with the study of Paul, and in particular of the letters generally agreed to be authentic: 1 Thessalonians, Galatians, Romans, 1 and 2 Corinthians, Philippians, and Philemon. These writings, which almost certainly antedate the earliest written Gospel, remain central for both the theology and the history of the period" (1988, p. 362).

2. Paul says that "when the fulness of the time came, God sent forth his Son, born of a woman, born under the law" (Galatians 4:4). Paul's intention here "was to bring out Jesus's similarity to other men, whereas the original purpose of the tradition about Jesus's virgin birth was to establish his very difference" (Pannenberg, 1972, p. 72). Pannenberg adds, as another indication that Paul did not regard Jesus as virgin born, that "he was certainly familiar with the idea of a miraculous birth. He mentions it in connection with the birth of Isaac through Sarah (Galatians 4:23, 27, 29); but he applies it *not* to Jesus, but in an allegorical sense to Christians as heirs of the promise (Galatians 4:28)". Thus Jesus's virgin birth is "legend", the motive of which was to explain "the title Son of God, which had already been conferred for other reasons" (pp. 73–74; cf. Wells 1989, Chapter 3). Pannenberg thinks that, as modern man may acquiesce to this motive (p. 76), he can continue to recite 'born of the virgin Mary' in the creed without compunction.

3. See Wells 1982, in particular Chapter 1, Section 3 ('Jesus's Eucharistic Words'), and Chapter 8 ('New Testament References to Jesus's Family'). On the eucharistic words, cf. also Note 33 below. The Peter (Cephas) with whom Paul quarrelled (Galatians 2:11ff) was a leader of the Christian community which existed at Jerusalem about AD 60, and Paul does not suggest that he had been a companion of the historical Jesus, any more than he himself had been. Although, in Galatians, he is anxious to discredit Peter, he does not suggest that Peter had ever denied his master.

4.   Cf. Pannenberg 1972, p. 116: "The resurrection of Jesus was originally thought of itself as an exaltation to God from the grave. Hence the appearances of the risen Jesus were experienced as happenings sent from heaven. The temporal distinction between resurrection and ascension only seems to have come into being in a fairly late phase of the early Christian tradition, namely in the theology of Luke. Moreover, it resulted from the more pronounced stress on the quasi-earthly corporeality of the appearances of the risen Jesus: by this time these counted as meetings taking place on earth. But if the Easter appearances were understood as earthly encounters, then the carrying away of Jesus from earth had to be viewed as an additional, special event; and this is the way in which the story of Jesus's ascension is presented."

5.   See, for instance, Wedderburn's postscript to the volume he edited entitled *Paul and Jesus* where, summing up findings of the contributors, he says: "There are many cases where Paul is involved in arguments where his case would have been greatly helped by appeal to sayings of Jesus which we know; yet no use is made of them in such contexts. That should warn us against any too glib assumption that Paul knew much more than he actually quotes as sayings of the Lord" (Wedderburn 1989, p. 192). Cf. p. 136f above.

6.   At 2 Corinthians 5:16 Paul states that he once "knew Christ according to flesh", but no longer knows him, nor anyone else, in this way. The reference is not to 'Christ in the flesh', to the earthly Jesus: the 'according to flesh' qualifies the verb 'knew', not the noun 'Christ' (cf. Wolff 1989, p. 89, 97–98). The meaning is that he no longer regards Christ 'from a human point of view', and this is how the passage is translated in most English versions. Thus the RSV has: "From now on, therefore, we regard no one from a human point of view; even though we once regarded Christ from a human point of view, we regard him thus no longer".

7.   These early letters include Hebrews, 2 Thessalonians (dependent on the genuinely Pauline 1 Thessalonians), Colossians, Ephesians, and 1 Peter (each of the two latter being dependent on the previous one), and possibly also the letter of James and 1, 2, and 3 John (although these four may be of slightly later date than the others). On the Christology of 1 Peter, cf. p. 129 above.

8. Thus the Pastoral epistles (1 and 2 Timothy and Titus)—ascribed to Paul but generally agreed to be second-century works—link Jesus with Pontius Pilate, and 2 Peter (the latest document in the New Testament) alludes to his transfiguration. Non-canonical letters show the change of attitude equally clearly: 1 Clement (of about AD 96) mentions some of his teachings; Ignatius's letters (of about AD 110) mention the virgin birth, the baptism by John and the Crucifixion under Pilate. Later documents are even more explicit.

9. For a brief account, see Wells 1986B; fuller accounts in Wells 1982 and 1986A. Most of my theologian critics have failed to understand what it is that I am maintaining, and suppose, for instance, that I commit the "elementary error" of believing a writer to be ignorant of *anything* he fails to mention; that my case is based only on the silence of the Pauline letters; that in my view Jesus was, for Paul, not a historical personage at all; and that I exaggerate the gap between early epistles and gospels by dating the latter after AD 100. (For examples of these criticisms of my views, see Stanton 1989, pp. 3, 139 and France 1986, pp. 12, 88.) In fact, as the summary in my text (above, pp. 94f) makes clear, I maintain none of these positions. France is quite right to say that Paul provides "early evidence for the tradition of Jesus as a real live Jew who was crucified and rose again" (p. 91). But this does not, as he supposes, conflict with what I maintain. France is also right when he says that I weave the evidence I have taken from theologians' research into a total account with which none of those from whom I have quoted would agree (p. 12). In other words, while many New Testament scholars agree that I have stated the evidence correctly, they and I do not agree on what it all adds up to. A just account of my views is given by the non-theologians Ellegård (1990) and Martin (1991).

10. Bowden 1977, p. 40, says: "That the gospel accounts may not be taken apart and then harmonised into a single narrative may be commonplace knowledge to the student of the New Testament; it is not to the average congregation, who are still likely to have their Good Friday devotions arranged round such a composite picture of 'the seven last words from the cross'". The sayings from the cross are but a particularly crass example. Details of the discrepancies here between the gospels are given in Wells 1989, pp. 149–152.

11. Downing 1968, pp. 190–91; cf. above, Chapter 3, Note 4, for Downing's comment on the discrepancies between Paul's letters and the Acts of the Apostles. Cf. Drury 1985, p. 3:

"Historical inquiry after the actual Jesus has reached an impasse after more than a century of diligent and exacting work". Cf. also Nineham, above, p. 150.

12.   Satan is an old Hebrew word meaning 'adversary'. At first a common noun, designating an adversary in war or in a lawsuit, it came to be the name of one of Yahweh's specialist angels, whose function it was to thwart and punish evil-doers. Gradually, increasing powers were attributed to this angel, who became opposed even to Yahweh himself. Details in Caird 1956, Chapter 2.

13.   The term 'thrones', meaning supernatural entities, occurs in 'The Ascension of Isaiah' (on which see Note 18 below), where "the Elect one" is said to be "him alone, to whose voice all the heavens and thrones give answer" (8:7–8). Wink comments: "By 'heavens' the author clearly means the heavenly hosts in each of the seven heavens; by 'thrones', then, he must mean those seated on them" (1984, p. 19). Cf. also 2 Enoch (the Book of the Secrets of Enoch) 20:1 (as numbered in R.H. Charles's edition of *The Apocrypha and Pseudepigrapha of the Old Testament*, Oxford, 1913: Clarendon Press, volume 2, p. 441): Enoch is lifted into the seventh heaven and reports: "I saw there . . . fiery troops of great archangels, incorporeal forces and dominions, orders and governments, cherubim and seraphim, thrones and many-eyed ones".

14.   Cf. Jubilees 15:31–32: "There are many nations and many peoples . . . and he has set spirits in authority over all of them to lead them astray from him. But over Israel he appointed no angel or spirit, for he alone is their ruler". That God should want the nations' angels to "lead them astray" may, says Wink, be "merely hindsight that treats what happens in history as the determined plan of God". But the statement inevitably casts these angels in a negative light, and "the step from this to their demonization is very short" (1984, p. 29). The idea that each nation has its guardian angel is represented in the canon at Deuteronomy 4:19 and 32:8–9. The Septuagint reading of the latter passage (the Most High "fixed the borders of the peoples according to the number of *the sons of God"*—not "the children of Israel" as in the Hebrew text) has been confirmed by one of the Qumran texts; cf. Caird 1956, p. 5n, who also observes: "The Deuteronomist does not seem to have been disturbed by the knowledge that the pagan nations worshipped their angelic rulers in the place of God. These rulers had been allotted to them by

God and, provided that Israel was not seduced by their worship, the order of God's providence was not disturbed".

15. A faint echo of this doctrine appears at Luke 22:3, where Satan is said to "enter into" Judas and cause him to betray Jesus (cf. Werner 1941, p. 243).

16. This interpretation depends on taking (as many commentators do) 'Christ', not 'God' as the subject of the verb. The Greek allows either. Wink (1984, pp. 57–59) argues for the latter, so that the meaning could be: God "stripped off of himself the principalities and powers", that is (in Wink's phrase), he got them "off his back".

17. Carr (1981, pp. 63, 70–71, 77) has tried to controvert this interpretation of Colossians. He takes the "principalities and powers" to be, not hostile forces, but angel figures of the heaven of God; and he supposes that, if Chapter 2 Verse 15 of the epistle is rightly interpreted, it states that Christ did not 'strip them off from himself' and triumph over them, but led them as units forming his own triumphant armies. The statement (three verses later) that the Colossians should not heed people who insist on 'worship of angels' is taken to mean, not worship offered *to* angels by human beings, but worship offered *by* angels to God in the court of heaven. Carr supposes that the author of the epistle is criticizing the Colossians for wishing to participate in this. By means of such forced exegesis Carr is able to reach the conclusion that the standard English versions (RV, NEB, RSV) of these passages are completely misleading, and that there is no "obscure mythology" about demonic powers and hostile angels at the centre of the epistle's argument (pp. 175–76). He also regards the reference to "undoubtedly malevolent hostile powers" at Ephesians 6:12 as an interpolation "typical of second-century gnosticism" (pp. 104, 110, 123). Wink describes this excision as a "desperate expedient" (1984, p. 85n).

Carr's endeavour—to show that the New Testament itself is not committed to some of the traditional absurdities—is a not uncommon ploy. J.A.T. Robinson likewise expends a great deal of ingenuity in order to make it appear that, for instance, Jesus's pre-existence as a particular individual "before all worlds" and his virgin birth were introduced into Christian thinking only by the Fathers (1973, pp. 50ff, 151).

18. The text of 'The Ascension of Isaiah' is given in E. Hennecke, *New Testament Apocrypha,* edited by W. Schnee-

melcher, English translation edited by R. McL. Wilson, Volume 2, London: Lutterworth, 1965, 642–663. I discuss the relevance of this apocalypse to early Christian ideas of Jesus in Wells 1971, pp. 291–96.

19. See Best 1965, p. 15; cf. Wells 1989, p. 100.

20. Carr (1981, p. 76) quite arbitrarily takes the 'pleroma' of Colossians 2:8 to mean "the fullness of teaching in Christ".

21. Not until his imprisonment does Paul reckon with the possibility that he might die before the second coming (Philippians 1:21–23).

22. On late Jewish ideas of the coming kingdom, see Russell 1986, p. 123. He notes there that there is "no complete consistency" as to its character and fruits in the writings of this period. However, it was believed that "the power of the Gentiles will be curbed: they will be forced to pay homage to Israel or else will be utterly destroyed . . . Israel itself will be purified, the ungodly will be judged. . . . For the most part the kingdom will be established here on this earth, or else on a renewed earth or, in a few cases, in a new transcendent order. In the Book of Daniel it belongs to this earth. . . . Its coming is imminent; and the righteous dead will be raised in resurrection to share in its blessings".

23. Some commentators have made Jesus's words at Mark 7:27 less offensive by supposing him to have here called gentiles not 'dogs' but something more like 'little bow-wows', as a diminutive noun is used in the Greek. Haenchen however (1968, p. 275 and note) points out that the spoken Koine-Greek of the time had a preference for diminutives, which do not, however, alter the sense. He gives as an example the 'ear' cut from the servant of the high priest at Jesus's arrest. Mark and Matthew uses diminutives here, Luke does not; but the two former do not mean to speak of a 'tiny little ear'. Further on Mark 7:27, cf above, p. 142.

24. Any synopsis which prints corresponding gospel passages side by side will show of Matthew Chapter 10 that Verses 5–15 conflate Mark 6:8–11 with other material, whereas Luke (9:1–6 and 10:1–6) has kept the two separate; that Verses 17–22 have been taken from the apocalyptic discourse which Mark made Jesus deliver later in his career; and that verses 24ff have

material which occurs in various other contexts in Mark and Luke.

25. On Jesus's discourse in Matthew 10, cf. Wells 1982, pp. 119–124 and 1986A, pp. 73, 106–09.

26. Wells 1982, pp. 200f. T.W. Manson commented that "in spite of the moving eloquence with which the story is told by Schweitzer, there is no escape from the conclusion that its hero was a deluded fanatic" (1956, p. 216).

27. Cf. Wells 1971, pp. 101–02, 329–331; 1986A, p. 142 n.11; 1989, pp. 13–15.

28. On J.M. Robertson, see Wells 1987B.

29. On Paul's quarrel with Peter, and on the attestation of Paul's epistles, see Wells 1982, pp. 20, 153ff.

30. Cf. Finley (1968, p. 189), who says that the non-Christian evidence concerning Jesus from the first century or century and a half of Christianity consists of "a handful of sentences in pagan writers, wholly unilluminating, and a few passages in Josephus and the Talmud, tendentious when they are not forgeries. . . . It is no exaggeration to say that they contribute nothing".

31. See Schopenhauer's essay on history in his *Die Welt als Wille und Vorstellung,* Book 3, Chapter 38; in *Sämmtliche Werke,* ed. J. Frauenstädt, Volume 3, Leipzig: Brockhaus, 1873, p. 506.

32. Matthew Arnold notes (in his essay 'The Study of Poetry', 1880) that he who "overbusies himself" with a work "is prone to overrate it in proportion to the trouble which it has cost him" (p. 166 of the edition listed in the bibliography). This, although obvious, is too often forgotten.

33. Walter has noted that at 1 Corinthians 11:23–25 Paul is dealing with a tradition that existed in a fixed wording because of its use in liturgical rites or in catechetical instruction about such rites (1989, pp. 54, 60). The formula "functions as an aetiology for ritual" (p. 62); that is, it purports to explain the origin of the eucharist, and does not allow us to "draw conclusions as to the way in which Paul learnt and transmitted traditions about Jesus in general" (p. 55). Walter also insists that Paul's reference here

to "the night on which the Lord Jesus was offered up" (or 'handed over'—παρεδίδοτο) should not be taken as an allusion to the 'betrayal' by Judas—in spite of the rendering of English translations which speak here of Jesus's 'betrayal' (p. 63). On this, see Wells 1986A, pp. 132ff.

34. "The definite assertion 'He was the Christ' is . . . inconceivable in the mouth of anyone but a Christian"; and the sentence with 'On the third day he appeared to them' also "does not come from Josephus" (Winter 1973, pp. 435, 437). Winter also observes that "Josephus nowhere informs his pagan readers what is meant by the expression 'Christ' or 'Messiah'. It would have been necessary to elucidate the term to them", whereas "a Christian interpolator quite sure of what he himself meant by the word χριστός would not have felt an explanation necessary. His readers would be Christians, as he was" (p. 435).

35. At the very end of his *Antiquities,* Josephus says that he completed it in the thirteenth year of Domitian's reign.

36. Charlesworth asks: "What Christian would refer to Jesus's miracles in such a way that a reader could understand them as merely 'surprising works'?" (1989, p. 93)—"surprising feats" in the Loeb translation. But he admits in a note that the Greek here can mean 'wonderful works', and that that is how an early Christian would understand such an expression apropos of Jesus (p. 100 n.24). He also follows those who have amended '(Jesus taught) the truth' to '(he taught) the unusual' and who regard the former, i.e. what is in the extant manuscripts, as a scribal error resulting from misreading one letter. This emendation makes this portion of the text acceptably Jewish and not blatantly Christian. Finally, he takes "the tribe of Christians" (not then a derogatory expression) "has still to this day not disappeared" as meaning "is not (yet?) extinct", as if the implication were that it probably soon would be (pp. 91, 93). This would represent Jewish, not Christian thinking. But the Greek could, of course, be equally well understood as a triumphant assertion of Christianity's success in surviving the apparent set-back of the Crucifixion.

37. The Greek, literally rendered, is: 'those who first loved him did not cease', i.e. from doing so. Taking it to mean 'did not cease to cause trouble' is an expedient that goes back to Eisler. See Bruce 1974, p. 39.

38. Charlesworth seems to be trying to parry these objections when he says (p. 101 n.35) that 'he was perhaps the Messiah' could also be translated as "he was thought to be the Messiah"; and that in any case no Christian would give such a half-hearted appraisal of Jesus (p. 95). But in fact a Christian interpolator, aware that he was supposed to be expressing a Jewish view, might have checked his usual reverential way of speaking. And there remains Winter's objection (see Note 34 above) that 'Messiah' is left elucidated.

39. The text says that Jesus "won over" ($\epsilon\pi\eta\gamma\acute{\alpha}\gamma\epsilon\tau o$) many Jews and Greeks. Bammel thinks that what Josephus actually wrote was: Jesus "misled" ($\dot{\alpha}\pi\eta\gamma\acute{\alpha}\gamma\epsilon\tau o$) them. The emendation involves a change of only one letter. The next sentence reads: "He was the Christ". Bammel deletes the 'was' as a Christian addition, and alleges that the remainder then acquires "a mocking, ironical tone" which represents a credible attitude of Josephus to Christ. He further amends "those who had in the first place come to love him" ($o\dot{\iota}\ldots\dot{\alpha}\gamma\alpha\pi\acute{\eta}\sigma\alpha\nu\tau\epsilon$s) to "those who had in the first place deceived themselves": i.e. $\dot{\alpha}\gamma\alpha\pi\acute{\eta}\sigma\alpha\nu\tau\epsilon$s is changed to $\dot{\alpha}\pi\alpha\tau\acute{\eta}\sigma\alpha\nu\tau\epsilon$s (a change of two letters, the second and the fourth), but an $o\ddot{\upsilon}\tau o\upsilon$s (themselves) has additionally, and very questionably, to be supplied, so that the sense becomes: "those who had initially deceived themselves went on doing so". The sequel "on the third day he appeared to them" etc. is then understood not as a statement of fact, but as specification of their delusions. Thus amended and re-interpreted, the text accuses Jesus only of misleading people, and the really culpable persons are the disciples who deluded first themselves and then others (Bammel 1974B, pp. 11, 14, 19).

40. Augstein 1972, p. 95. "The point of this book", he says (pp. 401, 403), "is not to deny the existence of a man named Jesus who . . . was killed during the prefecture of Pontius Pilate", but rather to show that the Jesus of earliest Christianity can be of no interest to us today, and that the Jesus of modern theology is a construct bearing no relation to the Jesus the first Christians believed in. He concludes: "He did exist, even if the evangelists have twisted many of his words to mean their opposite, and have foisted many other pronouncements onto him" (pp. 16, 149).

41.   An eleventh-century Muslim scholar reproved another because, in refuting the doctrines of a heretical sect, he had first given a full account of them (Details in Watt 1988, p. 29). The views of many ancient Christian writers which were eventually declared heretical have been allowed to survive only in so far as hostile orthodox presentations allude to them.

42.   It is in his preface to the work that Locke uses the phrase "attentive and unbiassed search". The results of such a search, as stated in the work itself, include the claims that Jesus sufficiently manifested himself "to be the Messiah in all the particulars the Scriptures had foretold of him", and that the evidence of his mission from heaven "is so great, in the multitude of miracles he did before all sorts of people, that what he delivered cannot but be received as the oracles of God" (Sections 117 and 166 of *The Reasonableness of Christianity,* as numbered in the 1836 edition published in London by Hatchard as Volume 25 in the Series *The Sacred Classics,* where the work is divided into 179 sections. In some editions there are no such divisions).

43.   On the arbitrariness of 'Christological' interpretation of Old Testament passages, Barr's account (1966, especially pp. 125, 151) is very informative. Apologists today often claim no more than that a number of such passages vaguely 'point to' Jesus. Barr finds this standpoint "very unconvincing", for "it at once leads us into questions of purpose and intention, and purpose and intention cannot really be otherwise expressed than as the purpose and intention of the writers at the time of writing"; and "there is no actual prediction or prophecy of which we can say that Jesus is the intended content" (pp. 152–53). I noted above (p. 207) a tendency among modern writers to say that one thing points to another when they wish to allege some kind of relationship between them, but are quite unable to say wherein this relationship consists.

CHAPTER 5:   THE NEW TESTAMENT ON HUMAN DESTINY AND HUMAN NATURE

1.   The article on 'The Apostles Creed' in *The Oxford Dictionary of the Christian Church,* edited by F.L. Cross, Oxford University Press, 1971, states that the title of this creed "is first found c. 390, and soon afterwards the legend appears that it was a joint composition by the twelve Apostles."

2. Details concerning how the after-life is portrayed in the Wisdom of Solomon and in 4 Maccabees are given by Evans 1970, pp. 17–19. He notes too that the Dead Sea Scrolls have also been taken to "reflect a belief in the immortality of the soul rather than in the resurrection of the whole person, body and soul together" (p. 28). Badham observes that, "as in any pluralistic society, the Jews of the first century were thoroughly confused in their own minds about what to believe" on this subject (1978, p. 39).

3. *Seventh-day Adventists Believe. . . . A Biblical Exposition of 27 Fundamental Doctrines,* Chapter 25, 'Death and Resurrection', p. 358. The book is published by the Ministerial Association, General Conference of Seventh-day Adventists, Washington DC, 1988.

4. According to Romans 5:18, as one man's (Adam's) trespass led to condemnation for all men, so one man's (Jesus's) act of righteousness leads to acquittal and life for all. But in the next verse these two 'alls' are immediately modified to 'many': many were made sinners by Adam's trespass, and many will be made righteous by Christ's obedient death. And in Verse 15 it is said that, if many died by the trespass of one, by much more did the grace of God abound to the many (cf. Sanders 1977, p. 473).

5. Schopenhauer, 'Fragmente zur Geschichte der Philosophie', in Volume 1 of his *Parerga und Paralipomena.*

6. Maury, a Calvinist admired by Karl Barth, said we must allow that the mystery of predestination is "inaccessible to our reason" (1960, p. 57). Kelly discerns a "tension" between predestination and human responsibility which raises "baffling problems", to the solution of which no New Testament writer provides a clue (1969, p. 94). Milne, having pointed out that both doctrines are taught in scripture, says that "both are to be believed" and that mystery is inevitable "where the transcendent God relates himself to us" (1982, p. 184).

7. St. Augustine's comment on Matthew 25:46 is perfectly just: "What a fond fancy it is to suppose that eternal punishment means long-continued punishment, while eternal life means life without end, since Christ in the very same passage spoke of both in similar terms in one and the same sentence" (*City of God,* Book 21, Chapter 23.)

8. The Catholic exegete Hans Küng declares that Jesus's

descent into hell, "in the restricted sense of an activity between death and resurrection, is . . . nowhere attested in the New Testament". There is, he allows, the "enigmatic" statement at 1 Peter 3:18–20 (a "late" and "unauthentic" epistle) that Christ, alive in the spirit after his death in the flesh, went and preached in the spirit to "the spirits in prison" who had been disobedient at the time when Noah was building the ark. But he points to recent research which seems to have established that the reference is not to activity of Jesus in the underworld, but to what he did as he rose up to heaven at his resurrection. Two verses later we meet the statement that he has "gone into heaven", angels and other supernatural powers "being made subject to him". Küng comments on all this:

> Christ, transfigured by the Spirit, risen like a new Enoch, on his way to heaven (not to hell) proclaims to the fallen angels in the lower regions of the air (not in the depths of the earth) their definitive condemnation. (1984, p. 160)

The idea that Jesus conquered hostile supernatural powers in the air at his resurrection is represented in other epistles (see above, pp. 98ff).

At 1 Peter 4:6 we learn—immediately after having been told that both the living and the dead will be judged—that "he (or it) was preached even to dead persons, so that they might be judged according to men in flesh, but according to God in spirit". (I have given a rendering that is as literal as possible). That they were 'judged in flesh' probably means simply that they died, death being God's judgment on all flesh as punishment for sin. 'Dead persons' may mean: persons who are now dead after having in their lifetime heard Christian evangelists. The author is expecting the final judgment very soon—the next verse says: "the end of all things is at hand"—and on this interpretation his purpose was to give an assurance that even those Christians who have already died will not be excluded from the possibility of redemption. There is a likely connection with the practice of baptism on behalf of the dead—a practice taken for granted by Paul (1 Corinthians 15:29). Some commentators, however, take the author of 1 Peter to mean that all dead persons will have had a chance to hear the Christian message, and that he is trying to answer what Pannenberg calls the "urgent question" of what is happening to those who died knowing nothing of it (1972, p. 94). But this is more likely to be an 'urgent question' for the modern humane apologist than for the author of the epistle. It is of course quite possible that reflection on the enigmatic statements in it have had a lot to do with the growth of a legend about Jesus's descent into hell.

9. Rowell says, apropos of nineteenth century discussions of eternal punishment, that "many became uneasy about a doctrine which was so clearly retributive in an age whose understanding of punishment was increasingly influenced by the theories of Bentham and the Utilitarians, with their emphasis on deterrance and reformation" (1974, p. 13).

10. Brandon 1962, pp. 244–45. Cf. p. 320 of the English translation of the Koran published in Everyman's Library (London: Dent, and New York: Dutton, 1909 or later reprint): "God will mislead whom He pleaseth, and whom he pleaseth He will place upon the straight path". "Had we [i.e. God] pleased, we had certainly given to every soul its guidance. But true shall be the word which hath gone forth from me—I will surely fill hell with Djinn and men together" (p. 191). Other passages, however, assure all who "love God" of salvation (e.g. p. 388).

11. Thus Allah's apparent tolerance of the wicked is explained by supposing that he is postponing their punishment "to an appointed term"; and "when their term is come, they shall not delay or advance it an hour" (The Koran, as cited, p. 204).

12. Reference in Walker 1964, p. 48. I owe a great deal to D.P. Walker's valuable book.

CHAPTER 6: IDEAS AND PSEUDO-IDEAS

1. Cf. Strawson 1963, p. 29: "A knowledge which is simply intellectual, based only on reason, cannot possibly be as full as knowledge received through faith, which arises out of total human experience". Cf. also what Richardson called "existential knowledge" (above, p. 192).

2. "Scientific theories . . . begin as imaginative constructions. They begin, if you like, as stories, and the purpose of the critical or rectifying episode in scientific reasoning is precisely to find out whether or not these stories are about real life. . . . It follows that scientific and poetic or imaginative accounts of the world are not distinguishable in their origins. They start in parallel, but diverge from one another at some later stage. We all tell stories, but the stories differ in the purposes we expect them to fulfil and in the kinds of evaluations to which they are exposed" ('Science and Literature' in Medawar 1984, p. 53).

3. In a later publication Richardson specifies expertise in theology as including knowledge of Greek, Latin, Hebrew, Aramaic, French, and German; the expert must also "learn how to decipher an ancient codex and how to collate manuscripts", "understand the principles and methods of textual criticism and also of literary and historical criticism", "possess a background knowledge of ancient, medieval and modern history", and "know something of the development of human society and thought from the earliest times". It follows that "the observations of a jockey or a journalist on the subject of religion" will be worth little (1950, pp. 39–40).

4. This position—that the progress of the early Church is proof that its beliefs were sound—has repeatedly been asserted. It was adequately answered by J.M. Robertson (see Wells 1987B, pp. 169ff); cf. my discussion of the origin of the Resurrection faith in Wells 1989, Chapter 2.

5. Nineteenth-century writers such as Herbert Spencer and John Tyndall insisted on the 'gulf' between psychic and physical phenomena (Their strong expressions on the subject are quoted by James 1901, pp. 146–47). They would have scorned the idea of any transformation of matter into energy; but we soon get used to such ideas. Psychic and physical phenomena can surely be regarded as different aspects of one and the same person, just as visible motion and audible sound are aspects of the same thing: it is the same process which gives to us the sensation of motion through our eyes and of sound through our ears.

6. Wickham 1989, p. 200: "Church councils at any level are improbable organs of the Holy Ghost, subject, as they are, to the same failings and mischances as beset annual general meetings of amateur dramatic societies, the proceedings of Faculty Boards and even more august assemblies. They are composed of the few who speak much, and the many who sit silent save when roused to chorus approval or outrage. When they meet, some members will turn up late; most will have only an imperfect understanding of the business". Wickham's paper is concerned particularly with the Council of Ephesus (AD 431) as "an excellent example of the genus at its worst."

7. Kaufman 1985, p. 56. Kaufman does not entirely free himself from the traditional view of God as something external to the cosmos; for he calls God "that reality which has brought us into being, which continues to sustain us, and which draws us

onward toward a fuller and more profound humanity" (p. 42); "that ecological reality behind and in and working through all of life and history" (p. 45).

CHAPTER 7:   THE ORIGIN AND DEVELOPMENT OF POETRY AND DANCE

1. W. Wordsworth, Essay Supplementary to the Preface to the second edition of the 'Lyrical Ballads' (1800); in *The Poetical Works of William Wordsworth,* Edinburgh: Paterson, Volume 4, 1883, pp. 334–35.

2. Preface to the second edition of the 'Lyrical Ballads', *vol.cit.,* p. 292. For full discussion of such "vices of literary criticism", see Englefield 1990, Chapter 2.

3. I. Kant, *Kritik der Urteilskraft,* 1790; Part 1, Book 1, § 6.

4. Wells 1987A, pp. 18–20; Englefield 1985, pp. 129–130.

5. Gummere (1901, p. 96) says: "Rhythm is an affair of instinctive perception transformed into a social act as the expression of social consent". He thinks it pertinent to ask "how rhythm in poetry may stand to rhythm in nature, to the breath or the pulse of man, to periodic movements of tide, of star" (p. 99). He refers (p. 109) to Carl Bücher's *Arbeit und Rhythmus* (Leipzig, 1897) for the view that the rhythmic movements of the early craftsman are instinctive: "energetic and continual movements of an instinctively rhythmical nature beget 'not only the form but the material' of poetry". (The words in single quotation marks are from Bücher).

6. Details as to how the devices employed vary in different languages are given by Englefield 1985, p. 132: "The verse of the ancient Hebrews lacks both metre and rhyme but displays a rhythm produced by parallel clauses . . . Chinese poetry also lacks metre but relies on rhyme to mark the end of each line and provide the ear with a resting place. Greek and Latin could do without rhyme because they had such clear metres. English poetry can also do without it where the metre is uniform and clear, as in iambic verse. . . . In French poetry metrical rhythm has practically disappeared, but rhyme is important". The arguments of the next five paragraphs of my text are taken from Englefield's article 'The Origin, Functions, and Development of

Poetry', *Trivium* (University of Wales Press), 10 (1975) where he discusses the origins of poetry more fully than in the brief summary given in his book of 1985.

7. Cf. Lorenz 1966, p. 60: "If one does not know which details of the whole performance are essential for its success as well as for its safety, it is best to cling to them all with slavish exactitude. The principle, 'You never know what might happen if you don't' is fully expressed in such superstitions."

8. On Condillac, Voltaire, and Herder, see Wells 1987A, pp. 14–15, 32. De la Grasserie said that rhythm entered poetry as "un instrument de mémoire" (1892, p. 41f). Schumann and Müller's article is called 'Experimentelle Beiträge zur Untersuchung des Gedächtnisses' and was published in the *Zeitschrift für Psychologie und Physiologie der Sinnesorgane,* Volume 6 (1894). They state that their experiments "inevitably" seem to lead up to the question of the extent to which speech formation according to metrical rules, often peculiar to poetry, owes its origin to the fact that "a rhythmically constructed verbal sequence is more easily impressed upon and committed to memory; a circumstance which was obviously most important at a time when writing did not yet exist, or was only rarely practised" (pp. 282–83).

9. Eduard Norden (1898, p. 31) held that forms of magic, the language of the laws, ceremonial religious rites were "spoken in measured, solemn tones, and so became rhythmical", and that these utterances were furnished "for emphasis and for the help of memory, with certain vocal expedients, such as alliteration and rime". All this existed as a "kind of prose . . . before there was any artistic poetry".

10. Vansina 1965, pp. 35, 56; 1985, pp. 46–47, 70.

11. Finnegan 1988, pp. 158, 172. The religious function of the early stages of oral compositional traditions is stressed by Peabody, who says that such conditions "seem necessary for the birth of an oral tradition and for its continuation beyond nascent beginnings"; for something more is required than "a casual or occasional desire for public entertainment" (1975, p. 31).

12. Peabody (1975, p. 18) says that "from all we know, the immediate origins of the Greek epos lie within a period of total

illiteracy. . . . We now believe that the tradition to which Homer belonged was an oral tradition". Denys Page (1962, p. 9) held that Greek epic poetry was "preserved by memory and handed down by word of mouth". This kind of poetry, he adds, "can only be composed and . . . preserved if the poet has at his disposal a ready-made stock of traditional phrases". The Homeric poems are composed of sequences of such phrases: "In 28,000 lines there are 25,000 repeated phrases, large or small". Russo thinks that, although Homer wrote in an extremely traditional style, his repetitions, like the "familiar thematic content and traditional subject matter", may merely be his means of helping his listeners: "Communication is served by the lucidity and predictability of a diction that depends on traditional patterns" (1976, p. 49).

13.   Wundt notes, as a kindred phenomenon, the mania for flagellation which spread through Europe from Italy in the thirteenth and fourteenth centuries, and owed its prevalence to fears of epidemics and particularly of the plague (1923, p. 480). George Grote, speaking of the Dionysian and other orgies, says that they mostly "obtained their admission and their influence at periods of distress, disease, public calamity or danger, or religious terror or despondency, which appear to have been but too frequent in their occurrence" (*History of Greece,* 10-volume edition, London: John Murray, 1903, i, 25).

14.   Englefield 1977, Chapter 11, and 1985, Chapter 15.

15.   It may seem absurd to suggest that gestures and pantomime could have been credited with unreal powers. But although men had invented language, they did not all understand why it worked, because, as always, there are those who invent and those—the great majority—who can only use the inventions without understanding any more than is necessary for their practical application.

16.   Englefield gives a full discussion of play (1985, Chapter 13).

17.   Friedrich Hebbel, apropos of the public's rejection of his play *Der Rubin;* in *Werke,* Munich: Hanser, 1965, iii, 614.

18.   Franz Grillparzer, Diary entry of 1836, in *Sämtliche Werke,* Munich: Hanswer, 1964, iii, 316.

19. R.M. Rilke, first of the *Briefe an einen jungen Dichter,* dated February, 1903.

CONCLUSION

1. See W. Montgomery Watt 1987, p. 246.

2. Heinrich von Treitschke, essay on Cavour, 1869: p. 40 of the 1939 edition listed in the bibliography.

3. E.A. Freeman complained of Mommsen's "unblushing idolatry of mere force" (*Historical Essays,* second series, London: Macmillan, 1873, p. 270). This certainly seems to be a phase of thought through which many German writers passed in the last century.

4. James, *Varieties of Religious Experience,* Doubleday edition, as listed in the bibliography, pp. 255f.

5. Locke believed that those who, through no fault of their own, have never heard of Christ, will not be condemned for their ignorance, but judged according to the use they have made of their natural reason, "this candle of the Lord", in ascertaining what was their duty and in finding the path to "reconciliation and forgiveness" when they had failed in it. He met the objection that Acts 4:12 denies any possibility of achieving salvation without Christ, by appealing to "the wisdom of God" which is beyond our understanding (*The Reasonableness of Christianity as delivered in the Scriptures,* Sections 163–66, as numbered in the 1836 edition published by Hatchard in London). Byrne (1989, p. 46) calls this "a collapse into mystery", and comments: "Locke's claim is that the Christian dispensation, once expounded properly by reference to the true meaning of Scripture, will be seen to be reasonable. An appeal to mystery is, however, a way of saying it cannot be so expounded."

6. Richardson says that secular humanists and Marxists "have been deeply influenced by Christian teaching and ideals", and therefore "cannot be said to be . . . totally bereft of the illumination of the Sun of Righteousness . . . The touch of Christ's hand has begun but has not finished its healing work upon their blind eyes" (1947, pp. 27–28).

BIBLIOGRAPHY

Adam, Karl, 1934. *Das Wesen des Katholizismus,* seventh edition. Düsseldorf: Schwann.

Andreski, S., 1987. 'Robertson, Historian and Sociologist', in *J.M. Robertson, 1856–1933, Liberal, Rationalist and Scholar,* edited by G.A. Wells. London: Pemberton, 66–78.

Arnett, Willard E., 1968. *George Santayana,* in the series 'Great American Thinkers'. New York: Twayne.

Arnold, Matthew, 1880. 'The Study of Poetry', in *The Complete Prose Works of Matthew Arnold,* Volume 9 (English Literature and Irish Politics), edited by R.H. Super, Ann Arbor: University of Michigan Press, 1973, 161–188.

Augstein, R., 1972. *Jesus Menschensohn.* Munich: Bertelsmann.

Badham, P., 1978. *Christian Beliefs about Life After Death.* London: SPCK.

—— and Badham, Linda, 1984. *Immortality or Extinction?,* second edition. London: SPCK

Bain, Alexander, 1894. *The Senses and the Intellect,* fourth edition. London: Longmans, Green, 1894.

Baker, John A., 1970. *The Foolishness of God.* London: Darton, Longman and Todd.

Baker, T.G.A., 1988. 'Is Liturgy in Good Shape?', in James, Eric (editor), 1988, as cited below, 1–14.

Bammel, Ernst, 1974A. Review of S. Pines's *An Arabic Version of the Testimonium Flavianum and Its Implications,* Jerusalem, 1971, in *The Epositary Times,* 85 (1974), 145–47.

——, 1974B. 'Zum Testimonium Flavianum', in *Josephus-Studien,* edited by Otto Betz et al. (Festschrift for O. Michel). Göttingen: Vandenhoeck and Ruprecht, 9–22.

Barr, J., 1966. *Old and New in Interpretation. A Study of the Two Testaments.* London: SCM.

Bass, B.M., 1981. *Stogdill's Handbook of Leadership. A Survey of Theory and Research. Revised and Expanded.* London: Collier-Macmillan.

Beare, Francis W., 1962. *St. Paul and his Letters.* London: Black.

——, 1981. *The Gospel According to Matthew. A Commentary.* Oxford: Blackwell.

Beeson, Trevor, 1973. *The Church of England in Crisis.* London: Davis-Poynter.

Bell, Daniel, 1950. 'Notes on Authoritarian and Democratic Leadership', in *Studies in Leadership,* edited by Alvin G. Goulder. New York: Harper, 395–408.

Berkeley, George, 1710. *Treatise Concerning the Principles of Human Knowledge.*

Bernard, L.L., 1924. *Instinct. A Study of Social Psychology.* London: Allen and Unwin.

Best, Ernest, 1965. *The Temptation and the Passion.* Cambridge: Cambridge University Press.

———, 1967. *The Letter of Paul to the Romans,* in the series 'The Cambridge Bible Commentary on the New English Bible', Cambridge: Cambridge University Press.

Bezzant, J.S., 1963. 'Intellectual Objections', in *Objections to Christian Belief,* with an introduction by A.R. Vidler. London: Constable, 79–111.

Bicknell, E.J., 1955. *A Theological Introduction to the Thirty-Nine Articles of the Church of England,* third edition, revised by H.J. Carpenter. London: Longmans.

Blackmore, John T., 1972. *Ernst Mach: His Life, Work, and Influence.* Berkeley: University of California Press.

Bowden, John, 1970. *Who is a Christian?* London: SCM.

———, 1977. *Voices in the Wilderness,* London: SCM.

———, 1988. 'Honesty is not Enough', in James, Eric (editor), 1988, as cited below, 43–52.

Bowra, C.M., 1943. *The Heritage of Symbolism.* London: Macmillan.

———, 1962. *Primitive Song.* London: Weidenfeld and Nicholson.

Brandon, S.G.F., 1962. *Man and his Destiny in the Great Religions.* Manchester: Manchester University Press.

Brinson, Peter, 1985. 'Anthropology and the Study of Dance', in *Society and the Dance,* edited by Paul Spencer, Cambridge: Cambridge University Press.

Brown, David, 1989. *Invitation to Theology.* Oxford: Blackwell.

Brown, Laurence, 1988. *The Psychology of Religion. An Introduction.* London: SPCK.

Brown, Thomas, 1830. *Lectures on the Philosophy of the Human Mind.* Edinburgh.

Bruce, F.F., 1974. *Jesus and Christian Origins Outside the New Testament.* London: Hodder and Stoughton.

Bultmann, R., 1968. *Theologie des Neuen Testaments,* sixth edition. Tübingen: Mohr.

Burke, Edmund, 1757. *A Philosophical Inquiry into the Origin of our Ideas of the Sublime and the Beautiful,* Cassel edition, with an Introduction by Henry Morley, London etc., no date.

Bury, J.B., 1913. *A History of Greece,* second edition. London: Macmillan.

———, 1923. *History of the Later Roman Empire,* Volume 1. London: Macmillan.

———, 1930. *History of the Papacy in the Nineteenth Century, 1864–1878.* London: Macmillan.

Byrne, Peter, 1989. *Natural Religion and the Nature of Religion.* London and New York: Routledge.

Cadbury, H.J., 1937. *The Peril of Modernizing Jesus.* New York: Macmillan.

Caird, George B., 1956. *Principalities and Powers.* Oxford: Clarendon Press.

———, 1980. *The Language and Imagery of the Bible.* London: Duckworth.

Campbell, George, 1814. *The Philosophy of Rhetoric* (first published 1776). Edinburgh: Constable and Fairbairn.

Carr, A.W., 1981. *Angels and Principalities.* Cambridge: Cambridge University Press.

Charlesworth, J.H., 1989. *Jesus Within Judaism: New Light from Exciting Archaeological Discoveries.* London: SPCK (first printed in the U.S. by Doubleday in 1988, as part of the Anchor Bible Reference Library).

Coleman, Francis X.J., 1986. *Neither Angel nor Beast: The Life and Work of Blaise Pascal.* London and New York: Routledge.

Collingwood, Robin G., 1924. *Speculum Mentis.* Oxford: Clarendon.

———, 1934. *Roman Britain.* Oxford: Clarendon Press.

———, 1946. *The Idea of History.* Oxford: Clarendon.

Crawshay-Williams, R., 1947. *The Comforts of Unreason.* London: Kegan Paul.

Croce, B., 1941. *History as the Story of Liberty,* English translation by Sylvia Sprigge. London: Allen and Unwin.

———, 1949. 'Why We Cannot Help Calling Ourselves Christians', in *My Philosophy.* London: Allen and Unwin, 37–47.

Cross, F.L. (editor), 1971. *The Oxford Dictionary of the Christian Church.* Oxford: Oxford University Press.

Cullmann, O., 1962. *Christ and Time,* revised edition. London: SCM.

Davey, Graham, 1981. *Animal Learning and Conditioning.* London: Macmillan.

Davis, Caroline Franks, 1989. *The Evidential Force of Religious Experience.* Oxford: Clarendon Press.

Dibelius, Martin, 1909. *Die Geisterwelt im Glauben des Paulus.* Göttingen: Vandenhoeck and Ruprecht.

Dilthey, W., 1923. *Einleitung in die Geisteswissenschaften,* second edition, in *Gesammelte Schriften,* Volume 1. Leipzig: Teubner.

Dingle, H., 1931. *Science and Human Experience.* London: Williams and Norgate.

Dodds, E.R., 1951. *The Greeks and the Irrational.* Berkeley: University of California Press.

———, 1965. *Pagan and Christian in an Age of Anxiety.* Cambridge: Cambridge University Press.

Downing, F. Gerald, 1968. *The Church and Jesus.* London: SCM.

Draper, John W., 1923. *History of the Conflict Between Religion and Science,* new edition. London: Pioneer Press.

Driver, Tom F., 1988. 'The Case for Pluralism', in *The Myth of Christian Uniqueness,* edited by John Hick and Paul Knitter. London: SCM, 203–218.

Drury, John, 1985. *The Parables in the Gospels.* London: SPCK.

Dupont-Sommer, A., 1961. *The Essene Writings from Qumran,* translated by G. Vermes. Oxford: Blackwell.

Edwards, David L., 1988. 'Why the Conservative Backlash?' in James, Eric (editor), as cited below, 81–95.

Ehrenfeld, David, 1981. *The Arrogance of Humanism.* Oxford: Oxford University Press.

Eliot, T.S., 1951. *Selected Essays,* third, enlarged edition. London: Faber and Faber.

Ellegård, Alvar, 1990. 'Jesus, Paul, and Early Christianity', *Lychnos,* 1–47.

Engels, Friedrich, 1894. *Herrn Eugen Dührings Umwälzung der Wissenschaft,* third edition.

Englefield, F.R.H. (Ronald), 1977. *Language: Its Origin and Its Relation to Thought.* London: Elek/Pemberton; New York: Scribner.

———, 1985. *The Mind at Work and Play.* Buffalo: Prometheus.

———, 1990. *Critique of Pure Verbiage.* La Salle: Open Court.

Evans, C.F., 1970. *Resurrection and the New Testament.* London: SCM.

Fabre, J.H., 1912. *The Life of the Caterpillar,* English translation by A.T. de Mattos. London: Hodder and Stoughton.

Feldman, Louis H., 1984. *Josephus and Modern Scholarship, 1937–1980.* Berlin and New York: De Gruyter.

Finley, M.I., 1968. 'Christian Beginnings', in *Aspects of Antiquity.* London: Chatto and Windus, 177–196.

Finnegan, Ruth, 1988. *Literacy and Orality.* Oxford: Blackwell.

Foote, Peter, 1977. 'Oral and Literary Tradition in Early Scandinavian Law', in *Oral Tradition, Literary Tradition,* a symposium edited by Hans Bekker-Nielsen et al. Odense: Odense University Press.

Forster, Roger, and Marston, Paul, 1989. *Reason and Faith.* Eastborne: Monarch Publications.

France, R.T., 1986. *The Evidence for Jesus.* London: Hodder and Stoughton.

Galton, Francis, 1951. *Inquiries into Human Faculty* (first published 1883). London: the Eugenics Society.

Gibb, C.A. (editor) 1969. *Leadership. Selected Readings.* Harmondsworth: Penguin Books.

Gilkey, Langdon, 1988. 'Plurality and Its Theological Implications', in *The Myth of Christian Uniqueness,* edited by John Hick and Paul Knitter. London: SCM, 37–50.

Glasson, T.F., 1980. *Jesus and the End of the World.* Edinburgh: St. Andrews Press.

Goodall, Jane van Lawick, 1971. *In the Shadow of Man.* London: Collins (Fontana Books).

Grant, F.C., and Rowley, H.H., eds., 1963. *Dictionary of the Bible,* second edition. Edinburgh: T. and T. Clark.

Grant, R.M., 1990. *Jesus after the Gospels. The Christ of the Second Century.* London: SCM.

Grasserie, R. de la, 1892. *Essai rhythmique comparée.* Louvain.

Guilford, J.P., 1939. *General Psychology.* London: Chapman and Hall.

Gummere, Francis B., 1901. *Beginnings of Poetry.* London and New York: Macmillan.

Guyau, J.M., 1927. *L'irréligion de l'avenir,* twenty-third edition. Paris: Alcan.

Haenchen, Ernst, 1968. *Der Weg Jesu,* second edition. Berlin: De Gruyter.

Hanson, A.T., and Hanson, R.P.C., 1989. *The Bible Without Illusions.* London: SCM.

Harvey, Van A., 1967. *The Historian and the Believer.* London: SCM.

———, 1986. 'New Testament Scholarship and Christian Belief' in *Jesus in History and Myth,* as cited under Wells 1986B below, 193–200.

Hatch, Edwin, 1895. *The Influence of Greek Ideas and Usages upon the Christian Church* (Hibbert Lectures of 1888), fifth edition. London: Williams and Norgate.

Herder, J.G. von. *Ideen zur Philosophie der Geschichte der Menschheit.* 4 volumes, 1784–1791.

Hewitt, Douglas, 1969. 'Getting into the Creative Act', *Times Literary Supplement*, 27 March.

Hick, John, 1973. *God and the Universe of Faiths*. London: Macmillan.

———, 1985. *Death and Eternal Life*, second edition. London: Macmillan.

Hinde, Robert A., 1966. *Animal Behaviour*. New York: McGraw Hill.

Hoskyns, Edwyn, and Davey, Noel, 1958. *The Riddle of the New Testament* (first published in 1931). London: Faber and Faber.

Hume, David, 1738. *A Treatise of Human Nature*, Everyman's Library edition in two volumes. London: Dent; New York: Dutton, 1911.

———, 1751. *An Inquiry Concerning the Principles of Morals*, edited by C.W. Hendel. New York: Bobbs-Merrill, 1957.

Hutten, K., 1957. *Die Glaubenswelt des Sektierers*. Hamburg: Furche.

Huxley, T.H., 1894. *Science and Christian Tradition*. London: Macmillan.

James, Eric, 1965. 'Reflections on the Conference', in *Crisis for Baptism: The Report of the Ecumenical Conference*, edited by Basil S. Moss. London: SCM.

James Eric, ed., 1988. *God's Truth: Essays to Commemorate the Twenty-Fifth Anniversary of the Publication of 'Honest to God'*. London: SCM.

James, William, 1901. *The Principles of Psychology*, Volume 1. London: Macmillan.

———, *The Varieties of Religious Experience* (Gifford Lectures on Natural Religion, delivered at Edinburgh, 1901–1902). Dolphin Books edition, Gorden City, New York: Doubleday, no date.

Jessop, T.E., 1960. *An Introduction to Christian Doctrine*. London: Nelson.

Kaufman, Gorden D., 1985. *Theology for a Nuclear Age*. Manchester: Manchester University Press, and London: Westminster Press.

Kee, H.C., 1977. *Jesus in History*, second edition. New York: Harcourt Brace.

Kelly, J.N.D., 1969. *A Commentary on the Epistles of Peter and of Jude*. London: Black.

Kiparsky, P., 1976. 'Oral Poetry: Some Linguistic and Typological Considerations', in *Oral Literature and the Formula*, edited by B.A. Stolz et. al. Ann Arbor: University of Michigan Press.

Knox, D.B., 1967. *Thirty-Nine Articles*. London: Hodder and Stoughton.

Köhler, Wolfgang, 1921. *Intelligenzprüfungen an Menschenaffen*, second edition. Berlin: Springer.

———, 1927. 'Some Contributions to the Psychology of Chimpanzees', published as an Appendix to *The Mentality of Apes* (English translation of Köhler 1921), second edition. London: Kegan Paul, 271–329.

Küng, Hans, 1984. *Eternal Life?* English translation by E. Quinn. London: Collins.

Lamprecht, K., 1897. *Zwei Streitschriften*. Berlin: Gaertner.

———, 1899. *Die historische Methode des Herrn von Below*. Berlin: Gaertner.

Lang, Andrew, 1899. *Myth, Ritual, and Religion*, new edition, Volume 1. London: Longmans, Green.

Lecky, William E.H., 1897. *History of the Rise and Influence of the Spirit of Rationalism in Europe* (first published in 1865), new edition in two volumes. London and Bombay: Longmans, Green.

Leivestad, R., 1954. *Christ the Conqueror*. London: SPCK.

Lewis, H.D., 1981. *Jesus in the Faith of Christians*. London: Macmillan.

Locke, John, 1690. *An Essay Concerning Human Understanding,* new edition. London: Routledge; New York: Dutton, no date.

——, *The Reasonableness of Christianity as Delivered in the Scriptures,* first published 1695.

Lofmark, Carl, 1977. 'The Higher Kinds of Truth', *Question* 10 (1977), 3–17.

Lorenz, Konrad, 1966. *On Aggression,* English translation by Marjorie Latzke. London: Methuen.

Macgregor, G.H.C., 1954/55. 'Principalities and Powers. The Cosmic Background of Paul's Thought', *New Testament Studies,* I, 17–28.

Mach, Ernst, 1926. *Erkenntnis und Irrtum,* fifth edition. Leipzig: Barth.

Manson, T.W., 1956. 'The Life of Jesus. Some Tendencies in Present-Day Research', in *The Background of the New Testament and its Eschatology,* edited by W.D. Davies and D. Daube (C.H. Dodd Festschrift). Cambridge: Cambridge University Press, 211–221.

Marshall, Michael, 1988. *Church at the Crossroads.* London: Collins.

Martin, Michael, 1991. *The Case Against Christianity,* Philadelphia: Temple University Press.

Mascall, E.L., 1965. *The Secularisation of Christianity.* London: Darton, Longman and Todd.

Maspero, Gaston, 1916. *The Dawn of Civilization,* English translation by M.L. McClure, edited by A.H. Sayce, fourth edition. London: SPCK.

Maury, Pierre, 1960. *Predistination and Other Papers.* London: SCM (from the French *La Prédestination.* Geneva: Labor et Fides, 1957).

McDougall, William 1920. *An Introduction to Social Psychology,* fifteenth edition. London: Methuen.

Medawar, Peter B., 1984. *Pluto's Republic.* Oxford: Oxford University Press.

Merivale, Charles, 1853. *The Fall of the Roman Republic.* London: Longman.

Meyer, Eduard, 1924. 'Zur Theorie und Methodik der Geschichte', in *Kleine Schriften,* Volume 1. Halle (Saale): Niemeyer.

Milgram, S., 1974. *Obedience to Authority.* London: Tavistock.

Mill, John S., 1872. *An Examination of Sir William Hamilton's Philosophy.* London: Longmans, Green.

Milne, Bruce, 1982. *Know the Truth: A Handbook of Christian Belief.* Leicester: Inter-Varsity Press.

Mitchell, Basil, 1973. *The Justification of Religious Belief.* London: Macmillan.

Moberly, Walter, 1990. 'Political Wellbeing in Biblical Perspective', *Studies in Christian Ethics,* III No. 1, 14–29.

Montagu, M.F. Ashley, 1968. *Man and Aggression.* New York: Oxford University Press.

Muggeridge, M., 1969. *Jesus Rediscovered.* London: Collins.

——, 1975. *Jesus. The Man Who Lives.* London: Collins (reissued in new format in 1988).

Munson, T.N., 1962. *The Essential Wisdom of George Santayana.* New York: Columbia University Press.

Murray, Gilbert, 1933. *Aristophanes.* Oxford: Clarendon.

Neill, Stephen, 1984. *Crises of Belief: The Christian Dialogue with Faith and No Faith.* London: Hodder and Stoughton.

Neill, Stephen, and Wright, Tom, 1988. *The Interpretation of the New Testament, 1861–1986,* second edition. Oxford: Oxford University Press.

Neuner, J. and Roos, H., 1958. *Der Glaube der Kirche,* fifth edition, edited by K. Rahner. Regensburg: Pustet.

Nickelsburg, G.W.E., 1981. *Jewish Literature Between the Bible and the Mishnah.* London: SCM.

Nineham, Dennis, 1976. *The Use and Abuse of the Bible.* London: Macmillan.

———, 1977. 'Schweitzer Revisited', in Nineham's *Explorations in Theology,* I. London: SCM, 112–133.

———, 1988. 'What Happened to the New Reformation?' in James 1988, 152–160.

Norden, Eduard, 1898. *Die antike Kunstprosa.* Leipzig: Teubner.

O'Neill, John C., 1975. *Paul's Letter to the Romans.* Harmondsworth: Penguin.

O'Neill, Judith, 1975. *Martin Luther.* Cambridge: Cambridge University Press.

Page, Denys, 1962. 'The Homeric World', in *The Greeks,* edited by H. Lloyd-Jones. London: Watts, 1–14.

Pannenberg, Wolfhart, 1972. *The Apostles' Creed in the Light of Today's Questions.* London: SCM (from the German original, also of 1972).

Paulhan, F., 1930. *The Laws of Feeling,* English translation by C.K. Ogden. London: Kegan Paul.

Pavlov, I.V., 1927. *Conditioned Reflexes,* English translation by G. V. Antrep. Oxford: Oxford University Press.

Peabody, Berkeley, 1975. *The Winged Word: A Study in the Technique of Ancient Greek Oral Composition.* Albany: State University of New York Press.

Popper, Karl R., 1957. *The Poverty of Historicism.* London: Routledge and Kegan Paul.

———, 1972. *Conjectures and Refutations: The Growth of Scientific Knowledge,* fourth edition. London: Routledge and Kegan Paul.

———, 1975. *Objective Knowledge. An Evolutionary Approach.* Oxford: Clarendon.

Premiger, A. (ed.), 1965. *Encyclopedia of Poetry and Poetics.* Princeton: Princeton University Press.

Rahner, K., 1961. 'Current Problems in Christology', in Rahner's *Theological Investigations.* London: Darton, Longman, and Todd, 149–200.

Randell, Keith, 1988. *Calvin and the Later Reformation.* London: Hodder and Stoughton.

Ranke, Leopold von, 1896. *History of the Popes,* English translation (Bohn edition), Volume 1. London: Bell.

Raven, Charles E., 1943. *Science, Religion, and the Future.* Cambridge: Cambridge University Press (reprinted 1968).

Read, Carveth, 1925A. *Man and his Superstitions,* second edition. Cambridge: Cambridge University Press.

———, 1925B. *The Origin of Man,* second edition. Cambridge: Cambridge University Press.

Rees, R. J., 1949. *Background and Belief.* London: SCM.

Richardson, A., 1947. *Christian Apologetics.* London: SCM.

———, 1950. *Science, History, and Faith.* London: Oxford University Press.

———, 1957. *Science and Existence.* London: SCM.

———, 1963. 'The Rise of Modern Biblical Scholarship', in *The Cambridge History of the Bible,* edited by S.L. Greenslade, Volume 3, Cambridge: Cambridge University Press, 294–338.

———, 1966. *Religion in Contemporary Debate.* London: SCM.

Rickert, H., 1913. *Die Grenzen der naturwissenschaftlichen Begriffsbildung,* second edition. Tübingen: Mohr.

Rignano, Eugenio, 1923. *The Psychology of Reasoning*, English translation. London: Kegan Paul. (The French original, *Psychologie du Raisonnement*, was published in Paris by Alcan in 1920.)

Ringgren, Helmer, 1967. 'Islamic Fatalism', in *Fatalistic Beliefs in Religion, Folklore, and Literature*, edited by H. Ringgren. Stockholm: Alquist and Wiskell, 52–62.

Robbe-Grillet, A., 1961. 'The Case for the New Novel', *New Statesman*, 17 February.

Robertson, Edwin, 1989. *Bonhoeffer's Heritage*. London: Hodder and Stoughton.

Robertson, John M., 1891. *Modern Humanists*. London: Swan, Sonnenschein.

———, 1895. *Buckle and his Critics*. London: Swan, Sonnenschein.

———, 1912. *The Evolution of States*. London: Watts.

———, 1926. *The Dynamics of Religion* second, revised edition. London: Watts.

Robinson, H. Wheeler, 1926. *The Christian Doctrine of Man*, third edition. Edinburgh: T. and T. Clark.

Robinson, John A.T., 1963. *Honest to God*. London: SCM.

———, 1972. *The Difference in Being a Christian Today*. London: Collins.

———, 1973. *The Human Face of God*. London: SCM.

Rowell, G., 1974. *Hell and the Victorians*. Oxford: Clarendon.

Russell, B., 1948. *Human Knowledge*. London: Allen and Unwin.

Russell, D.S., 1986. *From Early Judaism to the Early Church*. London: SCM.

Russo, J.A., 1976. 'Homer's Formulaic Style', in *Oral Literature and the Formula*, edited by B.A. Stolz et al. Ann Arbor: University of Michigan Press.

Sanders, Ed.P., 1977. *Paul and Palestinian Judaism*. London: SCM.

Sanders, Ed.P., and Davies, Margaret, 1989. *Studying the Synoptic Gospels*. London: SCM.

Santayana, George, 1900. *Interpretations of Poetry and Religion*. London: Black.

Sargant, William, 1957. *Battle for the Mind: A Physiology of Conversion and Brain-Washing*. London: Heinemann.

———, 1967. *The Unquiet Mind*. London: Heinemann.

Schopenhauer, Arthur, 1873. *Über die vierfache Wurzel des Satzes vom zureichenden Grunde*, in *Sämmtliche Werke*, edited by J. Frauenstädt, Volume 1, Leipzig: Brockhaus. English translation, *On the Fourfold Root of the Principle of Sufficient Reason*. La Salle: Open Court, 1974.

Schrage, Wolfgang, 1988. *The Ethics of the New Testament*. Edinburgh: T. and T. Clark (from the German of 1982).

Schweitzer, Albert, 1913. *Geschichte der Leben-Jesu Forschung*. Tübingen: Mohr.

———, 1954. *The Quest of the Historical Jesus* (English translation of Schweitzer's *Von Reimarus zu Wrede*, 1906), third edition. London: Black.

Shaw, Graham, 1983. *The Cost of Authority: Manipulation and Freedom in the New Testament*. London: SCM.

Sherwin-White, A.N., 1963. *Roman Society and Roman Law in the New Testament*. Oxford: Oxford University Press.

Smith, Henry P., 1921. *Essays in Biblical Interpretation*. London: Allen and Unwin.

Smith, Morton, 1972. Review of S. Pines's *An Arabic Version of the Testimonium Flavianum and Its Implications*, Jerusalem, 1971, in *Journal of Biblical Literature*, 91 (1972), 441–42.

Spencer, Herbert, 1872. *Principles of Psychology* (first published in 1855), second edition, Volume 2. London: Longman.

Staal, Fritz, 1986. 'The Fidelity of Oral Tradition and the Origins of Science', *Mededelingen der koninklikje Nederlandske akademie von Wetenschappen,* 49 n.8 (1986).

Stanton, G.N., 1989. *The Gospels and Jesus.* Oxford: Oxford University Press.

Stark, R.S. and Glock, C.Y., 1970. *American Piety: The Nature of Religious Commitment.* Berkeley University of California Press.

Stendahl, Krister, 1953. 'The Called and the Chosen: An Essay on Election', in *The Root of the Vine: Essays in Biblical Theology,* by A. Fridrichsen et al. London: Black, 63–80.

Stogdill, R.M., 1977. *Leadership, Abstracts, and Bibliography, 1904–1974.* Columbus: Ohio State University.

Strahler, Arthur N., 1987. *Science and Earth History: The Evolution/Creation Controversy.* Buffalo: Prometheus.

Strawson, William, 1963. *The Christian Approach to the Humanist.* London: Edinburgh House Press.

Swinburne, R., 1981. *Faith and Reason.* Oxford: Clarendon.

Taylor, A.E., 1945. *Does God Exist?* London: Macmillan.

Toynbee, A.J., 1934. *A Study of History.* Oxford: Oxford University Press.

Treitschke, Heinrich von, 1939. *Cavour* (first published 1869), edited by F. Endres. Ebenhausen bei München: W. Langewiesche-Brandt.

Trotter, Wilfred, 1953. *Instincts of the Herd in Peace and War.* Oxford: Oxford University Press.

Tylor, E.B., 1891. *Primitive Culture,* third, revised edition, Volume 1. London: John Murray.

Van Harvey. See above: Harvey, Van A.

Vansina, Jan, 1965. *Oral Tradition.* London: Routledge.

———, 1985, *Oral Tradition as History.* London: James Currey.

Volney, C.F., 1822. *Les ruines, ou méditations sur les révolutions des empires,* tenth edition. Paris: Bossange.

Walker, D.P., 1964. *The Decline of Hell: Seventeenth-Century Discussions of Eternal Torment.* London: Routledge.

Walker, Stephen, 1987. *Animal Thought.* London: Routledge.

Walter, Nikolaus, 1989. 'Paul and the Early Christian Jesus-Tradition', in Wedderburn 1989, 51–80.

Watt, W. Montgomery, 1987. 'The Muslim Tradition in Today's World', in *Religion in Today's World,* edited by Frank Whaling. Edinburgh: T. and T. Clark, 230–249.

———, 1988. *Islamic Fundamentalism and Modernity.* London: Routledge.

Weber, Max, 1949. *The Methodology of the Social Sciences,* English translation and edition by E.A. Shils and H.A. Finch. New York: Free Press.

Wedderburn, A.J.M., ed., 1989: *Paul and Jesus: Collected Essays.* Sheffield: Sheffield Academic Press.

Wells, George A., 1956. 'The Critics of Buckle', *Past and Present* (1956), 75–84.

———, 1959. *Herder and After: A Study in the Development of Sociology.* The Hague: Mouton.

———, 1971. *The Jesus of the Early Christians.* London: Pemberton.

——, 1982. *The Historical Evidence for Jesus,* Buffalo: Prometheus (reissued in 1988).

——, 1985. 'Paul Valéry on the Importance of the Poet', *Modern Languages,* 66 (1985), 186–191.

——, 1986A. *Did Jesus Exist?,* second edition. London: Pemberton.

——, 1986B. 'The Historicity of Jesus', in *Jesus in History and Myth,* edited by R.J. Hoffmann and G.A. Larue. Buffalo: Prometheus, 27–45.

——, 1987A. *The Origin of Language: Aspects of the Discussion from Condillac to Wundt.* La Salle: Open Court.

——, 1987B. 'Robertson as Critic of Christianity', in *J.M. Robertson, 1856–1933, Liberal, Rationalist, and Scholar,* edited by G.A. Wells. London: Pemberton, 123–196.

——, 1988. *Religious Postures.* La Salle: Open Court.

——, 1989. *Who Was Jesus? A Critique of the New Testament Record.* La Salle: Open Court.

Werner, Martin, 1941. *Die Entstehung des christlichen Dogmas.* Bern: P. Haupt. (An abbreviated English translation by S.G.F. Brandon is entitled *The Formation of Christian Dogma.* London: Black, 1957).

White, Amber B., 1948. *Ethics for Unbelievers.* London: Routledge and Kegan Paul.

Whiteley, D.E.H., 1974. *The Theology of St. Paul,* second edition. Oxford: Blackwell.

Whittaker, John H., 1990. *The Logic of Religious Persuasion.* New York: Lang.

Wickham, Lionel, 1989. 'Pelagianism in the East', in *The Making of Orthodoxy: Essays in Honour of Henry Chadwick,* edited by Rowan Williams. Cambridge: Cambridge University Press, 200–213.

Wiles, M., 1967. *The Making of Christian Doctrine,* Cambridge: Cambridge University Press.

——, 1974. *The Remaking of Christian Doctrine.* London: SCM.

——, 1987. 'The Reasonableness of Christianity', in *The Rationality of Religious Belief,* Basil Mitchell Festschrift, edited by W.J. Abraham et al. Oxford: Clarendon, 39–51.

Wilkinson, A., 1988. 'Three Sexual Issues', *Theology,* 91, 122–131.

Wilson, S.G., 1984. 'From Jesus to Paul: the Contours and Consequences of a Debate', in *From Jesus to Paul,* studies in Honour of F.W. Beare, edited by P. Richardson and J.C. Hurd. Waterloo (Ontario), W. Laurier University Press, 1–21.

Wimsatt, William K., and Brooks, Cleanth, 1957. *Literary Criticism: A Short History.* New York: Knopf.

Wink, W., 1984. *Naming the Powers.* Philadelphia: Fortress Press.

Winter, Paul, 1973. 'Josephus on Jesus and James', in Schürer, Emil, *The History of the Jewish People in the Age of Jesus Christ,* a new English version revised and edited by Geza Vermes and Fergus Millar, Volume 1. Edinburgh: T. and T. Clark, 428–441.

Wolff, Christian, 1989. 'True Apostolic Knowledge of Christ: Exegetical Reflections on 2 Corinthians 5:14ff', in Wedderburn 1989, 81–98.

Wood, H.G., 1955. *Belief and Unbelief Since 1850.* Cambridge: Cambridge University Press.

Wootton, Barbara, 1950. *Testament for Social Science.* London: Allen and Unwin.

Wundt, Wilhelm, 1910. *Völkerpsychologie,* Volume 4, second edition. Leipzig:
    Engelmann.
————, 1923. *Völkerpsychologie,* Volume 3, fourth edition. Leipzig: Kröner.
Xénopol, A.D., 1899. *Les principes fondamentaux de l'histoire.* Paris: Leroux.
Ziesler, John, 1989. *Paul's Letter to the Romans.* London: SCM; Philadelphia:
    Trinity Press International.

INDEX OF NEW TESTAMENT REFERENCES

GENERAL INDEX (See also Table of Contents on p. v above)

NT = The New Testament
OT = The Old Testament

Page numbers in parentheses following references to notes indicate pages where an author is quoted (or his views alluded to), but not named. Thus Bicknell 264 n3 (84) means that this author is alluded to on p. 84, where superscript 3 directs the reader to the note on p. 264, where Bicknell is named.